Chas. R. Moore

Christian Doctrines

A Compendium
of Theology

By JAMES MADISON PENDLETON

PHILADELPHIA
THE JUDSON PRESS

CHICAGO   LOS ANGELES

Copyright in 1878
Copyright in 1906
by the
American Baptist Publication Society

Twenty-fifth Printing, 1952

Printed in U.S.A.

To

MRS. SALLIE L. CROZER

for many years the loving and devoted wife of

JOHN P. CROZER,

who since his death has exemplified the dignity of Christian widowhood; whose years have been prolonged till her children and grandchildren have risen up to call her "Blessed"; whose uniform courtesy and kindness have had much to do in making my Upland pastorate pleasant; regarding her character with exalted admiration, and wishing her name to be favorably known wherever I can, in any way, make it known,

I very respectfully and very affectionately dedicate this volume.   —THE AUTHOR

PREFACE.

For several years I have thought that a small work treating theological topics in an abridged form would be useful, and have at last undertaken to prepare such a vol ime. My plan has been to present in a concise manner the chief subjects usually discussed at length in works on Systematic Theology.

The work lays no claim to originality. While a few ideas are my own, the substance of the volume is not new. The same ideas may be found in books written within the last three hundred years, and these ideas are expressed in my own words, except in extracts for which due credit has been given. No man who has made Theology a study for nearly half a century can possibly tell the measure of his indebtedness to the authors he has read. I can make nothing more than a general acknowledgment of my obligations.

But it has been my purpose to present the views of theologians so far only as those views accord with the teachings of the Scriptures. The Bible is the only authoritative standard in matters of faith and practice

The questions in the writing of every chapter have been. "What saith the Scripture?" "How readest thou?" Of course, the views here presented seem to me to be in accordance with the word of God, but, having had so many proofs of the fallibility of my opinions, it will not be surprising if it should be necessary to modify some of them.

Every page has been written in the interest of scriptural truth, and for its maintenance. I trust that it has not been written in vain, but that the blessing of God will go with the volume which is now sent forth.

My days are passing away, and I shall be soon numbered with the dead. I would not be entirely forgotten when I die. Still, my desire of posthumous fame comes within narrow limits: it amounts only to this—a wish that some, profited by the Compendium of Theology, may, when their kindness prompts them to go to my grave, thank God that I lived.

J. M. P.

Upland, Pa., April 15, 1878

CONTENTS.

CHAPTER VIII.

CHAPTER IX.

CHAPTER X.

CHAPTER XI.

CHAPTER XII.

CHAPTER XIII.

CHAPTER XIV.

CHAPTER XV.

CHAPTER XVI.

CHAPTER XVII.

CHAPTER XVIII.

CHAPTER XIX.

CHAPTER XX.

CHAPTER XXI.

CHAPTER XXII.

CHAPTER XXIII.

CHAPTER XXIV.

CHAPTER XXV.

CHAPTER XXVI.

CHAPTER XXVII.

CHAPTER XXVIII.

CHAPTER XXIX.

CHAPTER XXX.

CHRISTIAN DOCTRINES:

A

COMPENDIUM OF THEOLOGY.

CHAPTER I.

THE BEING OF GOD.

THE first words in the Bible are these: "In the beginning God created the heaven and the earth." Gen. i. 1. Here the important fact of creation is declared, and the sublimest of all truths—namely, the existence of God—is taken for granted. There is no array of arguments to prove that there is a God, but it is simply assumed. Moses, under divine inspiration, had no doubt the best reasons for the course he adopted, and it would probably have been better for the interests of truth had some speculative theologians copied his example. To attempt to be "wise above what is written" is great folly.

The existence of God is the greatest of mysteries. Neither man nor angel can comprehend it. There must be heights and depths in the Infinite that can never be measured by the finite. "Canst thou by searching find out God? Canst thou find out the Almighty unto perfection? It is as high as heaven; what canst thou do? deeper than hell; what canst thou know? The measure thereof is longer than the earth and broader than the sea." Job xi. 7, 8, 9.

But while we are lost in wonder in contemplating a Being who has existed from eternity, all the causes of whose existence are in himself, we should give glad welcome to the truth that there is such a Being, and say with Paul, "For of him, and through him, and to him. are all things: to whom be glory for ever." Rom. xi. 36.

The existence of God has been referred to as the greatest mystery, but it furnishes a key to unlock a thousand other mysteries. How many things can be accounted for on the supposition that there is a God, which can be understood on no other supposition! If there is a God, man can know something about himself, whence he came; something about the world, whence it sprang; something about the universe, why it exists. If there is no God, nothing can be satisfactorily known, and all things, whether they exist by fate or chance, are in hopeless confusion and darkness.

Philosophers have generally admitted that there are "first truths" or "first principles" from which all reasoning must proceed. Among these first truths may be classed our belief of the connection between cause and effect. That this belief is entertained by every sane mind is beyond question. But if it should be asked why we thus believe, there is but one answer to the question, which is—that the belief is in accordance with the constitution of our minds. If any one should say that the answer is not sufficient, we can only reply that no other answer can be given. We are so constituted as necessarily to believe that causes produce effects, and that effects proceed from causes. It may be said that there are secondary causes, which stand in the relation of effects to other and prior causes. This is true, but the chain of causation, however many its links, may be traced back to the source of power. These links, being finite, can be numbered; for there is not and cannot be an endless succession of them. Tracing effects and secondary causes as far as possible, we reach the First Cause. Here we stop, for we can go no further. The constitution of the human mind finds its limits at this point. The First Cause is another name for God. All secondary causes are dependent on the First Cause, but the First Cause is absolutely independent. Jehovah is "God over all, blessed for ever."

The capacity of man to know that there is a God is recognized by Paul in these words: "Because that which may be known of God is manifest in them; for God hath shewed it unto them. For the invisible things of him from the creation of the world are clearly seen, being understood by the things that are made, even his eternal power and Godhead; so that they are without excuse." Rom. i. 19, 20. It is worthy of special notice that the apostle in this language refers to idolatrous heathen nations. He tells us that they know enough of God to render them inexcusable in their idolatry. Whence comes their knowledge? Evidently from their ability to infer from the works of creation the existence of a Creator. This inference has been drawn in all ages— "from the creation of the world." It should perhaps be said that some of the best scholars give to *from* in this passage the meaning *since*. The translation of Dr. Noyes is this: "For, ever since the creation of the world, his invisible attributes, even his eternal power and divinity, being perceived from his works, are clearly seen, so that they might be without excuse."[1] The idea, according to this translation, is that at all periods since the world

[1] *The New Testament: Translated from the Greek Text of Tischendorf* By George R. Noyes, D. D The general excellence of this translation is unquestionable

was made the human mind has been able to recognize the invisible attributes, the "eternal power and divinity," of the Creator. These "invisible things" are perceived or understood by "the things that are made," so that it is undeniably true that things made suggest a Maker, and works imply a Worker. It is also beyond question that man, in inferring the existence of a Creator, must attribute to him "eternal power." Creation in the absence of power is equally impossible and absurd. There can be no higher view of power than that suggested by the production of something out of nothing. This power, too, is manifestly eternal. That is to say, it must have existed before it was exerted and manifested in creation. Its existence clearly antedates creation, and everything before creation is eternal. In our conceptions of duration we can go back through intervening centuries to creation, but beyond that demonstration of Almighty power our thoughts are lost in the recesses of eternity. The power which created all things must be eternal power.

Nor is this power impersonal. Paul refers to the "invisible things of him" to whom he applies the term "Godhead"—a term suggestive of personality. If there is a Godhead, there is a God, and he is a personal being. The simplest idea of power is that of ability to do something; and the ability is either inherent or in actual exercise—that is, it exists in a quiescent state, or it is developed in action. In popular speech the word power is used with some latitude of meaning. We speak of the power of wealth, the power of government, the power of gravitation, or the power of Nature. A little reflection, however, will convince us that there is in wealth no power apart from those who possess and use it. There is in government no power independent of those who govern. There is no power of gravitation or power of Nature which God has not given. Witnessing some of the movements of matter—for example, the operation of machinery which turns ten thousand spindles, or the train of cars obediently following the dashing locomotive—we thoughtlessly exclaim, "What power!" We forget how long intellect was at work before the way to turn those spindles was invented and the majestic running of a railroad train became an actual thing. It was mind that arranged and controlled matter so wondrously as to excite the admiration of the world. I present this illustration to show that power, in its inferior operations, belongs to mind, or spirit, and not to matter. Much more does power, in the highest meaning of the word, belong to the Supreme Spirit. David well says that "power belongeth unto God." Ps. lxii. 11. I cannot so well express my view of the superiority of mind to matter as by quoting from Robert Hall's sermon on "The Spirituality of the Divine Nature."[1] He says: "There is a vulgar prejudice in favor of matter and against spirit, as if the former were possessed of great force, while the latter is only invested with a feeble degree of energy. Hence, in contemplating the operations of the elements of Nature, producing great and important changes, we are apt to think of matter, and of matter in its most gross and palpable form. This prejudice arises from our mistaking secondary and remote effects for causes, allowing them therefore to terminate our view, instead of ascending from those laws of Nature which God has established to himself the Supreme Cause. These changes certainly indicate the existence of great power, which, at the first view, we are apt to connect with the material part of the system. We are also acquainted in a measure with the mechanical forces, and, seeing that these are exerted through the

[1] *Hall's Works*, Harpers' edition, vol. iii., pp. 296–298.

medium of matter, we are thence led to suppose that to be the source of power. We find that we are incapable of operating on matter, of moving even an atom, by a mere act of our will; a material medium is necessary to enable us to produce the slightest change on the objects of Nature; and if a material substance is brought to bear upon them, the most important effects are produced. We have no power of operating on the objects immediately around us but by means of our bodies; and the changes that take place are always connected with certain motions in them, which enable us to come into contact with the visible world. Hence, we are apt to terminate our ideas of power in matter. But in these cases it is *mind*, and mind alone, which is the seat of power. The influence which our bodies have upon other bodies, whereby their relative position is changed, is merely a secondary effect— an effect of that act of will which produces the motion of our bodies. The power by which all changes are effected through the instrumentality of the body resides immediately in the mind. It is that mysterious principle, called Will, which the Divine Being has invested with a control over the various parts of our bodies; nor have we power to alter the state of a single external thing, in the least degree, except by means of volition, which is a mental power operating immediately upon the body. No other account can be given of this capacity but that the Divine Being has endowed us with instantaneous control over the muscular parts of our bodies. We can conceive nothing intermediate between the act of the will and the movement of the muscles. So complete, indeed, is the dominion of mind over matter that the moment we will a certain motion in the body it takes place, and thus only are we enabled to effect changes in the system of surrounding Nature. We probably derive our idea of power from the changes we see effected in this manner, but all these changes resolve themselves into acts of the will. It is therefore plain that power resides in the *mind*, and that matter is in these respects only the instrument of mind, which in the first instance acts, which alone properly acts, and becomes the author of all the subsequent changes. Mind, indeed, to a certain extent and within a certain sphere, is absolute power, and whatever motions it wills instantly take place. Though we are far from supposing for a moment that the Divine Being is the soul of the universe, or that he bears the same relation to the visible world as the soul does to the body—a notion replete with absurdity and impiety—yet the power which the mind exerts over the whole of our corporeal system may afford an apt illustration of that control which the Deity exercises over the universe. We will a certain motion in the muscles of our body, and immediately it takes place · nothing is perceived to intervene between the act of the will and the subsequent motion. By the mysterious constitution of our nature we are capable, from a very early period of life, of putting into instantaneous motion the right set of muscles for producing a certain change, but nothing intervenes between the volition and the change. In vain do we inquire how this takes place, because we can find nothing which comes between the operation of the will and the change produced in our corporeal frame.

"Conceive the Divine Being as a Spirit, having the same dominion over the invisible universe, in every part of space, as that which our minds possess over every portion of our bodies; and then you will perceive, faintly at least, the origin of that power the indications of which are so visible throughout the universe. He has only to will the most important changes, and they are instantly

2 *

accomplished. 'He speaks, and it is done; he commands, and it stands fast.' He said, 'Let there be light and there was light.' No causes intervene between the volition and the change which ensues, for the will of the Deity is itself the effect. Being an Infinite Spirit and coming into immediate contact with all the parts of the universe, he is capable, by a mere act of will, of effecting all possible changes in the same manner, but in an infinitely higher degree, as we are capable, by an act of our will, of causing certain motions in the muscular parts of our body, and thus producing changes in the external objects around us.

"We shall find it impossible to give any account of innumerable changes which are continually taking place in the visible world, without tracing them up to mind. There cannot be a clearer proof of a Deity than the existence of motion. This evident.y appears not to be essential to matter, because we see a very great portion of the material universe without it. Not being, therefore, an original state of matter, but merely an incident, it must be an effect. But since matter, not being intelligent, can not be the cause of its own motion—and yet we cannot conceive of any atom beginning to move without a cause—that cause must be found out of itself. Whatever may be the nearest cause or the number of secondary causes, though innumerable portions of matter may be reciprocally moved—though the series of links in the chain through which motion is propagated may be indefinitely multiplied—we must, in order to arrive at the origin of these various phenomena, ascend to mind, terminate our inquiries in spirit nor can we account for the beginning, much less for the continuance and extension, of motion, unless we trace it to the will of that Being who is the Cause of all causes—the great Original

Mover in the universe. Power is, therefore, the attribute
of mind; instrumentality, that of body. When we read
in the Old Testament of the most exalted achievements
ascribed to angelic spirits, we cannot suppose that it is
owing to any gross materialism which they possess; on
the contrary, they have no bodies capable of being investigated by our senses; and in proportion as they are more
attenuated do they possess greater power. We have
reason to believe that all finite minds are under the
direction of the Supreme Power, who, without destroy-
ing their accountability or interfering with their agency
makes all their operations subservient to the accomplishment of his counsels. Hence all opposition to the Deity
is beautifully represented by Isaiah, as if the instrument
should rebel against him that wields it, as if 'the rod
should shake itself against them that lift it up.' . .
All created beings in this respect are but instruments in
the hand of the Deity, whose will is sovereign over them.
The Divine Being, as the great Father of spirits, combines within himself all the separate energies of the
universe. He is the source, origin, and fountain of all
power diffused through creation. The very minds which
he has formed are kept in mysterious subordination, and
can never overstep the bounds he has assigned them.
'Once have I heard this, that power belongs unto God.'"

It is needless to call special attention to this quotation
from the writings of one of the most eloquent men of
modern times, for the view presented is too striking to
pass unnoticed. The prominent thought is that mind, or
spirit, is the residence of power. In a subordinate sense
this is true of finite spirits, and in the highest sense it is
true of the Infinite Spirit. This Spirit we call God, the
great First Cause of all things, himself uncaused. He is,
therefore, self-existent; for there can be no reasons why

he exists that do not inhere in himself. He existed before there were any angels, any men, any worlds, and consequently none of the causes of his existence could be external to himself. They are intrinsic causes, found in himself alone ; and if all created things should sink into the abyss of nothingness, such a disaster would affect the existence of the Supreme Spirit as little as the quenching of the glow-worm's spark would affect the sun in the heavens. What a Being is God! How incomprehensible! The idea of self-existence overwhelms us, but the constitution of the human mind is such as to require us to believe that there is a self-existent Being, the cause of all finite existence. Paul, as we have seen, refers to his "eternal power and Godhead," the indications of which are so evident from the works of creation that idolaters among heathen nations are without excuse.

There is a God. In this fact we find an explanation of many things otherwise inexplicable. The mind reposes on this fact, and finds satisfaction. It can be satisfied in no other way. It revolts from the doctrine of fate—that all things exist, and have existed from eternity, by inevitable necessity, so that there has been no creation at all. The mind of man in its normal state cannot accept this doctrine, but protests against it as entirely unsatisfactory, because utterly unreasonable. Nor is the human mind satisfied with the opposite doctrine of chance. That all things exist by chance is a theory that had its advocates in ancient times, and it is virtually defended by men now living. There is a denial of creation in the proper sense of the term—fate is ridiculed—and it is supposed that the material universe was constructed out of atoms fortuitously coming together from realms unknown, and giving no account of themselves. Now, these two systems—Fate and Chance—equally excite the revulsion of the well-balanced intellect. The capital objection to both is that they exclude God from the universe. They have no use for the existence of a Supreme Being to control all things, from the revolution of a planet to the fall of a sparrow. They are far as the poles apart in their distinctive teachings, but they are agreed in endorsing what, in David's day, the fool said in his heart, "There is no God." There is no satisfactory way of accounting for the existence of this world or any other world unless we admit that there is a God, the Omnipotent Creator of all things. What the mind of man calls for and presents as its first postulate is, Let there be a God.

While it is true that we cannot satisfactorily explain why the world exists if there is no God, it is also true that the indications of design are unaccountable if a Supreme Intelligence does not preside over all things. We see evidences of adaptation all around us. The world seems to be adapted to man and to other animals, and they seem to be suited to the world. The soil is adapted to such productions as are necessary to the support of physical life. The lungs and the air are adapted each to the other. Birds are fitted for the air, and fishes for the sea. There is adaptation everywhere and in every thing; and adaptation, so far as we are capable of judging, indicates intelligence and design. Intelligence and design are not properties of matter, but attributes of spirit. Where there is intelligence there is mind, and where there is design it must be the result of intelligence, and there must be a Designer. If, then, the many instances of adaptation visible everywhere are suggestive of design, the question arises, "Who is the Designer?" and the only answer is, "God, the Creator and Ruler of all things." One of the most obvious indications of design is to be seen in the provision made for the perpetuity of the human race. The two sexes are about equal in numbers, and it is utterly incredible that this is the result of accident. There must be design, and when we look into the matter in the light of the Bible, we shall see that the existence of the two sexes is the basis of the marriage relation; which relation contemplates the promotion of human happiness, the preservation of social order, and the continuance of the race. All this shows purpose, and where there is purpose affecting the condition, and even the existence, of the human race, who will say that there is not an intelligent and almighty Purposer?

These are suggestions rather than elaborate arguments in favor of the existence of a God, the First Cause of all things, infinite in power and boundless in wisdom. To this God we may say, in the reverent language of Scripture, "Thou, Lord, in the beginning hast laid the foundation of the earth; and the heavens are the works of thine hands. They shall perish, but thou remainest; and they all shall wax old as doth a garment; and as a vesture shalt thou fold them up, and they shall be changed; but thou art the same, and thy years shall not fail." Heb. i. 10-12.

CHAPTER II.

THE BIBLE A REVELATION FROM GOD.

FOR many centuries there has been in the world a book claiming to be *The Bible*—that is, *The Book*. There is no book like to it. It has had, and still has, more earnest friends and more bitter enemies than any other. Multitudes have submitted to martyrdom rather than abjure its teachings, and have been cheered by its promises when earth has receded from their view. On the other hand, greater efforts have been made to destroy the Bible than were ever put forth for the destruction of any other book. Its foes have persistently attempted to arrest its influence. Criticism has assailed it and ridicule has derided it. Science and philosophy have been invoked to discredit it. Astronomy in the disclosure of its heavenly wonders has been asked for some fact to disparage it, and geology in its researches in the earth has been importuned to throw suspicion on it.

The Bible, however, yet has a place in the world. There are more copies of it in circulation to-day than ever before. Written originally in Hebrew and Greek, it has been translated into hundreds of languages, so that poetry breathes historical truth in the words,

> " Dialects unheard at Babel or at Jewish Pentecost
> Now first articulate divinest sounds,
> And swell the universal anthem."

In view of these facts, whatever men may think of the Bible, it must be conceded that it is a wonderful book—wonderful in its effects and in its history. But different opinions are entertained as to the origin of the Bible. Some do not hesitate to assign to it a human origin. This is the position of Deists, who, as their designation denotes, believe in the existence of God. They believe also in his wisdom and goodness, but they suppose that the volume of Nature and the teachings of reason are sufficient, without such a revelation as Christians consider the Bible to be. This is a very weak point in Deism, for the system not only grants that God is good to men, but glories in it. If this be so, then it is surely reasonable to expect from him a supernatural revelation of his will. The reasonableness of this expectation grows out of the insufficiency of the light of Nature to teach men all that they need to know. The rational inference from the goodness of God is that he will not leave his creatures in comparative darkness. It is more accordant with his benevolence to believe that he has given his word to be "a lamp to their feet and a light to their path."

It is scarcely necessary to make a distinction between Deists and Rationalists. The latter are so excessively addicted to the inculcations of reason, and attach so much importance thereto, that they reject the teachings of the Bible unless its doctrines accord with their Rationalistic views. Admitting, as some of them do, that God has spoken in his word, they, in the plentitude of their self-conceit, attempt to decide how much of what he has said harmonizes with reason. The attitude they assume is fatal to a fair and candid examination of the Bible.

In opposition to the views of Deists, Rationalists, and all kindred errorists, I maintain that the Bible is a super-

human production—that it is the book of God, properly
so called, because it contains a revelation from him.
Before attempting to show that the Bible is a revelation
from God it may be well to refer to the necessity of such
a revelation. The necessity, it may be argued, does not
prove that the revelation has been given. Even so,
but it creates an antecedent probability in favor of a
revelation.

The necessity of a divine revelation is suggested by
such considerations as the following:

1. *Without it, there cannot be such knowledge of God as is
essential to acceptable worship.* While it is true, as has been
seen in the preceding chapter, that heathen nations are
not ignorant of the existence of a Supreme Being, it cannot be maintained that they have sufficient knowledge
of his character to render them intelligent and acceptable
worshippers. The existence and the character of God are
distinct from each other. His existence may be recognized when there is no satisfactory knowledge of his character. To know that God exists does not determine how
he is to be worshipped. There must be knowledge of his
character. His character is what he is, and we must
know his character to render him acceptable service.
Can his character be known without a revelation from
himself? Let us see. As we may know something of
what are called God's natural attributes from the proofs
of his existence around us, it may be said that we are not
ignorant of what may be termed his intellectual character. This is true, for we have conceptions of his wisdom,
power, greatness, and of other natural attributes. But
what can we say of his moral character, made up of his
moral perfections? The light of Nature does not reveal
it, and the deductions of man's reason do not disclose it.
This, too, is the very point on which information is need

2

ed; for God, if worshipped at all, must be worshipped in
his moral character. His natural perfections may excite
our intellectual admiration, but cannot awaken our love.
Love, however, is the central idea of worship, and there
can be no true worship without it. The injunction,
" Thou shalt love the Lord thy God," commends itself
to every man's common sense. But those excellences
of the divine character which excite love cannot be
known without a divine revelation. Surely, then, the
necessity of such a revelation cannot be denied.

2. *Without a revelation, it is impossible to fix the standard
of moral right and wrong.* This point, considered in its
relation to the foregoing, is too plain to need much elab-
oration. Every one can see that ignorance of the moral
character of God renders the adoption of a correct rule
of morals impossible. What is right or what is wrong
must ever depend on what God is. In his nature are
found the elements of all that is right. The origin of
right is traceable to the *nature* rather than to the *will* of
God, though his will must be in accordance with his nature What I mean to say is, that things, strictly speaking, are not right because God wills them, but that he
wills them because they are right. Whatever is in
harmony with the moral character of God is right, and
whatever is in conflict with it is wrong. Here, then, we
see how the standard of duty is to be established among
men, for their duties to one another grow out of their
duties to God. The second commandment, " Thou shalt
love thy neighbor "—that is, thy fellow-creature—" as thyself," is like the first, " Thou shalt love the Lord thy
God." Obligations grow out of relations. The highest
relation is that between the creature and the Creator, and
therefore in this relation obligation shows its supreme
strength; but there is a subordinate relation between

creatures themselves, out of which mutual relation mutual duties arise. It must not be forgotten, however, that we should love our fellow-creatures primarily because they are the *creatures of God*, and secondarily because they are our fellow-creatures. Love to God inspires love to men, and prompts the performance of the duties we owe to men in the various relations of life. This we see where the influence of the Bible is felt; but if God had not given us the Bible, how could the standard of duty be known? Ignorant of his moral character, we should be utterly unable to settle the question of right and wrong. This view receives confirmation from the inadequate and variable standards of morals among ancient, and also among modern, heathen nations. Even the ancient Egyptians, Greeks, and Romans, with all their mental cultivation, were very ignorant on moral subjects —a fact which shows that there is no necessary connection between intellectual culture and moral rectitude. As to modern heathen nations, our missionaries tell us that in them is exemplified the repulsive depravity described by Paul in the first chapter of his Epistle to the Romans. The more their deplorable condition is studied, the more manifest will be the necessity of a revelation from God.

3. *Without a revelation, a future state must be a matter of conjecture.* Ancient philosophers speculated concerning it, some professed to believe it, some wished to believe it, and others denied it, while others still ridicued it. Julius Cæsar said in a speech in the Roman Senate— for he was an orator as well as a warrior—"To those that live in sorrow and misery death is a repose from their calamities, not a torment: it puts an end to all the evils that mortals are subject to, and beyond it there is nc place left for anguish or joy." Pliny, who lived some time after Cæsar, expressed himself thus: "All

men are in the same condition after their last day as before their first; nor have they any more sense, either in body or soul, after they are dead than before they were born." [1]

These two great men were doubtless representative men Others espoused the views they advocated, and before them all was the gloomy abyss of annihilation. Some of the Greek philosophers had held substantially the same views, and one of the Greek poets had eloquently exclaimed in language which has been translated thus:

> " Alas! the tender herbs and flowery tribes,
>   Though crushed by winter's unrelenting hand,
>   Revive and rise when vernal zephyrs call.
>   But we, the brave, the mighty, and the wise,
>   Bloom, flourish, fade, and fall; and then succeeds
>   A long, long, silent, dark, oblivious sleep—
>   A sleep which no propitious power dispels,
>   Nor changing seasons, nor revolving years."

Thus hopeless was the future to many of ancient times, and others, according to the testimony of Cicero, while reading the arguments in favor of the immortality of the soul, accepted the doctrine, and laying down their books gave it up. If there is a future state, doubtless there will be in it rewards for the righteous and punishments for the wicked. How important, then, to be assured of such a state! Most men who think at all will ask, "Whither do we go?" as well as, "Whence did we come?" The restless spirit wants an answer to such questions. Surely it is desirable to have some assurance concerning the mysterious future; and how can it be obtained apart from revelation? "Faith is a conviction of things not

[1] Quoted in Leland's *Advantage and Necessity of the Christian Reve-lation*, vol. ii. p. 387.

seen."[1] But faith rests on testimony, and testimony implies a revelation from God; for he alone can testify to a future state, he being "the high and lofty One who inhabits eternity," with whom "one day is as a thousand years, and a thousand years as one day."

With regard to a future state of rewards and punishments, it may be said that a belief in such a state supplies strong motives to stimulate to the doing of that which is right and to the avoidance of that which is wrong. For, whatever theorists may say, it is practically true that self-interest appeals to men, while hope and fear are the two powerful springs of human action. A belief that the rewards and punishments of a future state will be distributed according to the characters that men form and the courses they pursue in this life cannot be otherwise than influential and salutary. But the future is dark without a revelation from God, and hence the necessity of a revelation.

4. *Without a revelation there is not an intimation of a way of salvation for sinners.* I have referred to the fact that a correct standard of right is impossible unless there is a divine communication on the subject. Light is needed from heaven. It must be remembered, however, that heathen nations have their imperfect standards of right and wrong, and that they universally fail to come up to these standards. They are therefore self-condemned. Conscience pronounces its censure and stings with its accusations. In accordance with this view, Paul says: "For when the Gentiles, which have not the law, do by nature the things contained in the law, these, having not the law, are a law unto themselves: which show the work of the law written in their hearts, their conscience also bearing witness, and their thoughts the mean while

[1] Noyes's translation

accusing or else excusing one another." Rom. ii. 14, 15. The excusing or approving operation of conscience is dependent on conformity to the recognized standard of right, while a departure from that standard is followed by self-accusation. That the departure and the self-accusation are universal among the heathen is evident from the universality of sacrifices. Offerings are made to propitiate their gods, and in these offerings there is a recognition of sin and of the necessity of appeasing the wrath of these gods " which are yet no gods." I think it may be said that the benighted heathen labor under the consciousness that some moral disaster has come upon them, that some wreck has befallen their moral nature. They are aware that their moral constitution is infected by disease, but they know not of a remedy. They grope in darkness. That we may, as far as it is possible, place ourselves in their condition, let us shut out all the light we have received from the gospel on the subject of salvation. Then what could we learn from the light of Nature? There are many things recorded in the volume of Nature, but there is nothing concerning the salvation of a sinner. In the wide realm of Nature no discoveries can be made touching this infinitely important matter. No word comes from the abysses of the deep; for " The depth saith, It is not in me: and the sea saith, It is not with me." No price paid for a knowledge of salvation can procure it; for " It cannot be gotten for gold, neither shall silver be weighed for the price thereof." Not a syllable is heard from the blue heavens above us nor from the green earth beneath us. The whistling winds say nothing, the rolling thunders utter nothing, the fiery lightnings disclose nothing. All Nature is, as to the salvation of sinners, as silent as the grave.

Nor can human reason, in its amplest researches, find

a way in which a sinner can be saved. We have seen that the moral character of God cannot be known by the discoveries of reason, but his moral character is specially concerned in saving sinners. As moral Governor of the world he must exercise pardoning mercy if it is exercised at all, but reason cannot tell whether there is mercy in God. The truths involved in the salvation of a sinner are beyond the jurisdiction of reason. The science of redemption is a supernatural science. Without the light of a divine revelation it defies comprehension. We must not forget that salvation is a subject of infinite moment. It is invested with an importance which language was not invented to describe. This we see in listening to such questions as these: Shall I be saved or lost? Shall I go to heaven or hell? Shall I spend eternal ages in the beatific presence of God or in hopeless exile from him. These questions will appear far more important ten thousand centuries hence than they do now. If salvation thus affects and involves man's supreme interests—interests which overleap the horizon of time and measure years with eternity—and if there is no intimation of a way of salvation for sinners without a revelation from God, the necessity of a revelation is incontrovertible.

Having attempted to show the necessity of a divine revelation, I shall now endeavor to show that the Bible contains such a revelation. The two things are distinct. What reasons justify the belief that the Bible is the word of God, a revelation from heaven? In answer to this question the following things may be said:

1. *The human intellect could not produce such a book as the Bible.* It is cheerfully conceded that the capacity of man's intellect is great. The extent to which the mind may be strengthened and expanded is an unsettled question. It is unsettled, because no man can say to the

mind in its high career of improvement, "Hitherto shalt thou come, but no farther." It is equally foolish and false to deny that the capabilities of the human intellec' are wonderful. But these capabilities can be exercised only in their proper spheres. There are doc- trines taught in the Bible of which the unaided intellect of man could have formed no conception. We may take for example, what the Scriptures say of God's omni- presence. They teach that he is everywhere—not that he is in different places at different times, but that he is in all places at all times. They teach that he has control of matter and of spirit, and that he is present with both that his presence displaces neither matter nor spirit; and that there is in the vast realms of space no spot from which he is absent. He himself asks, " Am I a God at hand, saith the Lord, and not a God afar off? Can any hide himself in secret places that I shall not see him? saith the Lord. Do not I fill heaven and earth? saith the Lord." Jer. xxiii. 23, 24. David, solemnly impressed with the doctrine of the divine omnipresence, exclaimed, "Whither shall I go from thy Spirit? or whither shall I flee from thy presence? If I ascend up into heaven, thou art there: if I make my bed in hell, behold, thou art there. If I take the wings of the morning, and dwell in the uttermost parts of the sea, even there shall thy hand lead me, and thy right hand shall hold me." Ps. xxxix. 7–10.

Were not these grand ideas divinely communicated to David? Was it possible for his unaided intellect to origi- nate a conception of them? Now that they are revealed, the mind can comprehend them only in part, and surely they did not have a human origin.

Again: What the Bible says of redemption by Christ is obviously above the invention of the human intellect

We are told that "God so loved the world that he gave
his only-begotten Son, that whosoever believeth in him
should not perish, but have everlasting life." "When the
fulness of the time was come, God sent forth his Son
made of a woman, made under the law, to redeem them
that were under the law, that we might receive the adoption of sons." "But we see Jesus, who was made a little
lower than the angels for the suffering of death, crowned
with glory and honor, that he by the grace of God should
taste death for every man. For it became him, for whom
are all things, and by whom are all things, in bringing
many sons to glory, to make the Captain of their salvation perfect through sufferings." John iii. 16; Gal. iv.
4, 5; Heb. ii. 9, 10.

Can any man read these passages and say that they
are the production of the human intellect? Could the
thought have originated in the mind of man that God
loved this perishing world to such an extent as to give his
Son to become incarnate and suffer death, even the death
of the cross? Could man or angel have imagined that it
" became God," that it was worthy of him, to bring many
sons to glory under the leadership of a Captain of salvation fitted for his position by means of sufferings? That
the guilty creature should be saved at the expense of the
incarnation of the Creator; that life should come to the
sons of men through the death of the Son of God; that
heaven should become accessible to earth's distant population by the blood of a shameful cross,—was utterly re
mote from all finite conception. Even when the won
der was made known by the gospel, it excited the con
tempt of Jews and Greeks. To the former it was a
stumbling-block, an offence; to the latter it was foolishness. The Greeks were a highly cultivated people, acute in
intellect, profound in philosophy. and subtle in reason

ing, but they ridiculed the idea of salvation through one who was crucified. They may well be regarded as representing the possibilities of the human intellect—what it can do; and, so far from claiming the Christian doctrine of redemption as an invention of philosophers, they laughed at it as unworthy of philosophy. The facts of the gospel they rejected as incredible, because they seemed to be in positive conflict with their conceptions of reason. The point of the argument is, that as intellect, which was developed so favorably among the Greeks, did not recognize the doctrine of redemption through Christ as in harmony with their philosophy, we must conclude that the doctrine is above the invention of the human intellect.

2. *Man's heart would not prompt him to make such a book as the Bible.* He has a heart as well as an intellect, and even if he were mentally capable of making such a volume, he is morally incompetent. This will appear if we consider the universal depravity of the human race. Whether men accept or reject the Bible view of the origin, the transmission, and the history of sin, they are compelled to admit that man's moral nature rests under the blight of some disaster. It exhibits imper·fection and perversity from infancy to old age, and this it has done as far back as the records of history give us information. The power of human depravity does not exhaust itself by lapse of time and the succession of generations, but continues in undiminished strength from century to century. All the annals of the world's history bear testimony to this truth. The moral depravity of man shows itself in some diversity of manifestation, as we see in savage and in civilized lands, under different forms of government, but it is substantially the same in all climes and in all ages. It may surely be assumed as true that univer-

sal man is the subject of moral depravity, that his heart is not right with God, that he loves sin, and that his tendencies are in the direction of evil. This being the case, how is it possible to believe the Bible a human production? It commends everything that is right and condemns everything that is wrong. It puts the seal of its approval on all that is good, and pronounces its censure on all that is evil. It inculcates supreme love to God, and universal love to men as the creatures of God. It declares all human works to be without merit, and presents salvation as the gift of God's sovereign grace. It crucifies the pride of man, placing him in the dust; it exalts the Lord of glory, placing him on the throne.

Now the questions arise, Would man with his depraved heart be inclined to make such a book as the Bible? Would he produce a volume in condemnation of himself? Would he, though by nature under the influence of a self-justifying disposition, declare his righteousness to be "as filthy rags"? Would his natural self-love operate so strangely? Would he become the patron of every virtue and the censor of every vice? Would he urge holiness of heart and life by the glories of an eternal heaven and the miseries of an eternal hell? If so, it would be equivalent to the emanation of a sweet stream from a bitter fountain. In the one case, there would be a violation of a fixed analogy of Nature; in the other, one of the established analogies of the moral world would be nullified. It cannot be. The Bible is not a human production. Man's heart would not let him make such a book even if he had the intellectual ability. The latter, however, he does not possess. The argument in favor of the Bible as a divine revelation, as now presented, is in substance this: Man could not make such a book if he would, and would not if he could. The former is pre-

cluded by the condition of his intellect, the latter by the
state of his heart. If, then, the Bible is not a human production, it follows that it is the book of God. There is no
middle ground. The Bible tells us what no being in the
universe but God knew, and therefore it contains a revelation from him. I may thus illustrate my view: A husband, being absent from home, receives a letter purporting
to be from his wife. Some one, we will suppose, tries to
convince him that the letter is not genuine, that the hand-
writing of the wife has been counterfeited. The husband
knowing the expertness of counterfeiters, admits that some-
body may have learned to form letters and to write words
precisely as does his wife; but he says, "This letter is from
my wife, because it tells me what no one except herself
knows." Here he rests unmoved, feeling that he has the
most solid foundation for his belief. Our faith in the
Bible as a divine revelation may well and safely repose on
the fact that it tells us what God alone knows. It is the
word of the Lord, for the men who wrote it "spake as
they were moved by the Holy Ghost." 2 Pet. i. 21.

3. *The person and character of Christ as revealed in the
Bible prove the divine origin of the book.* As to the person
of Christ, it is unique—it stands alone—there is nothing
like it in the universe. The constitution of his person as
the Christ results from the mysterious union in him of
two natures, the divine and the human. As the Word,
who "in the beginning was with God and was God," he
was not the Christ. As man, possessing a human body
and a human soul, he was not the Christ. But as the
"Word made flesh," taking human nature into alliance
with supreme Divinity, he became the Christ, the Anointed One. As the Christ, he lived on the earth, suffered in
Gethsemane, died on Calvary, was buried, rose again, ascended to heaven, and there lives immortal. His person

will undergo no change through all the boundless future He will ever be the God-man, for the union of the two natures constituting him the Christ is indissoluble. Strange as it is, humanity is exalted and enthroned in the heavens. Such honor has never been conferred on the angelic nature. The person of Christ will be the wonder of wonders through all eternity. Who can believe that the thought of such a person as the Scriptures represent Christ to be could have entered into the mind of man, except by divine revelation? The origin of such a thought in the unaided human intellect would have been about as impossible as the creation of a world by human power.

The character of Christ is to be considered as well as his person. It was a perfect character. Nothing like it had been seen on earth. Imperfection cleaves to the best of men, and even in the strongest points of character weakness sometimes exhibits itself. For example, Abraham, remarkable for his faith, seems on some occasions not to have trusted in God fully; Moses, distinguished for his meekness, was not invariably meek; Job, proverbial for his patience, was not always patient; Peter, bold and impetuous, occasionally acted the coward; and Paul, most loyal of men to principle and truth, did a few things that are scarcely defensible. But the character of Christ was absolutely faultless and spotless. His friends, who for years were on intimate terms with him, who saw him in public places, in the social circle, and in the privacy of life, do not attribute to him a solitary imperfection. Their opinion of him obviously was that his character would bear the most scrutinizing inspection. Of Christ's twelve disciples, there were three, Peter, James, and John, who on several occasions were admitted to the intimacy of special friendship. The testimony of two of

4

the three has been handed down to us. Peter refers to his Lord as a "Lamb without blemish and without spot,' 'who did no sin, neither was guile found in his mouth ;" and John uses this language: "And ye know that he was manifested to take away our sins; and in him is no sin." The writer of the Epistle to the Hebrews says of him that he " is holy, harmless, undefiled, separate from sinners." Nor can we attribute this immaculate perfection to the absence of temptation. Good men have often yielded to temptation, falling before its power, but Jesus, though "tempted in all points like as we are," resisted and triumphed. "Without sin " are the significant words used in connection with his temptations—" tempted in all points like as we are, yet without sin." Heb. iv. 15. The tempter no doubt employed all his ingenuity in presenting inducements to lead him to sin, but failed in every instance. Jesus himself said, "The prince of this world cometh, and hath nothing in me." John xiv. 30. That is, the purity of his character was so perfect that there was in him absolutely nothing responsive to the suggestions of Satan. The temptations which Christ resisted proved his moral rectitude, and were the means of displaying his glory, even as the dark clouds from which the sun emerges cause his welcome face to appear more bright.

If the person and character of Christ are what the Bible declares them to be, then the Bible contains a revelation from heaven. The argument is, that the unassisted intellect of man could not have conceived of such a person and such a character, and therefore the portraiture of the person and character of Christ must be divine. If any man takes the opposite view and insists that the human intellect, without light and aid from heaven, could invent such a person and character, let him accept what follows; and this plainly follows: If the New Testament writers did, of themselves and without divine inspiration, conceive and present the person and character of Christ, they performed a greater miracle than any recorded in the Bible. He who assumes so unreasonable a position can never make a plausible objection to the most astounding miracles. It is not necessary to enlarge on this point.

The person and character of Christ, as revealed in the New Testament, prove the Bible to be of superhuman origin. If there were no other sources of proof, this would be sufficient. There is no rational way of accounting for what the Scriptures say of Christ, unless they are divinely inspired. While I have referred to the New Testament as specially revealing the person and character of Christ, it is to be remembered that the divine origin of the Old Testament is as undeniable as that of the New. The New Testament everywhere recognizes the Old Testament as the word of God. How often did Jesus in referring to the ancient Scriptures say, " It is written," " How readest thou ?" " As the Scripture hath said "! The Old Testament and the New are both parts of the same revelation of God to man. The Old anticipates the New, and the New presupposes the Old. Neither is complete without the other, but the two constitute God's book given to man. There is no other revelation; there is no intimation that there will be another while the world stands.

It is not worth while to go into the question of " degrees of inspiration." Nothing is said about lower or higher degrees in the Bible itself. Inspiration is a mystery. How God inspired men to speak and write his truth, " not in the words which man's wisdom teacheth, but which the Holy Ghost teacheth," and at the same time did not interfere with individuality of style, but left it undisturbed, we do not know. We do know, however that the style of Moses is not that of David, nor is the style of Isaiah like that of Jeremiah, nor the style of Matthew similar to that of John; and the style of Paul is plainly different from that of Peter. This diversity of style seems to us to result from individuality of character each writer using such words as he was acquainted with and accustomed to use; yet they were God's words as cer tainly as if the inspired men had known nothing of them Hence we read again and again, "Thus saith the Lord," and "The Lord spoke, saying." While revelation and inspiration are not precisely equivalent, the terms are often used convertibly. Thus we say "the volume of reve-lation" and "the volume of inspiration," meaning the same thing. Possibly a strict use of terms would require us to confine the word *revelation* to those things in the Bible which were not known, and could not be known, till God revealed them, while inspiration has to do with the whole Bible. For example, the coming of Christ in the flesh to save sinners was a matter of revelation; but that there were Pharisees and Sadducees at Jerusalem, and that the river Jordan ran through Judea, are unquestionable facts, though not supernaturally revealed. Still, all that is con-tained in the Bible concerning Pharisees, Sadducees, and the river Jordan was written under the inspiration of God. That is to say, God by his Spirit influenced the sacred penmen to write just what they did write, no more, no less; so that the Bible is as much the book of God as if he, without the intervention of men had written it himself.

I have thought proper to say as much as this concern-ing inspiration, as there will be no chapter of this work specially devoted to the subject. Indeed, such a chap-ter will hardly be necessary, for if the Bible is, as I have attempted to show, a revelation from God, its inspiration must be granted. Nor shall I dwell on what are called the external evidences of the truth of the Bible, such as miracles, prophecy, etc. The limits I have prescribed for myself will not permit; and, moreover, I have preferred to present some of the internal evidences of the truth of the Scriptures. Of these I have selected only a few, but if the trains of thought which they suggest are carried out, we shall see that in accepting the Bible as true " we have not followed cunningly-devised fables." 2 Pet. i. 16.

If the Bible is the word of God, its authority cannot be questioned. There must be no cavilings as to its teachings. What it says must be received as true, and its words must be candidly and faithfully interpreted. There must be docility of spirit—a willingness to " be taught of God," which will express itself in the language of the child Samuel: "Speak, Lord, for thy servant heareth." 1 Sam. iii. 9.

Recognizing the Bible as the word of God, I shall appeal to it in every part of this volume as the standard of truth and right.

4 *

CHAPTER III.

THE ATTRIBUTES OF GOD

THE term *attribute*, in its application to persons or things, means something belonging to persons or things. The attributes of a thing are so essential to it that without them it could not be what it is; and this is equally true of the attributes of a person. If a man were divested of the attributes belonging to him, he would cease to be a man, for these attributes are inherent in that which constitutes him a human being. If we transfer these ideas to God, we shall find that his attributes belong inalienably to him, and, therefore, what he is now he must ever be. His attributes are his perfections, inseparable from his nature and constituting his character. There have been many attempts made by theologians to arrange the attributes of God in classes. They have been styled natural and moral attributes, communicable and incommunicable, positive and negative, absolute and relative. To all these divisions and epithets of designation objections can no doubt be made. Possibly the classification of *natural* and *moral* attributes in God is as good as any. These have been defined thus:

"The natural are all those which pertain to his existence as an infinite, rational Spirit. . . . The moral are those additional attributes which belong to him as an infinite, righteous Spirit."[1] In the light of this defini-

[1] Hodge's *Outlines of Theology*, p. 104.

tion I will refer to some of the more prominent of the attributes of God.

I. His Natural Attributes.

1. *Self-existence.* This, of course, means that the causes of his existence are in himself. Jesus teaches this doctrine where he says that "the Father hath life in himself." John v. 26. The life is inherent. Unlike the life of creatures, it comes from no external source. If there were no creatures in the universe, their non-existence would not in the least affect the existence of God. It did not affect his existence before he performed the work of creation. He had "life in himself" when there was life nowhere else. In the total absence of life outside of himself all the possibilities of life were in himself. We are never to forget that in him creatures "live and move and have their being"—are dependent on him for life, motion, and existence; but his self-existence makes him absolutely independent. The causes of their existence not being in themselves, creatures are of necessity dependent on the Creator, to whose will the reasons of their existence are traceable. The reasons of God's existence are in himself alone, and his self-existence is an inalienable attribute of his nature. When he interposes his oath to confirm his word he swears by himself, saying, "As I live," leaving his oath to rest on the immutable basis of his self-existence. In the boundless range of human and angelic thought there will never be found a deeper mystery than the self-existence of God. It defies finite comprehension. God alone knows how he exists, why he exists, why he has always existed, and why he will exist for ever. "Great is the Lord, and greatly to be praised; and his greatness is unsearchable." Ps. cxlv. 3.

2. *Eternity.* The attribute of self-existence suggests that of eternity, or it may be said that the two attributes are suggestive of each other. For if the causes of God's existence are in himself, reason will admit that those causes have been in operation from eternity; and if he is an eternal Being, then he must be self-existent. As to the eternity of God, the Scriptures are plain. We read as follows: " And Abraham planted a grove in Beersheba, and called there on the name of the Lord, the everlasting God." Gen. xxi. 33. " The eternal God is thy refuge, and underneath are the everlasting arms." Deut. xxxiii. 27. " Before the mountains were brought forth, or ever thou hadst formed the earth and the world, even from ever-lasting to everlasting, thou art God." Ps. xc. 2. " Now unto the King eternal, immortal, invisible, the only wise God, be honor and glory for ever and ever." 1 Tim. i. 17 " And they rest not day and night, saying, Holy, holy holy, Lord God Almighty, which was, and is, and is to come." Rev. iv. 8.

These passages are sufficient to show that the God of the Bible is he who "inhabits eternity." He " was," and this includes all the past; he " is," and this includes the present; he " is to come," and this includes all the future. I may avail myself of the eloquent words of one of the most distinguished of American scholars.[1] Referring to God, he says: " His existence in space is an infinite *here;* his existence in duration is an infinite *now.* The waves of two eternities break upon his throne, and it rests unmoved above the flood." We are reminded by the words, " an infinite now," of the language of Peter: " But, beloved, be not ignorant of this one thing, that one day is with the Lord as a thousand years, and a thousand years as one day." 2 Pet. iii. 8. The finite mind is impressed

---

[1] Prof. A. C. Kendrick, D. D., of Rochester University

with the difference between a day and a week, but to the Infinite Mind the distinction between a day and a thousand years is obliterated. Points of time as far apart as the creation of the world and the last judgment are surveyed with the same glance, while intermediate centuries pass "as a watch in the night." This is the case, because God's "existence in duration is an infinite now.' The God of the Bible is the only Being who is absolutely eternal, his existence having neither beginning nor end. In this sense eternity is an attribute peculiarly his own, and on the throne which is "for ever and ever" he must ever sit in majestic isolation. There is no being like Jehovah.

3. *Unity.* The application of this term to God is designed to teach that there is one, and but one, God. The doctrine of God's unity is involved in his self-existence and in the eternity of his being. It is evident that there is need of only one self-existent being in the universe, for self-sufficiency is allied to self-existence. That is to say a self-existent being must be a self-sufficient being, able to do whatever needs to be done and whatever he chooses to do. One self-existent being for ever supersedes the necessity of another; and not only so, but renders the existence of another impossible. There cannot be two self-existent beings, for the very good reason that self-existence implies the possession of *all* perfections. If, then, there could be two such beings, they would each possess all perfections, and would therefore be essentially one and the same. They would fill one and the same sphere—a thing impossible if they were two, and not one. The existence of more than one God comes not within the limits of possibility. The attribute of self-existence establishes this position, and the attribute of eternity fortifies it. For if one God has existed from eternity, there

has been no place for another. The eternity of God is a conclusive proof of his unity. As illustrative of the divine unity I might refer to the system of Nature as indivisible, bearing the impress of one Almighty Agent in all its wide realm, from the revelations of the telescope to the wonders of the microscope, with all intervening displays of oneness of design. But it is time to ask, What do the Scriptures say? Let the earth listen: "Hear, O Israel: The Lord our God is one Lord." Deut. vi. 4. "For thou art great, and doest wondrous things: thou art God alone." Ps. lxxxvi. 10. "Is there a God besides me? Yea, there is no God; I know not any." "Look unto me, and be ye saved, all the ends of the earth: for I am God, and there is none else." Isa. xliv. 8; xlv. 22. "The Lord our God is one Lord." Mark xii. 29. "And this is life eternal, that they might know thee the only true God, and Jesus Christ, whom thou hast sent." John xvii. 3. "For there is one God." 1 Tim. ii. 5. "Thou believest that there is one God; thou doest well." James ii. 19. These passages abundantly prove the doctrine of the divine unity, and the one God claims for himself exclusive worship and service.

4. *Immutability.* Creatures change, everything earthly changes, but God changes not. He is and must be eternally the same, for he is infinitely perfect, and infinite perfection precludes change. There can be no change which does not imply imperfection. It is needless to say that imperfection is implied in a change for the worse, for such a change would indicate imperfection before, and greater imperfection after, its occurrence. It is also true that a change for the better denotes previous imperfection, for such a change is toward perfection. Now, God, whether we consider him as possessing natural or moral attributes, is absolutely perfect. There can be no addi-

tion to the number of his natural attributes, and there can be no increase of their capacity and power. There can be no change in these respects. It would be absurd to suppose that God can be *more* self-existent, *more* eternal, *more* omnipotent than he is. It is equally absurd to suppose that his natural attributes can be alienated from him, or that he can lose them in any way. He must retain them and as his attributes are immutable, he changes not.

As to the moral attributes of the divine character, they also are unchangeable. They bear the stamp of perfection. If God, however, could change in his moral attributes, it would imply imperfection in his moral character If, for example, he could become a better being than he is, it would imply that he is not perfect in goodness. If he could be more just, then justice has not reached its climax in him. If he could be more faithful to his word, his veracity is not perfect. If he could be more holy, it follows that he is not infinitely holy now. I present these suppositions, and the consequences resulting from them if true, to show that they cannot possibly be true. God in his moral as well as in his natural attributes is immutable, and therefore his character is unchangeable. This conclusion is sustained by the following Scriptures: "But thou art the same, and thy years shall have no end." Ps. cii. 27. "For I am the Lord, I change not; therefore ye sons of Jacob are not consumed." Mal. iii. 6. "Every good gift and every perfect gift is from above, and cometh down from the Father of Lights, with whom is no variableness, neither shadow of turning." James i. 17.

The doctrine of God's immutability is replete with joy to his people. They see indications of change in everything around them. They are constantly in the midst of changing scenes; their spiritual emotions change; soon the

mode of their existence will change—for their spirits will
go forth and .leave their bodies to fall into the grave—but
the God of their salvation is unchangeable in his purposes
of love, and says to each one of his children, "The mountains shall depart, and the hills be removed; but my kindness shall not depart from thee, neither shall the covenant
of my peace be removed, saith the Lord, that hath mercy
ᴿ˙ thee." Isa. liv. 10.

5. *Omnipresence.* This is one of the essential attributes
of God. It is his prerogative to be everywhere. Some
make a distinction between the omnipresence and the immensity of God. This distinction will be sufficiently denoted by the following words: "When we call his essence
immense, we mean that it has no limits; when we say
that it is omnipresent, we signify that it is wherever
creatures are."[1] We can imagine remote tracts of space
where creatures are not and have never been, but God is
there. In those places the doctrine of his immensity is
exemplified, but we, for obvious reasons, are more interested in his omnipresence. He is emphatically present
wherever his creatures are. We are lost in wonder in
contemplating this fact. We know that there are hundreds of millions of human beings in the world. They
are on the land, and on the sea, and in the isles of the
sea. Some of them are in high and some in low positions, some rich and others poor, some wise and others
ignorant, some righteous and others wicked—all hasten-
ing to eternity; but the presence of God is with every
one of them. There is no place on this planet where
God is not. If we leave this world and go in our con-
templations to heaven, to "the innumerable company of
angels," to the various orders of the celestial hosts, we
shall find that God is present with them all. Even if the

[1] Dick's *Theology*, Lecture 19.

theories of some astronomers be true, and there are so many worlds that their number cannot be computed, and all peopled with rational beings, God is in all those worlds and present with every one of those beings. Well did David say, "Whither shall I go from thy Spirit, or whither shall I flee from thy presence? If I ascend up into heaven, thou art there; if I make my bed in hell, behold, thou art there. If I take the wings of the morning, and dwell in the uttermost parts of the sea, even there shall thy hand lead me, and thy right hand shall hold me. If I say, Surely the darkness shall cover me, even the night shall be light about me. Yea, the darkness hideth not from thee, but the night shineth as the day; the darkness and the light are both alike to thee." Ps. cxxxix. 7–12.

How transcendently great is God! How deeply should his omnipresence impress us! The practical influence of the doctrine should ever be seen in restraining from sin. God is everywhere. How absurd to suppose that sin can be committed where he is not! He is in every place. He knows every act performed, every word spoken, every thought entertained, every feeling indulged.

> "Oh, may these thoughts possess my breast
> Where'er I rove, where'er I rest!
> Nor let my weaker passions dare
> Consent to sin, for God is there."

6. *Omnipotence.* By this attribute of God is meant his unlimited power, his power to do whatever he chooses to do. Finite beings can form nothing more than a feeble conception of this power. They exercise what power they have in contracted spheres and under necessary limitations. It is a secondary power derived from God the Source of supreme power. Accustomed to manifesta

tions of imperfect power among men, we are amazed in contemplating the almighty power of God. His omnipotence, however, is conceded by all who believe in his existence. There is no more striking proof of divine power than the work of creation. The central idea in the term "creation" is the production of something out of nothing. To create is not to select and adjust pre-existent materials, but to give existence to that which did not exist before. A created thing springs of necessity from the abyss of nothingness. It follows, therefore, that omnipotence alone was adequate to the work of creation as described in the divine word. God was able to perform this work, because the attribute of omnipotence belongs inalienably to him. Hence we read, " In the beginning God created the heaven and the earth." Gen. i. 1. He said, "Let there be light, and there was light." Gen. i. 3. The ease with which this majestic work was done seems to be indicated by the Psalmist: "He spake, and it was done; he commanded, and it stood fast." Ps. xxxiii. 9. The almighty power of God is seen, not only in the creation of all things, but also in their preservation. He is said to " uphold all things by the word of his power," and "by him all things consist." Heb. i. 3 ; Col. i. 17. The preservation of all things requires the constant exertion of the power employed in their creation. When we remember that God created things visible and invisible; that the invisible are far more numerous than the visible; and that all these things, seen and unseen, are kept in existence by him,—we are filled with reverential awe. We recognize the truth of the words addressed to Abraham: "I am the Almighty God." Gen. xxvii. 1. The Scriptures, both of the Old Testament and the New, ascribe omnipotence to Jehovah. We therefore read, "Thou, even thou, art Lord alone; thou hast made heaven, the heaven of heavens, with all their host, the earth and all things that are therein, the seas and all that is therein, and thou preservest them all; and the host of heaven worshippeth thee." Neh. ix. 6. "Behold, thou hast made the heaven and the earth by thy great power and stretched out arm, and there is nothing too hard for thee." Jer. xxxii. 17. "With God all things are possible." Matt. xix. 26. "The Lord God omnipotent reigneth." Rev. xix. 6.

Those who love God may well rejoice in the thought that all power is his, that he sits on the throne, sways a universal sceptre, controls all things, and exercises his omnipotence in behalf of those who trust in him.

7. *Omniscience.* This term denotes the infinite intelligence of God—his knowledge of all things. Like every other attribute we have considered, the omniscience of God defies our comprehension. We know very little, and while in this world will probably not turn over the first page of the book of knowledge. How impossible, then, to take in the idea of universal knowledge! The little knowledge we acquire is usually gained by laborious study. We learn one thing, and infer from it another, and thus we proceed, drawing conclusions which we lay down as premises from which to draw other conclusions. How, then, can we comprehend the Infinite Mind, which knows all things by intuition? We speak of knowledge as of the past, the present, and the future. What shall we say of God, to whom the past and the future are not distinguished from the present, and whose knowledge, therefore, is not successive, but perfectly simultaneous? The Psalmist's words at once suggest themselves: "Such knowledge is too wonderful for me; it is high, I cannot attain unto it." Ps. cxxxix. 6. The omniscience of God is in harmony with his omnipresence and his omnipotence. Being every

where in all parts of his vast dominions at al. times, he knows what needs to be done, and his omnipotence is equal to any exigency that may arise. What a blessing that the universe has an omnipresent, omnipotent, and omniscient God!

The theory which some hold concerning the omniscience of God is an absurdity—namely, that as God's omnipotence is his ability to do all things he pleases to do, but he does not please to do all things; so his omniscience is his ability to know all things, but he does not choose to know all things. To banish this theory from the world it is only necessary to say that, even in accordance with it, God must first know all things before he could decide which to know and which not to know.

The doctrine of God's omniscience is clearly revealed in the Bible, as the following passages show: "The Lord searcheth all hearts, and understandeth all the imaginations of the thoughts." 1 Chron. xxviii. 9. "His understanding is infinite." Ps. cxlvii. 5. "I am God and there is none like me, declaring the end from the beginning, and from ancient times the things that are not yet done." Isa. xlvi. 9, 10. "Oh, the depth of the riches both of the wisdom and knowledge of God!" Rom. xi. 33. "All things are naked and opened unto the eyes of him with whom we have to do." Heb. iv. 13. "For if our heart condemn us, God is greater than our heart, and knoweth all things." 1 John iii. 20. "And all the churches shall know that I am he who searcheth the reins and hearts." Rev. ii. 23.

Reflections on the omniscience of God should afford his people comfort and joy at all times, but especially when their motives are misconceived, their words misinterpreted, and their acts misconstrued. It is a source of high satisfaction on such occasions to think that God, who knows all things, looks approvingly on his persecuted children.

II. THE MORAL ATTRIBUTES OF GOD.

1. *Goodness.* The disposition in God to impart happiness to his creatures is called his goodness. Whether the term *happiness* can be properly applied to irrational creatures may be questioned; but they experience what is called animal enjoyment. Of this, the gambols of lambs and the singing of birds are proofs. There is, perhaps, much more of this enjoyment among the various orders of animals than we suppose. According to their different capacities, they find satisfaction, and even pleasure, in the spheres in which they move. Their eyes wait on God, and he giveth them their meat in due season. Thus he displays his goodness, but this is the lower grade of his goodness; its higher manifestations have reference to rational and accountable beings.

God is good to angels. His love is in constant exercise toward them, and is included in his goodness. This love is expressed in their preservation and in the bestowal of all the blessings which render their existence a perpetual joy. They derive their happiness from God, for he is the "blessed" or "happy God," the fountain of felicity, and it is his delight to communicate of his blessedness to all the angelic hosts. He is ever displaying his goodness and manifesting his love. It has been his pleasure to give to angels a nature which, so far as we know, is exclusively spiritual. If we ask why, the answer is to be found in the words of Jesus: "Even so, Father, for so it seemed good in thy sight." Matt. xi. 26.

God's goodness to men has been differently manifested. They are complex beings, made up of body and spirit

5 *

The divine goodness is seen in their twofold organization. The constitution of their bodies is such that their senses are inlets of great pleasure and enjoyment. Who does not say with Solomon, "Truly the light is sweet, and a pleasant thing it is for the eyes to behold the sun"? Eccles. xi. 7. Who has not enjoyed the fragrance of flowers? Who has not been thrown into ecstasy by the sweet strains of music? God might have made the senses the medium only of pain and disgust: he might have rendered every object of sight as repulsive as the loathsome serpent, every object of taste as bitter as wormwood, every object of smell as offensive as a putrefying carcass, every object of touch as painful as the piercing of the thorn, and every sound as doleful as the wail of sorrow. God's goodness is seen in the formation of our bodies with a view to physical enjoyment.

So also of our mental constitution. How elevated are the pleasures of the intellect! The powers of the mind, if rightly improved, are sources of much enjoyment. Who in the acquisition of knowledge has not been made glad? Who has not felt the impulse to strive after higher and larger attainments? It is the possession of intellect which raises man above the beasts that perish and allies him to the angels of God. Indeed, so far as his intellectual nature is concerned, man, even since his fall, is made after the similitude of God. James iii. 9. He is a rational creature; and when we think of the pleasures resulting from rationality, we see plainly the goodness of God in man's mental constitution.

His moral organization likewise indicates the goodness of God. This is inseparable from his mental constitution. He is a moral, accountable agent, because he is a rational creature. His rational nature makes him a proper subject of moral government, and his moral nature enables him to appreciate his relations to God and to hold fellowship with him. Evidently, man was made that he might glorify God and enjoy him for ever, and the adaptation of his moral nature to these ends shows the goodness of God.

Time would fail in referring to the providential blessings which God bestows on men. From the cradle to the grave there is a constant succession of providential kindnesses which proclaim the goodness of God. Thus are we reminded of the words of David: "The Lord is good to all." Ps. cxlv. 9. The goodness or love of God in redemption is supremely worthy of notice. This phase of divine goodness has to do, not with angels, but with men. It is peculiar to sinners of Adam's fallen race. It is therefore written, "God commendeth his love toward us, in that, while we were yet sinners, Christ died for us." Rom. v. 8. "Herein is love, not that we loved God, but that he loved us, and sent his Son to be the propitiation for our sins." 1 John iv. 10. To a certain point the goodness or love of God to angels and men is identical and coincident, but beyond that point it may be said, so far as men are concerned, to diverge into grace and mercy. That is to say, grace and mercy are terms not applicable to holy angels, but to sinful men. Grace always implies unworthiness in its recipients. They are unworthy, because they are sinners. Their sinfulness creates their un-worthiness. If saved, they must be saved as unworthy, and therefore saved by grace. There is no salvation to the unworthy but by grace, and grace implies the justice of the condemnation of the unworthy; for if they are not justly condemned, they may claim deliverance from condemnation as a matter of right and of debt. The capital fact of the gospel is that grace reigns in the salvation of the unworthy. While grace regards men as unworthy

mercy contemplates them as miserable and wretched. It
therefore means all that is included in pity, compassion
and kindred terms. The goodness of God, assuming the
form of mercy, commiserates sinners in their ruin and
wretchedness. This mercy will be glorified in the sal
vation of unnumbered millions in heaven.

2. *Justice.* This attribute may be considered in two
aspects—internal and external. In the former sense, it
refers to the moral uprightness and excellence of the
divine character; in the latter, to the inflexible rectitude of the divine conduct. God is infinitely just. In
his bosom justice has its seat and its throne. Because of
the perfect righteousness of his character it is infallibly
certain that he will do right—that is, act in accordance
with the principles of justice. He can make no compro-
mise with wrong, nor can he connive at evil in any of its
forms. The thought of injustice is infinitely remote from
him. Being perfectly just, he is just in all he does. The
Bible therefore says, " The Lord is righteous in all his
ways." Ps. cxlv. 17. He himself says, " Judgment also
will I lay to the line, and righteousness to the plummet "
(Isa. xxviii. 17), and Paul declares that God " will judge the
world in righteousness." Acts xvii. 31. A reference to the
day of judgment suggests that on that day the ways of
God will be vindicated, and it will be clearly seen that in
his government of the world, and in the distribution of
the rewards and punishments of eternity, there has not
been the slightest deviation from the great principles of
justice. God not only administers the affairs of his vast
empire in accordance with righteousness, but he intends
that all the subjects of that empire shall see and acknowledge it.

The justice of God sustains so important a relation to
sin that it has been considered by some as the perfection

which is specially displayed in the punishment of sin. It certainly requires the punishment of sinners, and they should be punished on account of their ill-desert. No other theory of punishment is defensible. Two theories have been earnestly advocated: The one affirms that punishment should be inflicted with a view to the reformation of the guilty; and the other, with a view to the prevention of crime. According to the former opinion, if the guilty are too bad to be reformed, they need not be punished; so that the more wicked a criminal is, the less propriety there is in punishing him. This is too absurd to think of. According to the latter opinion, it would follow that there is no reason why the guilty alone should suffer punishment. It might, according to this theory, be applied to any person whatever, if there were any danger at all that he might be led into sin. It would be merciful to inflict the punishment beforehand, and prevent him from incurring guilt. Neither opinion will stand examination. The reformation of criminals and the prevention of crime are only secondary objects in punishment. The primary, the supreme, reason for the infliction of punishment is found in the fact that there is inherent ill-desert in sin, and therefore the guilty *deserve* to be punished.

The death of Christ furnishes the most impressive and even appalling exhibition of divine justice. An able writer has forcibly said, "If God could have permitted sin to escape with impunity, if the determination to punish it had not proceeded from his nature, but merely from his will, he would not have subjected his own Son to a cruel and ignominious death. . . . No; the unavoidable conclusion is, that the death of Christ was the indispensable condition of the redemption of the world; that the designs of mercy, abstractly considered, were at variance with the demands of justice; and that, to establish harmony between them, it was necessary that justice should be satisfied. This was the most solemn display of justice —the highest proof that it is as truly an attribute of the divine nature as power and wisdom. It no longer admits of a doubt that there is a necessary connection between guilt and punishment. Who can hope for impunity if the Son of God did not escape?"[1]

3. *Veracity.* Writers on theology usually employ the term "truth" in this connection. I prefer veracity, because it is more applicable to persons, while truth more properly refers to things. A man of veracity makes a true statement. Veracity is, therefore, a personal moral attribute, and truth is a property of things. This being the case, veracity is that perfection in God which renders all his judgments according to truth, which prompts him to say what is true, and which makes it impossible for him to lie. The impossibility is moral, not natural. That is, God has the natural ability to say what is not true, but the infinite excellence of his character, including his veracity, makes it morally impossible for him to lie. Jesus in praying for his disciples addressed his Father thus: "Sanctify them through thy truth: thy word is truth." John xvii. 17. The word of God is true, because veracity is one of the attributes of his moral character. Whatever that word says as to the past, the present, or the future is true, for the truth of God endures to all generations. "A God of truth and without iniquity, just and right is he." Deut. xxxii. 4. Truth, in the highest sense of the word, is a correct representation of things as they have been, as they now are, or as they will be for ever. In this view the term truth is fully applicable to all that God says, for, though heaven and earth shall pass away, his words will not pass away.

[1] Dick's *Theology*, Lecture xxv.

The veracity of God comprehends his faithfulness, and his faithfulness includes the fulfilment of his promises and the execution of his threatenings. The certain performance of the divine promises may be argued from the omniscience of God. Men make promises, not knowing the future; and the occurrences of the future make the doing of what they had promised impossible. It is not so with God. When he made his promises, he knew all the future; and if he had seen anything to prevent their accomplishment, they would not have been made. The promises are given in Christ: Paul says, "For all the promises of God in him are yea, and in him Amen, unto the glory of God by us." 2 Cor. i. 20. As the promises are in Christ, God in fulfilling them will, if I may so say, draw on the exhaustless mediatorial resources of his beloved Son. Then, too, as the promises are to the divine glory, whatever considerations prompt God to take care of his glory will prompt him to fulfil his promises. This of itself is a sufficient reason for believing that God will do what he has promised. The promises of God, giving his people assurances of blessings on earth and in heaven, open to view a sacred realm too large to be explored. I do not enter it, but only say that the day will doubtless come when all the redeemed from the heights of glory will say, as did Joshua on his dying day, "Not one thing hath failed of all the good things which the Lord your God spake concerning you." Josh xxiii. 14.

God shows his faithfulness to his word in executing his threatenings. His veracity makes the execution of his threatenings as certain as the performance of his promises. His incorrigible enemies cannot escape his wrath "There is no darkness, nor shadow of death, where the workers of iniquity may hide themselves." Job **xxxiv**

22. On the very day when the Lord Jesus shall come "to be glorified in his saints" we are told that he "will be revealed from heaven with his mighty angels, in flaming fire taking vengeance on them that know not God, and that obey not the gospel of our Lord Jesus Christ: who shall be punished with everlasting destruction from the pre nce of the Lord, and from the glory of his power." 2 Thess. i. 7–9. Fidelity to his word, whether it be word of promise or word of threatening, is included in God's veracity.

4. *Wisdom.* There is a distinction between omniscience and wisdom. We may conceive of knowledge so vast as to imply acquaintance with all things, and we may imagine such knowledge as unused or not used for valuable purposes. In this there would be no wisdom, for wisdom always makes use of knowledge for some good end. Wisdom implies knowledge. To this extent .t may be classed among the natural attributes of God. But there is something in wisdom additional to knowledge; and wisdom in this sense, as using knowledge for purposes worthy of the moral character of God, may be regarded as one of his moral attributes. Or it may be considered as a divine attribute partly natural and partly moral. The proofs of God's wisdom in creation, providence, and redemption justify this view. It has been said so often as to be quite familiar, that wisdom consists in the choice of proper ends, and proper means to accomplish them. The two things must be united. Unworthy ends, whatever the means to effect them, would exhibit no wisdom; and worthy ends with means so unsuitable as to defeat their accomplishment would be no proof of wisdom. In the works of God we have worthy ends and proper means. David, in referring to these works, said, "O Lord, how manifold are thy works in wisdom hast thou made them all." Ps. civ. 24. In an exhaustive work on this subject specific references would be made to his various works as showing the wisdom of God. It would be interesting thus to dwell on the formation of the earth, the constitution of the atmosphere, the tides of the ocean, the position of the sun, the instincts of animals, the bodily organism of the human frame, man's intellectual powers, his consciousness of accountability and free agency, and all the works of creation opened to our view. But we can only make to these this brief reference. The providence of God also opens a large volume illustrative of his wisdom. Into this volume we must not look even far enough to see how wisely God preserves and governs what he has made.

Redemption through Christ is a luminous display of the wisdom of God. Wisdom appears in rendering the glory of God and the salvation of man compatible; in harmonizing law and justice with mercy; in manifesting divine love to sinners and hatred of their sins; in the manner in which the conscience is tranquillized; in providing for the interests of practical holiness; in humbling and elevating the saved; and in making the Saviour's death, instigated by Satan, the means of overturning Satan's empire. Who can contemplate topics like these without adopting the words of Paul?—" Wherein he hath abounded toward us in all wisdom and prudence." Eph. i. 8. Who does not exclaim?—" Oh, the depth of the riches both of the wisdom and knowledge of God!" Rom. xi. 33. It is not strange that angels are students of the science of redemption, for we are told that they desire to look into the things reported in the gospel.

5. *Holiness.* The holiness of God is often assigned a place among the moral attributes of the divine nature; yet, strictly speaking, it is not a single attribute, but

rather a combination of all the moral attributes of God. If we consider this combination, this aggregation, of moral perfections, and gaze on the glory radiating there-from, we shall probably have the scriptural idea of "the beauty of holiness." The definition of the term holiness, as now given, will enable us to understand several passages of Scripture in which there seems to be a manifest purpose to ascribe all moral excellence to God, and yet he is not referred to as good and just, but only as holy. The following is a specimen of these passages: " Who is like unto thee, O Lord, among the gods? who is like thee, glorious in holiness, fearful in praises, doing wonders?" Ex. xv. 11. " Holy, holy, holy is the Lord of hosts: the whole earth is full of his glory." Isa. vi. 3. " Be ye holy, for I am holy." 1 Pet. i. 16. " Who shall not fear thee, O Lord, and glorify thy name? for thou only art holy." Rev. xv. 4. It would be absurd to suppose that in these passages goodness, justice, and veracity are not attributed to God, but they are not mentioned. They are, however, comprehended in the holiness, which is evidently referred to as inclusive of the moral excellences of the divine character. The view now expressed concerning the holiness of God is substantially the view of Andrew Fuller. He uses the following words: "There are certain perfections which all who acknowledge a God agree in attributing to him; such are those of wisdom, power, immutability, etc. These, by Christian divines, are usually termed his *natural* perfections. There are others which no less evidently belong to Deity, such as goodness, justice, veracity, etc., all which may be expressed in one word—*holiness;* and these are usually termed his moral perfections." [1]

A profound American theologian uses these words

[1] *Complete Works*, vol. ii. p. 9.

" Goodness, truth, and justice are moral attributes of God. Holiness is not an attribute distinct from these, but a name which includes them all, in view of their opposition to contrary qualities. It implies the perfection of the assemblage—the absence of everything in it contrary to either of the properties included." [1]

Dr. A. A. Hodge expresses himself very forcibly as follows : " The holiness of God is not to be conceived of as one attribute among others ; it is rather a general term representing the conception of his consummate perfection and total glory. It is his infinite moral perfection crowning his infinite intelligence and power. There is a glory of each attribute, viewed abstractly, and a glory of the whole together. The intellectual nature is the essential basis of the moral. Infinite moral perfection is the crown of the Godhead. Holiness is the total glory thus crowned." [2]

Such is holiness, rendering the divine character the bright centre in which all the lines of moral perfection and beauty and glory meet.

[1] Dr. Dagg's *Theology*, p. 86.   [2] *Outlines of Theology*, pp. 127 128.

CHAPTER IV.

THE TRINITY.

WHILE the Bible teaches the unity of God—that there is one and only one God—it also teaches that in the one Godhead there is a distinction of persons. The distinction is threefold. It is such as to justify the use of the terms Father, Son, and Holy Spirit. The recognition of these three persons as equally belonging to the Godhead is in theology styled the Doctrine of the Trinity. The idea intended to be conveyed by this term is that of *three in one.* It is not meant that the three divine persons are three in the sense in which they are one, or that they are one in the sense in which they are three. I have seen no better definition of the term Trinity than I find in Webster's Dictionary—namely, "The union of three persons (the Father, the Son, and the Holy Spirit) in one Godhead, so that all the three are one God as to substance, but three persons as to individuality." It must be admitted that the word *person* in its Trinitarian sense is not wholly free from objection, but it seems to be understood by orthodox writers that there is no better word. The objection is, that it cannot be used in its common acceptation as applied to human beings. It needs modification. For example, *person* in the ordinary use of the term means a distinct and independent being, so that one person is one being, and a hundred persons are a hundred

64

eings. But in the Godhead there are three persons and one Being. The dissimilarity in the two instances is manifest.

The doctrine of the Trinity is one of mysterious grandeur, which defies the comprehension of every finite mind, and must be received as true on the authority of the Bible. The wisest men have most readily confessed their inability to explain Trinity in Unity or Unity in Trinity. Prof. Moses Stuart well remarks, in his second letter to Dr. Channing: "What, then, you will doubtless ask, is the specific nature of that distinction in the Godhead which the word *person* is meant to designate? I answer, without hesitation, that I do not know. The fact that a distinction exists is what we aver; the specific definition of that distinction is what I shall by no means attempt to make out. By what shall I, or can I, define it? What simile drawn from created objects, which are necessarily *derived* and *dependent*, can illustrate the mode of existence in that Being who is underived, independent, unchangeable, infinite, eternal? I confess myself unable to advance a single step here in explaining what the distinction is. *I re ceive the* FACT *that it exists, simply because I believe that the Scriptures reveal the* FACT. And if the Scriptures do reveal the fact that there are three *persons* in the Godhead; that there is a distinction which affords grounds for the respective appellations of Father, Son, and Holy Ghost; which lays the foundation for the application of the personal pronouns, *I, Thou, He;* which renders it proper to speak of *sending* and *being sent;* to speak of Christ as *being with God, being in his bosom,* and of other things of the like nature in the like way, and yet to hold that the divine nature equally belongs to each,—then it is, like every fact revealed, to be received simply on the credit of divine revelation."[1]

[1] *Miscellanies,* p. 23.

It has by some been made an objection to the **doctrine** of the Trinity that the word is not to be found in the Bible. This is true, but there is no weight in the objection if what is meant by the term is there; and this I shall attempt to show. I merely notice, without enlarging on the fact, that in the Old Testament, in several places, when God speaks the plural number is used, as in the following passages: " Let us make man in our image;" " Behold the man is become as one of us;" " Let us go down and there confound their language;" " Whom shall I send, and who will go for us?" Gen. i. 26; iii. 22; xi. 7; Isa. vi. 8. These forms of expression are certainly peculiar, and there is nothing incredible in the supposition that they were used as intimations of a plurality of persons in the Godhead—a fact to be distinctly revealed in the New Testament. The teachings of Christ and his apostles are too plain to be misunderstood. In Matthew **xxviii.** 19, Jesus says, " Go ye therefore, and teach [disciple] all nations, baptizing them in the name of the Father, and of the Son, and of the Holy Ghost." I shall enter into no critical examination of the import of the phrase " in the name," nor inquire whether it might be more properly rendered " into the name." It is enough for my present purpose to notice that baptism is connected with the name of every person in the Godhead. There is no consistent interpretation of the language which does not place on equality the Father, the Son, and the Holy Spirit. If the Deity of one of these persons is recognized, there is a recognition of the Deity of the three. It is impossible to make a valid distinction as to equality and sameness of nature. The Deity of the Father will be acknowledged by all who believe there is a God. This point, then, is settled. Now, as to the Son and the Holy Spirit, who could without a shudder hear of the name of angel or archangel as substituted in place of the name of either ? Why ? Because of the blasphemous inconsistency of exalting creatures to an equality with God.

But the name of the Son and the name of the Holy Spirit are joined with the name of the Father, and the conjunction is so important that the validity of baptism is inseparable from it. The doctrine of the Trinity must be true.

Some, conceding the personality of the Father and of the Son, have supposed the Holy Spirit to be an "energy" or an "influence." To show the absurdity of this view it is only necessary to point to the absurdity of baptizing in the name of an " energy " or an " influence " in connection with baptism in the name of the Father and of the Son. It is plain that the reference, in the last commission of Christ, to the Father, the Son, and the Holy Spirit, is a reference to persons, and not to energies or influences.

The doctrine of the Trinity is distinctly brought to view in 2 Cor. xiii. 14: " The grace of the Lord Jesus Christ, and the love of God, and the communion of the Holy Ghost be with you all." These words constitute what is usually called the apostolic benediction, and they are an invocation. The love of God the Father is in voked. This is too manifest to be denied. The grace of the Lord Jesus Christ is also mentioned, as is the communion of the Holy Spirit. It transcends all belief that the grace of the Son and the communion of the Spirit are referred to in immediate connection with the love of God the Father if the three persons are not the same in substance and equal in glory. Should the names Gabriel and Michael, conspicuous among angelic spirits, be put in place of the names Lord Jesus Christ and Holy Spirit, all who reverence the Scriptures would revolt from the blasphemous substitution. They would protest against the elevation of the highest order of creatures to an equality with God. In the benediction, however, the Lord Jesus Christ and the Holy Spirit are invoked as well as God the Father—a fact which shows the equality of the three persons.

In Ephesians ii. 18 we read, "For through him we both have access by one Spirit to the Father." Here the three persons of the Godhead are referred to, and the passage confirms the view already presented. In Revelation i. 4, 5 we have this remarkable language : "Grace be unto you, and peace from him which is, and which was, and which is to come; and from the seven spirits which are before his throne ; and from Jesus Christ, who is the faithful Witness." As seven was the perfect number among the Jews, we are to understand by " the seven spirits " the Holy Spirit in the plenitude of his gifts, in the completeness and diversity of his beneficent operations. If this view is correct, the point to which special attention is called is, that grace and peace are sought from the Holy Spirit and from Jesus Christ, as well as from him " which was, which is, and which is to come." These last words indicate existence from eternity to eternity, one of the attributes of Supreme Deity ; and as Jesus Christ and the Holy Spirit are named in conjunction with him who was, is, and is to come, the irresistible inference is that they are equally divine.

The argument in favor of the doctrine of the Trinity supplied by the use of the personal pronouns, " *I, Thou, He,*" is worthy of some expansion. The passages in the Bible are almost numberless in which God, in referring to himself, says, *I, mine,* and *me :* "As I live, saith the Lord ;" "I am the Lord ;" "All souls are mine ;" "Every beast of the forest is mine :" " Besides me there is no Saviour ;' " Prove me now herewith, saith the Lord of Hosts." There are passages, too, in which the Father and the Son say to each other *thou, thee,* and *thine:* "Thou art my Son; this day have I begotten thee;" "Thou hast loved righteousness;" "As thou hast given him power over all flesh;" "All mine are thine, and thine are mine." While the Father and the Son address each other in the use of the personal pronouns, *thou, thee,* and *thine,* the Spirit is referred to as *he* and *him:* "But the Comforter, which is the Holy Ghost, whom the Father will send in my name, he shall teach you all things" (John xiv. 26); "He shall glorify me" (xvi. 14); "The Comforter whom I will send unto you." xv. 26. It is needless to multiply proofs that the Spirit was to be sent by the Father and the Son. The Father is said to have sent the Son into the world, but neither the Son nor the Spirit is ever said to have sent the Father. The Son is represented as becoming flesh and dying, but this is not true of the Father and the Spirit. In view of these significant facts it is obvious that there is such a threefold distinction of persons in the Godhead as to justify and to require the use of the terms Father, Son, and Spirit. Nor does this threefold distinction conflict with the unity of God, for the three persons are one in substance, while they are three in individuality. These two truths present unity in Trinity.

It may be well, before dismissing this topic, to notice that equality of nature may consist with inequality in office. The most zealous Trinitarian will admit that while the three persons of the Godhead are equal in nature and in essential glory, there is, on the part of the Son and the Holy Spirit, official inferiority. There are various scriptures in which the Father is represented as supreme in office. That is, the Son and the Spirit act in subordination to him. For this reason God is said to have sent his Son into the world, and the Son is said to have come in the flesh.   Here we have inferiority, in the sense that he who is sent is inferior to him who sends The Son is also recognized as the servant of the Father, for it is said, " Behold my servant whom I have chosen." Matt. xii. 18.   As the servant is subordinate to the master, so was the Son subordinate to the Father.   Christ said again and again, " I came to do the will of him that sent me."   As doing the will of another denotes inferiority, so Christ in doing the will of the Father appears as his inferior.   But the inferiority is in office, not in nature; the subordination is official, and does not touch the divine substance.   Here there is perfect, undisturbed equality.   What I have said of the second person of the Godhead may be said substantially of the third.   When God the Father says, " I will pour out of my Spirit upon all flesh," when he is said to "give the Holy Spirit," and when Jesus says, " The Comforter whom I will send unto you," there is manifest reference to inequality of office There is the sublimest equality of nature.   Official inferiority and natural equality may be easily illustrated. The President of the United States is officially superior to any and every man in the nation.   All the men who hold office are, so far as official position is concerned, inferior to him.   No one aspires to be his equal.   But in nature every citizen of the republic is his equal—that is, every citizen possesses the same human nature.   Equality in nature and inferiority in office are therefore exemplified in matters both human and divine.

In contemplating the doctrine of the Trinity as an unspeakable mystery we must ever guard against looking on it as a profitless speculation, without practical influence.   The very fact that the subject is so far above our comprehension should inspire us with reverential modesty and humility.   The highest flights of reason cannot reach it, yet the doctrine is among "the true sayings of God." Alas, how little we know! God is infinite—we are finite, and can know but little of him and the mode of his existence. Where we cannot understand, let us wonder and adore. The economy of redemption seems to have been arranged in recognition of a distinction of persons in the Godhead, and hence the three persons are represented as acting their respective parts in the great work. It is our privilege to consider the love which had been lodged in the Father's bosom from eternity as expressing itself in the gift of his Son; to contemplate the Son as pouring forth his soul unto death, thus procuring redemption by his blood; and to rejoice in the work of the Spirit in renewing the heart, sanctifying the soul, and fitting it for heaven. We should never forget that in baptism there is avowed consecration to the Father, the Son, and the Holy Spirit. The doctrine of the Trinity, as it is recognized in baptism, has much to do with experimental and practical piety. Far, far from us be the idea that the existence of three persons in the Godhead is a barren speculation. It is a truth both mysterious and grand, and its influence should be eminently salutary. One of its effects should be the stimulation of desire on the part of Christians to be one even as the three persons of the Godhead are one. Who can think of the Father, the Son, and the Holy Spirit as one—one in nature, one in love, one in purpose—and not hope for the day when the intercessory prayer of Christ will be answered in the union of all his followers?

CHAPTER V.

THE DEITY OF CHRIST.

If the argument presented in the foregoing chapter is conclusive in favor of the doctrine of the Trinity, the Deity of Christ must be admitted. That is, if Christ is the second person of the Godhead, he is divine, the same in essence with the Father and the Holy Spirit, to whom he is by a blessed necessity equal in power and glory. This being the case, some suppose that a special discussion of Christ's Deity is needless. This is a very plausible opinion, to which I should yield if the subject was not of transcendent importance. Being fully satisfied, however, that the supreme divinity of the Lord Jesus is the basis of the system of Christianity, and that without this basis the system has no saving value, I deem it proper to assign to the Deity of Christ a distinct prominence.

Before adducing proofs that Christ is God, I wish to present a few considerations to prepare the way for these proofs, and to induce a higher appreciation of them.

1. *Christ both in the Old Testament and the New is represented as acting the part of Substitute for those he came to save.* We therefore read, " But he was wounded for our transgressions, he was bruised for our iniquities, the chastisement of our peace was upon him, and with his stripes we are healed. . . . . The Lord hath laid on him the iniquity of us all." Isa. liii. 5, 6. "Even as the Son of man came

not to be ministered unto, but to minister, and to give his life a ransom for many." Matt. xx. 28. "The good Shepherd giveth his life for the sheep." John x. 11. "Christ hath redeemed us from the curse of the law, being made a curse for us." Gal. iii. 13. These are but a specimen of the passages which teach that Christ took the place of those whom he saves, and died in their stead. I might refer to other passages from which we learn that we are forgiven and saved for Jesus' sake, but it is not necessary It will be conceded that the gospel teaches that sinners are saved, because Jesus has done and suffered something for them. As to the specific nature of what he did and suffered, I do not now inquire. I only assume that he was the Substitute of those who are saved by him, and that they are saved through his mediation.

2. *If Christ is not divine, he could not have taken the place of sinners, so as to make atonement for their sins.* One creature cannot, in the government of God, take the place of another. An angel cannot act in the room of a man. Why? Because all that an angel can do is, on his own personal account, due to God. This is the universal law of creatureship. It asserts its claims in all worlds, and will assert them for ever. Now, suppose Christ to have been a created being. Take the Arian view, first espoused in the fourth century. Arius conceded that Christ was the most exalted of beings, next to God, but he said also, " There was a time when the Son was not." Thus he refused to accord to the Son the attribute of eternity, and there cannot be Deity without eternity of existence. If we suppose, for argument's sake, the doctrine of Arius to be true, and that Christ, however highly exalted in the scale of being, is not God, but a creature, then it follows that he was personally bound to serve God the Creator His creatureship must have imposed on him personal

obligations, rendering it impossible for him to act in the room of others. Creatureship and substitution are not consistent with each other. They cannot stand together. "Thou shalt love the Lord thy God with all thy strength" (Mark xii. 30), is the law which extends its jurisdiction over the whole realm of creatureship. If *all* the creature's strength is to be exerted in the love and service of God on account of the creature's personal relation to the Creator, then there is no remaining strength to be used in any other way or for any other purpose. If Jesus was merely a created being, he must, like other creatures, act for himself alone. It is plain, therefore, that if Christ is not divine, he could not have taken the place of sinners, so as to die for them and make atonement for their sins.

3. *If Christ, as a created being, could have taken the place of sinners, suffering in their stead, there would not have been saving merit in his sufferings.* We speak of the different orders of rational creatures, but they are substantially one. As compared with God, their diversity as to each other disappears. If one creature fails to meet his obligations to God, how can another creature atone for the failure by satisfying the law which has been violated? There must be merit to satisfy the claims of God's law. But where is merit to be found in anything a creature can do? When creatures have done all required of them, Jesus teaches them to say, "We are unprofitable servants: we have done that which was our duty to do." Luke xvii. 10. On the supposition that Christ, as a mere creature, died for sinners, what saving merit could there be in his blood? When creatures deserved perdition, could the death of a creature effect their salvation? The law of God can recognize merit in that only which does honor to its preceptive and penal claims. Nothing that a creature can do or

suffer can confer this honor. There is an absence of merit, and there can be no merit unless it is found in a Being in whom the divine element supplies it.

In view of these considerations it is perfectly clear that Christ, unless divine, could have done nothing in the matter of human salvation. It would not have been possible for him to act in the room of others; and had it been possible, he could not have saved them. There is absolutely no hope for any sinner of Adam's race unless the Word who in the beginning was with God was God. John i. 1. This eternal Word, the second person in the Trinity, being above law, free from the obligations of creatureship, was at his own disposal, and could, if so inclined, place himself under a law enacted for the government of creatures. This the advocates of Christ's Deity believe he has done, and that the fact is recorded in these words: "God sent forth his Son, made of a woman, made under the law, to redeem them that were under the law." Gal. iv. 4, 5. Obeying the precepts of the law in his life and suffering its penalty in his death, the divine nature in the twofold constitution of his person imparted infinite worth to his obedience and sufferings. The law was magnified and made honorable, while a way was opened for the consistent exercise of mercy in the salvation of the guilty. This was done if Christ was divine, but on no other supposition. We may now proceed to consider in order some of the more prominent proofs of Christ's Deity. They are such as these:

I. DIVINE NAMES ARE GIVEN TO HIM. Before establishing this by direct quotations from the New Testament, I will name some passages in the Old Testament which without doubt refer to God in the supreme sense of the term, and are by the New Testament writers applied to Christ. In Ps. xlv. 6 it is written, "Thy throne, O God, is for ever and ever: the sceptre of thy kingdom is a right sceptre." In Heb. i. 8 we read, " But unto the Son he saith, Thy throne, O God, is for ever and ever: a sceptre of righteousness is the sceptre of thy kingdom." It is worthy of special notice that these words, as used in the Epistle to the Hebrews, are found in the midst of an argument to prove the pre-eminent dignity of Christ by showing his superiority to angels. It would be difficult to explain why the inspired writer wished to prove Christ's superiority to angels if he did not intend to teach his equality with God. It is indisputable that the Father in addressing the Son applies to him the term God: " Thy throne, O God."

Isaiah in the sixth chapter of his prophecy records a wonderful vision, in which he saw the Lord " high and lifted up, and his train filled the temple." He saw the six-winged seraphim, and heard them cry with reverential awe, " Holy, holy, holy is the Lord of hosts: the whole earth is full of his glory." No one will deny that the Lord Jehovah of hosts is the supreme God. But in the twelfth chapter of the Gospel of John we are referred to this vision of the prophet; and the evangelist, with Christ as the theme of his discourse, says, " These things said Esaias, when he saw his glory and spake of him." John xii. 41. Nothing is plainer than that Isaiah, in seeing the glory of the Lord of hosts, saw the glory of Christ; and why? Because Christ is Jehovah of hosts.

We have in Isaiah xl. 3 these words: " The voice of him that crieth in the wilderness, Prepare ye the way of the Lord, make straight in the desert a highway for our God." John the Baptist said of himself, " I am the voice of one crying in the wilderness, Make straight the way of the Lord, as said the prophet Esaias." John i. 23. As the harbinger of Christ, John the Baptist was his messenger, as we learn from Mal. iii. 1; Mark i. 2, 3, and came to prepare his way. In the Old Testament the way of the Lord is the way of Jehovah, and in the New Testament the way of the Lord is the way of Jesus. The conclusion is irresistible that the Jehovah of the Old Testament is the Jehovah-Jesus of the New Testament.

I now proceed to quote from the New Testament a number of passages which obviously teach the Deity of Christ. It is natural to refer first to John i. 1, 2: "In the beginning was the Word, and the Word was with God, and the Word was God. The same was in the beginning with God." That by the *Word* is meant the Being who became incarnate, we are taught in the fourteenth verse of the same chapter: "And the Word was made flesh and dwelt among us." The words "In the beginning" no doubt mean what they do in Gen. i. 1 The reference is to the period at which "God created the heaven and the earth." The Word was then with him, and as God existed before he performed the work of creation, and as the Word was with him, it follows that the Word existed before creation, which is equivalent to eternity of being. Jesus, therefore, in one place refers to the glory which he had with the Father before the world was. John xvii. 5. "The Word was God" is the declaration to which special attention should be called, and which deserves the strongest emphasis. What could be more unequivocal? How could testimony in favor of Christ's Deity be more positive?

The language of Thomas in John xx. 28 deserves consideration. This apostle had expressed his incredulity in terms unreasonably strong, but when Jesus presented infallible proofs of his resurrection Thomas said, "My Lord and my God!" I am aware that some who deny Christ's divinity insist that the words of Thomas are those of exclamatory surprise, and do not attribute Lordship and

7 *

Deity to Christ. To adopt this view it would be necessary to believe that the apostle expressed his surprise in a very irreverent, not to say blasphemous, manner. Whatever surprise Thomas felt, his words were declarative of his faith in Christ as his Lord and his God, and the avowal of his faith was pleasing to Christ. It is manifest that Jesus did not disclaim the titles that Thomas gave him, but recognized their propriety. He is, then, Lord and God.

In the ninth chapter of Romans, Paul refers to the advantages enjoyed by the Israelites, " of whom, as concerning the flesh, Christ came, who is over all, God blessed for ever." v. 5. The words " as concerning the flesh," though they almost seem to have been thrown in incidentally, are very significant. They teach the descent of Christ, how he came, as to his human nature; but the language which follows shows him to be divine, for he " is over all, God blessed for ever." It can only be said of a Divine Being that he is over all; and it is therefore perfectly natural that the term God should be applied to him " who is over all."

In 1 Tim. iii. 16 occurs the expression, " God was manifest in the flesh." It is the part of candor to say that the correctness of this translation is disputed. The two prominent views of the passage are these : Some say that the authority of ancient manuscripts justifies the Common Version, while others insist that the best manuscript authority requires the substitution of *who* in the place of *God.* Dr. Noyes, taking the latter view, translates, as follows : " And confessedly great is the mystery of godliness in him who was manifested in the flesh." He says in a note that " the words ' in him ' are not in the Greek, but seem to be implied in the context." It is evident, then, whichever view we take, that there was a manifestation in the flesh and the manifestation of a being. Mr. Spurgeon, in his sermon on this verse entitled "The Hexapla of Mystery," has placed the matter in controversy in so clear a light that any one can understand it. He says: "There is very little occasion for fighting about this matter, for if the text does not say 'God was manifest in the flesh,' who does it say was manifest in the flesh? Either a man, or an angel, or a devil. Does it tell us that a man was manifest in the flesh? Assuredly that cannot be its teaching, for every man is manifest in the flesh, and there is no sense whatever in making such a statement concerning any mere man, and then calling it a mystery. Was it an angel, then? But what angel was ever manifest in the flesh? And if he were, would it be at all a mystery that he should be 'seen of angels'? Is it a wonder for an angel to see an angel? Can it be that the devil was manifest in the flesh? If so, he has been 'received up into glory,' which, let us hope, is not the case. Well, if it was neither a man, nor an angel, nor a devil, who was manifest in the flesh, surely he must have been God; and so, if the word be not there, the sense must be there, or else nonsense. We believe that if criticism should grind the text in a mill, it would get out of it no more and no less than the sense expressed by our grand old version: God himself was manifest in the flesh." To this striking interpretation of Mr. Spurgeon not a word needs to be added, and every objection will assail it in vain.

I refer to one passage more in which Christ is called God: "And we are in him that is true, even in his Son Jesus Christ. This is the true God, and eternal life." 1 John v. 20. Here Christ is not only designated God, but the true God. As there can be but one true God, the epithet *true*, in its application to Christ, makes him one in essence with the Father and the Holy Spirit, while it lays the axe at the root of polytheism and shows all idol gods to be vanity. The phrase " eternal life " claims attention. If full force is given to the article in the original, we must read, " This is the true God, and the eternal life.' In this case there would be a repetition of the idea in chapter i. 2: " For the life was manifested, and we have seen it, and bear witness, and show unto you that eternal life, which was with the Father, and was manifested unto us." Here eternity of life or being is ascribed to Christ, and he must be God. Or if we take the words as we have them, without the force of the article—" This is the true God, and eternal life"—then we must understand the beloved disciple to teach, by a figure of speech, that Christ is the Author of eternal life. If so, he is divine, for God alone can give eternal life to creatures. The argument from the ascription of divine names to Christ in favor of his Deity is by no means exhausted, but I pursue it no further. The Scriptures call him God, and he is God.

II. DIVINE ATTRIBUTES BELONG TO CHRIST. The preceding argument derives its power from the fact that names which in the highest sense are applied to God are also applied to Christ. The force of the present argument will be seen in Christ's possession of attributes unquestionably divine. I shall not attempt to give an exhaustive catalogue of these attributes, but merely name the following conspicuous ones:

1. *Eternity.* That the Word, who in the beginning was with God, had an eternal existence is proved by the following Scripture: " But thou, Bethlehem-Ephratah, though thou be little among the thousands of Judah, yet out of thee shall he come forth unto me that is to be ruler in Israel; whose goings forth have been from of old, from everlasting." Mic. v. 2. That this language refers

ьо Christ is manifest from Matt. ii. 6. It will be observed that while the "ruler in Israel" was to come out of Bethlehem—that is, bo born there—it is said that his "goings forth have been from of old, from everlasting." While the passage contains a clear intimation of the two-fold constitution of the person of the Messiah, it is here quoted to show that he who was born in Bethlehem had ex-isted from eternity : "His goings forth had been from ever-lasting." When it is said in Psalm xc. 2, "From ever-lasting to everlasting thou art God," it is universally understood that God has existed from eternity. Why, then, do not the words "from everlasting," when applied to the Lord Jesus, mean the same thing ? They must have the same meaning.

I refer to one other passage in proof of the eternity of Christ's existence. It is found in John xvii. 5, and has been mentioned in another connection : "And now, O Father, glorify thou me with thine own self, with the glory which I had with thee before the world was." The words "before the world was" are identical in import with "before the foundation of the world," as in Eph. i. 4. Bringing the world into existence is referred to as one of the creative acts of divine power, and there is no intimation that it was subsequent to any other creative act. Between the remotest depths of eternity and the creation of the world there is no epoch from which to date, and therefore whatever was before the foundation of the world was eternal. "Glory before the world was" must have been eternal glory, and as the glory of a being implies his existence, his eternal glory implies his eternal existence. That Christ existed "before the world was" is a strong argument for his eternity ; and if the posses-sion of unbeginning existence is not proof of Deity, there is no proof of anything.

2. *Omniscience.* To know all things is a divine prerogative. It is God who "searches all hearts and understands all the imaginations of the thoughts." 1 Chron. xxviii. 9. He is referred to in Acts xv. 8 as "knowing the hearts"—literally, "the heart-knower;" and in 1 John iii. 20 he is said to "know all things." If these things are true of God and also of Christ, it follows that Christ is God. Peter said to Jesus, "Lord, thou knowest all things; thou knowest that I love thee" (John xxi. 17); and if in Acts i. 24 the term Lord, as in most places in the New Testament, refers to Christ, he is designated "heart-knower." However this may be, we know that it is he who in Rev. ii. 23 says, "And all the churches shall know that I am he which searcheth the reins and hearts." Probably the strongest proof of Christ's omniscience is to be found in his own words in Matt. xi. 27: "No man knoweth the Son, but the Father; neither knoweth any man the Father, save the Son." A literal translation requires the substitution of *one* for *man*—no one, any one. It is not only said that man does not possess the knowledge referred to, but that no one, in any class of rational beings, possesses it. The knowledge is peculiarly divine, and as Christ is in possession of it in common with the Father, the Deity of the Son is as undeniable as that of the Father.

3. *Omnipresence.* In the chapter on the attributes of God it was shown in the light of Ps. cxxxix. 7–12 and other Scriptures that God is everywhere. Omnipresence is obviously a divine perfection. If, then, this perfection belongs to Christ, his Deity is unquestionable. What did he himself say in his conversation with Nicodemus?—"No man hath ascended up to heaven, but he that came down from heaven, even the Son of man which is in heaven." John iii. 13. Here we are plainly taught

that he who came down from heaven was in heaven. The only explanation is, that while his bodily presence was on earth his essential presence was in heaven. Christ also said, " For where two or three are gathered together in my name, there am I in the midst of them." Matt. xviii. 20.

It is quite observable that Jesus does not refer to large numbers of his disciples, but to two or three met in his name. However numerous and however widely separated these little companies may be, the Saviour's presence is with them all. If it is said that his gracious presence is specially meant, I grant it, but his gracious presence wherever two or three meet is possible only because he is omnipresent. For the same reason his words are true: " Lo, I am with you alway, even unto the end of the world." Matt. xxviii. 20. His presence everywhere is of necessity implied. The omnipresence of Christ is proof of his Deity.

4. *Omnipotence.* If omniscience and omnipresence are divine attributes, it is certain that omnipotence must be classed among the perfections of God. If, therefore, it can be shown that Christ possesses almighty power, there will be another argument in support of his divinity. It is manifest that in the exercise of power he claimed equality with God the Father. Referring to the Father, he said, " For what things soever he doeth, these also doeth the Son likewise." Prophecy spoke of him as the mighty God." Isa. ix. 6. Even while on earth, in the days of his humiliation, his superhuman power was recognized. Winds and waves obeyed him, disease loosed its grasp at his bidding, while death and the grave were in haste at his word to yield up their prey. So great and so beneficent is the power of Christ, that Paul considered it a special favor for this power to rest

on him, and he rejoiced in his ability to do all things through Christ strengthening him. Surely Christ is almighty, and he is therefore divine.

5. *Immutability.* When God says, "I am the Lord, I change not" (Mal. iii. 6), the form of expression denotes that his unchangeableness is proof of his divinity. This being the case, it must be admitted that, if Christ is immutable, he is God. In Heb. i. 10–12, Christ seems evidently referred to as the Maker of the heavens and the earth, which are to perish and be changed; but it is said, "Thou art the same, and thy years shall not fail." In the last chapter of the same Epistle we have the words, "Jesus Christ, the same yesterday, and to-day, and for ever." v. 8. Changes belong to things and creatures. Immutability belongs to God alone, and Jesus Christ is invariably the same, because he is God.

Thus does the Deity of Christ appear from the ascription of divine attributes to him.

III. CHRIST IS REPRESENTED AS PERFORMING DIVINE WORKS. No physical act displays omnipotence more strikingly than creation. The production of something out of nothing is everywhere in the Scriptures considered the exclusive work of God. I concede, therefore, that if Christ has not exerted creative power, one of the strongest, if not the strongest, proofs of his Deity is wanting. But what say the Scriptures?—"All things were made by him; and without him was not anything made that was made." John i. 3. I do not see how the universal and the particular can be more fully expressed than in this verse. "All things were made by him"—this is the universal; "without him was not anything [literally, *one* thing] made"—this is the particular. There is nothing that rises above "all things" and there is nothing that falls below the "one thing." Every created object is embraced

in this inspired account of creation, and the omnipotent
work is ascribed to Christ. We have similar language in
Col. i. 16: "For by him were all things created, that are
in heaven, and that are in earth, visible and invisible,
whether they be thrones, or dominions, or principalities,
or powers : all things were created by him, and for him."
Here, too, the existence of all things is ascribed to the
creative power of Christ. The statement of the apostle is
so positive and so forcible that all words of paraphrase
would weaken it. I therefore leave it without comment.
Nor shall I quote other Scriptures to prove that the work
of creation is attributed to Christ. The two passages now
before the reader are amply sufficient. Who but a Divine
Being has created all things? Christ is therefore God.

The work of preservation is also the work of Christ.
Of him it is said, "And he is before all things, and by
him all things consist." Col. i. 17. Being before all
things, he existed prior to the creation of all things by
his power, and since their creation he has preserved them
by the same power. "All things consist"—that is, they
stand together, are kept in place—by him who made them.
They would fall to pieces, there would be disintegration,
if Christ were not Conserver as well as Creator. In
Heb. i. 3 are these words: "Upholding all things by the
word of his power." Here the kindred idea of sustaining
is presented. The imagery employed supposes the universe to rest on the word of Christ's power, and he is in
finitely able to uphold the "all things" he has created.
Does not his work of providence prove his Deity?

The resurrection of the dead will be a glorious display
of the power of God. No sane mind can suppose that
anything but omnipotence can reanimate the dust of the
countless millions in the empire of the grave. Indeed,
some in apostolic times seem to have thought it " incred-

ible that God should raise the dead." Certainly, no one supposed that any being but God could perform such a work. There is, however, a special ascription of this work to Christ. He says himself, "The hour is coming in the which all that are in the grave shall hear his voice, and shall come forth." John v. 28, 29. What amazing power will this be, accompanying the voice of the Son of God, and causing all the dead to hear that voice! They will do more: "They will come forth." These are the words of "the faithful and true Witness.' Paul says of Christ, "Who shall change our vile body, that it may be fashioned like unto his glorious body, according to the working whereby he is able even to subdue all things unto himself." Phil. iii. 21. This passage refers to the resurrection of the saints, and teaches three things: that the vile body—literally, the body of our humiliation—is to be changed; that it is to be conformed to the glorious body of Christ; and that this is to be done by the power of Christ—a power so great that in its exercise he is able to subdue all things. It is needless to quote further to show that Jesus will raise the dead. Now, I ask if divine works—creation, preservation, and the resurrection of the dead—are not ascribed to Christ, and do they not prove his Deity? But there is other proof.

IV. CHRIST IS THE OBJECT OF WORSHIP. What is worship? When our translation of the Bible was made the term was used in two senses: in the lower sense of the word it meant civil respect and deference, as in Luke xiv. 10: "Then shalt thou have worship in the presence of them that sit at meat with thee." The term in this sense is now obsolete, but it is used in its highest scriptural sense to denote adoration paid to God because he is God. We have the authority of Jesus himself on this point. In repelling one of Satan's temptations he said, "For it is

w.itten, Thou shalt worship the Lord thy God, and him
only shalt thou serve." Matt. iv. 10. Here we are taught
that worship belongs exclusively to God. If, then, it can
be shown that, according to the Scriptures, Jesus Christ is
the object of worship, the doctrine of his Deity will be
established. In John v. 23 it is written, "That all men
should honor the Son, even as they honor the Father."
No one will deny that supreme honor is claimed for the
Father, and equal honor is claimed for the Son. This
honor surely implies worship. The first Christians were
designated as those who called on the name of the Lord.
Paul wrote, " Unto the church of God which is at Corinth,
to them that are sanctified in Christ Jesus, called to be
saints, with all that in every place call upon the name of
Jesus Christ our Lord, both theirs and ours." 1 Cor. i. 2.
To call upon the name of the Lord is to invoke his name,
and this implies prayer, whatever else it may imply.
Prayer is an act of worship. Nor is this all. Calling
on the name of the Lord is inseparably connected
with salvation. "For whosoever shall call upon the
name of the Lord shall be saved." Rom. x. 13. It is
here taken for granted that the Lord has power to save.
I need not say that it requires the power of God to save.
The Lord Jesus must be God. Not only did the first
Christians call upon the name of the Lord in their worship and service during life, but in death they invoked
his name and committed their departing spirits into his
hands. Of the latter truth, Stephen is the most conspicuous illustration : " And they stoned Stephen, calling upon
and saying, Lord Jesus, receive my spirit." Acts vii. 59.
This is the correct translation. There is no word in the
Greek text corresponding to God, and there is no pause
between the calling upon and the saying. The Redeemer
was invoked, and the words of invocation were, "Lord

Jesus, receive my spirit." This was the first Christian martyr. With eternity just before him he called on his Lord, commending to him the spirit struggling to escape from the murdered body. Did Stephen labor under a mistake in believing that Jesus, because divine, was able to receive his disembodied spirit? Strange time to make a mistake when he saw the glory of God shining brighter than ten thousand suns! There was no mistake. The dying martyr recognized the Deity of his Lord.

In Heb. i. 6 it is said, "And let all the angels of God worship him." This is the command of the eternal Father—a command implying the divinity of the Son and the equality of his claims to angelic adoration. If the Lord Jesus is worshipped by saints and angels, is not this a conclusive proof of his Deity? Saints on earth worship him, and saints in heaven sing a new song, saying, "Thou art worthy; . . . for thou wast slain and hast redeemed us to God by thy blood." Rev. v. 9. John heard this exalted song, and then he heard the angels, "and the number of them was ten thousand times ten thousand, and thousands of thousands, saying with a loud voice, Worthy is the Lamb that was slain, to receive power, and riches and wisdom, and strength, and honor, and glory, and blessing." Rev. v. 12. It will be observed that while the angels make no reference to personal redemption, as do the saints, they fully recognize the worthiness of the Lamb slain. Christ is worshipped by saints and angels on earth and in heaven. He accepts the worship. Peter was utterly unwilling to receive worship from Cornelius, but raised him up from his prostrate position, "Saying, Stand up; I myself also am a man." Acts x. 26. Paul and Barnabas "rent their clothes" at the very intimation that sacrifices were to be offered to them. Acts xiv. 14, 18. When John was so impressed by the glory of the angel who made known to him the wonderful things which he saw that he fell down to worship, mistaking the angel for the Lord of angels, the heavenly messenger rebuked him, saying, "See thou do it not; . . . worship God." Rev. xxii. 9. Thus we see that apostles on earth would not receive worship, nor would angels in heaven. But Jesus accepted worship on earth and in heaven. Why? Because he knew himself to be the proper object of adoration. This he could not know without a consciousness of Deity. Christ is God.

In closing this chapter it is proper to notice a strange declaration, sometimes made by those who deny the supreme divinity of Christ. It is in substance this: That, though Jesus is not God, he is the best man the world ever saw. Nothing can be further from the truth than such a statement. The alternative is not that Jesus is God *or* the best of men. No! the alternative is that Jesus is God *or* the worst of men. If he was not God, he was such an impostor, such a blasphemer, as the world never saw. He claimed for himself divine honors and divine worship. He said, "He that loveth father or mother more than me is not worthy of me; and he that loveth son or daughter more than me is not worthy of me" (Matt. x. 37); "If any man come to me, and hate not his father and mother and wife and children and brothers and sisters, yea, and his own life also, he cannot be my disciple." Luke xiv. 26. It is proper to say that in the latter passage the word "hate" means to love less, and the spirit of both passages is that love to Christ must be superior to that exercised in any of the relations of life. Think of it! Here is a man—if Jesus is only a man—who requires the husband to love him more than he does his wife, and the wife to love him more than she does her husband; who requires parents and children to love him more than they love one another, and who requires everybody to love him more than life itself! On the supposition that Jesus is a mere man, there is no language that can define the presumption that presents such claims. He gives orders that in baptism his name shall be used between that of the Father and of the Holy Spirit; that his death shall be commemorated till the end of the world; that repentance and remission of sins shall be preached through him; and says that he will come in the clouds of heaven on the last day, raise the dead, judge the world, welcome the righteous into the kingdom of glory, consign the wicked to eternal perdition, and will then be the light and the joy of the New Jerusalem. Imagine prophet or apostle as asserting such claims and saying such things: Would not the presumption and the blasphemy be intolerable? They are just as intolerable in the case of Jesus Christ if he is not divine.

I present these views to show how absurd it is to deny the Deity of Christ and insist that the world never saw so good a man. No, he is the worst of men if nothing more than man. But he is God. This is the glory of the system of Christianity, that its Author is divine. His Deity is essential to the value of his atoning sacrifice—essential to his ability to save. In view of the proofs of his divinity presented in this chapter, every Christian may say with Thomas, "My Lord and my God!" and with Paul, "I know whom I have believed, and am persuaded that he is able to keep that which I have committed unto him;" and in the dying hour the words of Stephen may well come into the heart and find expression through the quivering lips: "Lord Jesus, receive my spirit."

CHAPTER VI.

THE PERSONALITY AND DEITY OF THE HOLY SPIRIT.

THE subject discussed in the preceding chapter may be considered in some of its aspects the most important and vital in the system of theology. It is therefore wise to establish by conclusive proofs the Deity of Christ. When this is done, the doctrine of the Trinity is usually accepted without hesitation, while personality and divinity are accorded to the Holy Spirit. This being the case, it will be unnecessary for the subject of this chapter to receive a very elaborate investigation, but it should by no means be passed over. It divides itself into two parts:

I. THE PERSONALITY OF THE HOLY SPIRIT. By this is meant that the Spirit is a person, not a mere energy or influence or operation, but an intelligent person. What does Jesus say?—"And I will pray the Father, and he shall give you another Comforter, that he may abide with you for ever;" "But the Comforter, which is the Holy Ghost, whom the Father will send in my name, he shall teach you all things." John xiv. 16, 26. The Comforter here promised is said to be the Holy Spirit, and the plain meaning of the term is, one who administers comfort. This is clearly suggestive of personality; but if stronger proof is required, it is found in the fact that the Spirit is said to teach. Surely the office of teacher is inseparable from personality. When it is said of the Spirit, "He shall teach you all things," it is virtually declared that he is a person. The baptismal commission furnishes as strong proof of the personality of the Holy Spirit as of that of the Father and of the Son. " Baptizing them in the name of the Father, and of the Son, and of the Holy Ghost." The phrase " in the name " usually means " by authority of," and if this is its meaning here, the authority of the Spirit is equal to that of the Father and of the Son, and the Spirit must be a person. But this is not the meaning of " in the name " in the commission. Baptism is administered by authority of the Son, but, as it seems to me, " into the name of the Father, and of the Son, and of the Holy Spirit;" that is, there is an avowal of allegiance and consecration to the three persons of the Godhead : there is a profession of fellowship with God in his threefold unity. The personality of the Spirit is undoubtedly implied, for it would be absurd to associate an influence or energy with the Father and the Son in the ordinance of baptism. The Spirit has equal personality with the Father and the Son. To confirm the view now presented, I may say that the Spirit is referred to as doing what a personal agent alone can do. He is said to " testify " of Christ, to " glorify " him, to make " intercession for the saints," to distribute gifts " as he will," to " seal unto the day of redemption." John xv. 26 ; xvi. 14 ; Rom viii. 27 ; 1 Cor. xii. 11 ; Eph. iv. 30. The acts mentioned in these passages are personal acts. It requires a person to " testify," to " glorify," to " intercede," to " will," and to " seal." It is morally certain that the Holy Spirit is a Person.

II. THE DEITY OF THE HOLY SPIRIT. Not more evident is the personality than the divinity of the Holy Spirit. This will appear in view of such facts as these :

1. *He is called God.* " But Peter said, Ananias, why hath Satan filled thine heart to lie to the Holy Ghost, and

to keep back part of the price of the land? . . . **Thou hast not lied unto men, but unto God.**" Acts v. 3, 4. Here it is plain that to lie to the Holy Spirit is to lie to God. But why is it so? Because the Holy Spirit is God. The charge which Peter interrogatively makes is, that Ananias had lied to the Holy Spirit; and to show the greatness of the sin he said it was lying to God, the term God being no doubt better understood by the guilty man than the phrase Holy Spirit.

" Know ye not that ye are the temple of God, and that the Spirit of God dwelleth in you?" 1 Cor. iii. 16. The temple at Jerusalem was God's house, and he was said to dwell there. Availing himself of this form of speech, Paul told the members of the Corinthian church that they were the temple of God—that is, his habitation. What else does he say?—" Know ye not that your body is the temple of the Holy Ghost?" 1 Cor. vi. 19. We have, therefore, in the same Epistle the expressions " temple of God " and " temple of the Holy Ghost " applied to the same church. If a church or an individual Christian is the temple of God and the temple of the Holy Spirit, it must be because the Holy Spirit is God.

2. *Divine perfections are ascribed to the Holy Spirit.* If these perfections, when ascribed to Christ, prove his Deity, they also, when ascribed to the Spirit, prove his Deity. That the Spirit is represented as eternal, omniscient, omnipresent, and omnipotent is manifest from the following passages : " How much more shall the blood of Christ, who through the eternal Spirit offered himself without spot to God, purge your conscience from dead works to serve the living God?" Heb. ix. 14. " But God hath revealed them to us by his Spirit: for the Spirit searcheth all things, yea, the deep things of God." 1 Cor. ii. 10. " Whither shall I go from thy Spirit? or whither shall I

flee from thy presence?" Ps. cxxxix. 7. "Being put to death in the flesh, but quickened by the Spirit." "He that raised up Christ from the dead shall also quicken your mortal bodies by his Spirit that dwelleth in you." 1 Pet. iii. 18; Rom. viii. 11. As the attributes of eternity, omniscience, omnipresence, and omnipotence belong inalienably to God, and as they are ascribed to the Holy Spirit, the conclusion is irresistible that he is God.

3. *Divine operations are ascribed to the Spirit.* The most prominent of these operations are connected with creation and the working of miracles. "The earth was without form and void; and darkness was upon the face of the deep. And the Spirit of God moved upon the face of the waters." Gen. i. 2. Order and beauty were brought out of chaotic darkness by the Spirit; and in Job xxvi. 13, we read, "By his Spirit he hath garnished the heavens." These two passages sufficiently show the Spirit's connection with the work of creation, and by consequence his Deity. As to miracles, it is written, "But if I cast out devils by the Spirit of God, then the kingdom of God is come unto you." "For to one is given, by the Spirit, the word of wisdom; . . . to another the gifts of healing by the same Spirit; to another the working of miracles." Matt. xii. 28; 1 Cor. xii. 8–10. A miracle is a supernatural work which no created being can perform and therefore the working of miracles by the Holy Spirit proves him to be divine. The "laws of Nature," as they are called, God has established, and he alone can suspend them; but as a miracle is a suspension of some law of Nature, the Holy Spirit in working miracles vindicates his claim to divinity.

I may say also that what is said of blasphemy against the Holy Spirit furnishes conclusive proof of his Deity: "All sins shall be forgiven unto the sons of men, and blasphemies wherewithsoever they shall blaspheme: but he that shall blaspheme against the Holy Ghost hath never forgiveness, but is in danger of eternal damnation: because they said, He hath an unclean spirit." Mark iii 28-30. The intimation here seems to be that ascribing an evil spirit to Christ and saying that his miracles were wrought by such a spirit, and not by the Spirit of God, was blaspheming against the Holy Spirit. This sin was not to be forgiven, and this fact implies the divinity of the Holy Spirit. That is, if the Holy Spirit is not divine, we cannot see why a sin committed against him cannot be forgiven, especially as sins against the Father and the Son are forgiven. There is of course something peculiar in blasphemy against the Holy Spirit, rendering it unpardonable, but the peculiarity, so far as we can judge, is inseparable from the Deity of the Spirit.

It will be seen that I prefer the phrase Holy Spirit to Holy Ghost, though they are of the same import. The chief reason for the preference is that Spirit is a more familiar word than Ghost, and is therefore better understood, to say nothing of associations connected with the latter term. It is a singular fact that " Holy Ghost " is not to be found in the Old Testament, though it occurs frequently in the New.

There has been some curiosity felt as to the more frequent application of the epithet " Holy " to the Spirit than to the Father and the Son. As there is in the three persons of the Godhead equality of nature, there must be equality of holiness. The holiness is infinite, and in the infinite there are no degrees. The Father, the Son, and the Holy Spirit are equally and perfectly holy. It follows, therefore, that the Spirit is emphatically called Holy to denote official distinction. In other words, the Spirit is termed Holy because it is his office to make holy. It is his work to deposit the germ of holiness in the sinful heart of man. There is no holiness in any human heart till the Holy Spirit produces it. The germ of holiness implanted in regeneration is developed in sanctification; which is, equally with regeneration, the work of the Spirit. The third person in the Godhead is designated the Holy Spirit because he renovates the soul, purifies it, and prepares it for heaven.

CHAPTER VII.

THE PURPOSES OF GOD.

THE transition from the being and attributes of God to
his purposes is natural and easy. For if there is a God
infinite in wisdom and holiness and glory, he must act
according to a predetermined plan. The perfection of
his nature suggests this. If, as has been shown, there are
three persons in the Godhead, coequal and coeternal, it
accords with reason to suppose that in their triune com-
munings and consultations—to speak after the manner of
men—they decided from eternity on a programme to be
carried into effect to eternity. Such decision is embraced
in the purposes of God, and is in truth his all-comprehen-
sive decree. With regard to the divine purposes it may
be said—

1. *They are eternal.* The eternity of the divine purposes cannot be severed from the eternity of the divine
existence. We are utterly unable to conceive of God as
sitting in purposeless majesty on his throne. Could we
form such a conception it would be infinitely unworthy
of God. As we cannot think of the sun apart from the
light and heat which he sends forth, so we cannot think
of God apart from his purposes. But what do the
Scriptures say?—"Come, ye blessed of my Father, inherit the kingdom prepared for you from the foundation
of the world." Matt. xxv. 34. If we ask in what sense

the kingdom was prepared from the foundation of the world, the answer is, In the purpose of God. A purpose which can be traced back to the foundation of the world is the purpose of him who made the world, and must be as eternal as himself. In the Epistle to the Ephesians there are several passages which teach the eternity of God's purposes: "According as he hath chosen us in him before the foundation of the world." Eph. i. 4 "The fellowship of the mystery which from the beginning of the world hath been hid in God. . . . According to the eternal purpose which he purposed in Christ Jesus our Lord." iii. 9, 11. There could have been no choice, no election, before the foundation of the world if there had not been a purpose antedating the creation of the world; and such a purpose must have been eternal. While the "manifold wisdom of God" in the redemption of the church is made known to the inhabitants of heaven, it is according to his eternal purpose. In 2 Tim. i. 9 it is written, "Who hath saved us, and called us with a holy calling, not according to our works, but according to his own purpose and grace, which was given us in Christ Jesus before the world began." The grace was given in the purpose of God before the world began, and in this sense the grace was coeval with the purpose. Peter, in referring to Christ, says, "Who verily was foreordained before the foundation of the world, but was manifest in these last times for you." 1 Pet. i. 20. Christ was manifested by his incarnation, but the manifestation was in pursuance of the foreordination of God, which bore date before the foundation of the world—a form of expression equivalent to the words *from eternity.* These scriptures sufficiently show the purposes of God to be eternal.

2. *They are also full of wisdom.* God is infinitely wise, and therefore his purposes are wise. It would be absurd

to suppose a conflict between the nature of God and his plan of operation. In judging of the divine purposes we should ever remember that they are unfolded only in part, and for this reason the wisdom pertaining to them is disclosed but in part. Still, we have such indications of wisdom in the works and ways of God as to call forth the exclamatory words of an apostle: "Oh, the depth of the riches both of the wisdom and knowledge of God!" Rom. xi. 33.

Our attention has been directed in another place to some of the proofs of divine wisdom as seen in creation, providence, and redemption; nor should we forget that whatever proves the wisdom of God in his works is an argument in favor of the wisdom of his purposes. For all his works are performed in accordance with his purposes. The strongest proof of the wisdom of the divine purposes is to be found in the scheme of redemption, as we learn from Eph. iii. 10: "To the intent that now unto the principalities and powers in heavenly places might be known, by the church, the manifold wisdom of God." These orders of celestial beings had seen much of the wisdom of God in the wonders of creation and the revelations of providence, but the disclosures of redemption through Christ gave them new views of what is termed "the manifold wisdom of God." But redemption itself and all its disclosures are in pursuance of God's purposes, and these purposes must therefore be full of wisdom.

3. *They are likewise free.* God freely formed his purposes in himself. The reasons for their formation were all in himself, for there were no external influences to act on him. The freedom, too, with which God framed his decrees was in direct opposition to what has been called by some, "necessity of nature." He was not obliged to form the purposes which the Bible reveals, but might

have formed different purposes. To illustrate: He might have purposed the creation of a world ten or twenty times as large as the one we inhabit, to be illuminated by a plurality of suns by day and a plurality of moons by night. He might have decreed the formation of rational creatures alone or of irrational creatures alone. He might have purposed the salvation of some or all of the fallen angels, or the salvation of more or less of the human race than will be finally saved. These suppositions are designed to give emphasis to the idea that the divine purposes are free. God in forming them was infinitely at liberty to do his pleasure. He arranged the plan according to which he is carrying on the affairs of the universe, and of all the plans conceivable by his omniscient mind he adopted the one which seemed to him best. The adoption was not arbitrary, not without reason. There were the wisest and the best reasons controlling his purposes and making them just what they are. "Even so, Father; for so it seemed good in thy sight." The reasons of the divine purposes it is not given to men or angels to know, but they are treasured up in that which seems good in the sight of God. They are to be found in what is called "the good pleasure of his will," and if his purposes accord with his pleasure, his good pleasure, they are free. It is therefore written, "Who hath directed the Spirit of the Lord, or being his counsellor hath taught him? With whom took he counsel, and who instructed him, and taught him in the path of judgment, and taught him knowledge, and showed to him the way of understanding?" Isa. xl. 13, 14. "For who hath known the mind of the Lord? or who hath been his counsellor?" Rom. xi. 34. "For who hath known the mind of the Lord, that he may instruct him?" 1 Cor. ii. 16.

4. *The purposes of God are unchangeable.* The immuta

bility of God is a truth decisive of the immutability of his purposes. As *he* is unchangeable, it does not accord with reason that his plans and purposes should be variable. It may be said of men that they often change their purposes. Why is it so? Because in some cases they are too ignorant to form wise purposes, and in other instances they lack ability to execute purposes which are wise and good. When purposes are seen to be unwise, they should be promptly given up and other purposes should take their place. So also the purposes which cannot be executed should be superseded by those that are practicable. Thus, because men have so little wisdom and so little power, it is often the best thing they can do to change their purposes. But how is it with God? His wisdom is infinite. When he formed his purposes he knew all the future. Nothing, therefore, that occurs can take him by surprise. Knowing all things from the beginning, had he known that any event or combination of events would detract from the wisdom of a purpose, his knowledge would have prevented the formation of the purpose. It follows, therefore, that the infinite wisdom of God renders needless a change of his purposes. So also of his power; he can do anything which does not involve a contradiction, or antagonize with the perfection of his nature. It is morally certain that no divine purpose would, in its execution, require either of these impossible things to be done, and we may therefore say that no lack of power on the part of God will ever render it necessary for him to change his purposes. This reasoning, however, amounts to nothing unless the Bible sustains it. What, then, does the Bible say?—" The counsel of the Lord standeth for ever, the thoughts of his heart to all generations " (Ps. xxxiii. 11); " The Lord of hosts hath sworn, saying, **Surely** as I have thought, so shall it come to pass; and **as I have**

9 *

purposed, so shall it stand " (Isa. xiv. 24) ; " My counsel shall stand, and I will do all my pleasure " (Isa. xlvi. 10) ; " I am the Lord, I change not " (Mal. iii. 6) ; " With whom is no variableness, neither shadow of turning." James i. 17.

5. *His purposes do not make God the author of sin.* Here we are required to survey a field on which many a theological battle has been fought. It has been said and written a thousand times that if God has decreed from eternity whatever comes to pass, as sin is one of the things that have come to pass, God must be the author of sin. I suppose that all things which come to pass may be included in two classes ; namely, things which God does by his positive agency, and things which he permits to be done. Things belonging to the former class are embraced in his *efficient* purposes, while things belonging to the latter class are embraced in his *permissive* purposes. This distinction between the purposes of God must not be forgotten, if we would know the truth as the Bible reveals it. The distinction itself is recognized and variously illustrated in the Scriptures. It was no doubt among the efficient purposes of God to create the world, to make Adam the ancestor of his race, to endow him with free agency and place him in the garden of Eden. In pursuance of his efficient purposes God did all this, but did he in the same manner decree the sin of Adam ? Clearly he did not. His purpose in regard to Adam's sin was only permissive ; it was not efficient. I am aware that the word " permissive " is not wholly free from objection, but I know of no better word. The objection to it is that some persons will regard it as expressive of sanction, if not of approval. I protest against this understanding of the word. There was, on the part of God, no approval, no sanction of the sin of Adam, yet it was per-

mitted. God could have prevented the introduction of sin into the world, and would have done so had its non-introduction been among his efficient purposes, but it was not. Its introduction was among his permissive purposes; and Adam, in the exercise of his free agency, sinned. So it has been with Adam's descendants in every age. God has permitted them to sin; but, so far from giving sanction to their sins, he has expressed his abhorrence and condemnation of evil in the waters of the flood, in the fires of Sodom, in the calamities of war, in the hardships of captivity, in the destruction of Jerusalem, and in a thousand other ways. God is not the author of sin, neither has he " fellowship with any therein "—no fellowship with the devil who tempts men to sin, and no fellowship with men in yielding to temptation. "To the law and to the testimony;" "Let no man say when he is tempted, I am tempted of God: for God cannot be tempted of evil, neither tempteth he any man." James i. 13. So immaculate is his holiness that, in the sense of soliciting to evil, it is morally impossible for God to tempt any man, and equally impossible for him to be tempted of evil. None but pure influences can reach him, none but pure influences can emanate from him. Perish the thought that God is the author of sin! for it was in his "wise and *holy* counsel" that he decreed all things.

6. *In God's purposes* " *violence is not offered to the will of the creature.*" There are no truths more plainly revealed in the Bible than that God is sovereign and man is free. The King of Babylon, when saved from the calamity that came upon him and restored to reason, said of Jehovah, " He doeth according to his will in the army of heaven and among the inhabitants of the earth: and none can stay his hand, or say unto him, What doest thou?" Dan.

iv. 35. It is the glory of the universe that such a Being sits on the throne and sways his sceptre over all worlds. Supreme dominion belongs to God, and he exercises absolute control over things animate and inanimate over creatures rational and irrational. But the exercise of divine sovereignty does not conflict with human agency. It was, doubtless, among the purposes of God to make man a free agent. What is a free agent? I answer in the words of Andrew Fuller : " A free agent is an intelligent being, who is at liberty to act according to his choice, without compulsion or restraint." The question is not as to what prompts to action ; the point is that the action is free. Men have acted freely in all ages of the world. The purposes of God, whether efficient or permissive, have not prevented such action. Good men have acted freely, and bad men have acted with equal freedom. In the world's infancy, Abel, in the exercise of his choice, presented his offering to the Lord ; and Cain, without compulsion, became the murderer of his brother. Abraham, at the command of God, voluntarily left the land of his fathers ; and the brothers of Joseph voluntarily sold him as a slave to the Ishmaelites, in violation of their obligation to God and in disregard of the claims of fraternal duty. In these cases the obedience and the disobedience were equally free. " No violence was offered to the will " in either case.

Perhaps the most striking instance of the harmony between the purposes of God and the free agency of men is recorded in Acts ii. 23 : " Him, being delivered by the determinate counsel and foreknowledge of God, ye have taken, and by wicked hands have crucified and slain." The death of Christ occurred, without doubt, in pursuance of the purpose of God ; nor can we conceive how any divine purpose could be more properly formed than in connection with such an event. The Lamb was "slain from the foundation of the world,"—that is, slain in the purpose of God—but the Jews acted very wickedly in procuring the crucifixion of Christ. They never acted more freely. There was a perfect absence of compulsion. The purpose of God was executed, and in its execution there was such a murder committed as never took place before and will never take place again. There was "no violence offered to the will" of the murderers, but they acted with perfect freedom. If any one asks, How could these things be? I answer, The facts are as I have stated; the philosophy of the facts I do not attempt to explain. To make the attempt would be to add one more to the number of those who have "darkened counsel by words without knowledge."

Having presented these general views of the purposes of God, it is proper before closing this chapter to say something of Predestination as taught in the Scriptures. While there is nothing in the term itself which forbids its use in the sense of the foreordination of all events, it is commonly employed with reference to human beings. It comprehends the purpose of election, and also, as will be shown, the purpose of "reprobation," as it has been called, which, as has been well said, "is nothing more than withholding from some the grace which is imparted to others." [1] These two purposes may be expressed thus: "That God chose in Christ certain persons of the fallen race of Adam, before the foundation of the world, unto eternal glory, according to his own purpose and grace, without regard to their foreseen faith and good works, or any conditions performed by them;" and that from the rest of mankind he withheld his grace and left them to dishonor, and the just punishment of their sins. The

[1] Hill's *Divinity* p. 561.

ideas brought to view in this statement need and deserve expansion. I may therefore say—

1. *Election is personal.* The choice exercised is a choice of persons. It is a choice of persons as distinguished from nations. The Jews were in one sense an elect nation, but their election from among the nations had no special reference to eternal life, to which persons are elected; and in addition to this, they were the only elect nation the world ever saw. But to see that election is not national we need only turn to Rev. v. 9: "And they sung a new song, saying, Thou art worthy to take the book, and to open the seals thereof: for thou wast slain, and hast redeemed us to God by thy blood out of every kindred, and tongue, and people, and nation." Here we are plainly taught that salvation is not national deliverance, but that the saved are redeemed *out of* every nation. An eclectic operation is referred to—persons selected out of nations. The theory of *national* election cannot be maintained as the doctrine of the New Testament.

Election is not only personal as distinguished from national, but it is of individuals as distinguished from individuals. The line of discrimination runs between persons. When Paul says in Rom. xvi. 13, "Salute Rufus, chosen in the Lord," the reference must be to personal election, as also when he writes to the members of the Thessalonian church, "God hath from the beginning chosen you to salvation." 2 Thess. ii. 13. Peter, in writing to the "strangers scattered abroad," addressing them as "elect according to the foreknowledge of God the Father," must have meant personal election. If it is said that the election of some is the rejection of others, it may be remarked, Rejection is a term needlessly strong, and it is preferable to say that God has left others as they were. The decree of election leaves them where they would have been had there been no election of any No injustice is done them. The truth is, election is injustice to none, while it is an unspeakable blessing to some. It takes a multitude which no man can number but which God can number, out of the fallen race of Adam, and raises them up to hope and heaven.

2. *Election is eternal.* In proof of this the following passages may be quoted: "According as he hath chosen us in him before the foundation of the world, that we should be holy and without blame before him in love" (Eph. i. 4); "Who hath saved us and called us with a holy calling, not according to our works, but according to his own purpose and grace, which was given us in Christ Jesus before the world began" (2 Tim. i. 9); "God hath from the beginning chosen you to salvation through sanctification of the Spirit and belief of the truth." 2 Thess. ii. 13.

After what has been said on preceding pages concerning the eternity of God, and the consequent eternity of his purposes, it is not necessary to enlarge on a point so plain as that his election of his people is from eternity. Election, being inseparable from the divine purposes, is as eternal as they. As it has to do with eternal life, it is eternal, as going back to the unbeginning past and forward to the unending future.

3. *Election was not in view of foreseen faith and good works.* There are some who make faith and good works the ground of election. That is, they suppose that God elected his people because he foresaw their faith and good works. This view transposes cause and effect, for it makes election dependent on faith and good works, whereas faith and good works are scripturally dependent on election. When we read, "chosen . . . that we should be holy," it is obvious that the election is not

because of holiness, but in order to holiness. The purpose of election contemplates the sanctification of the
elect, and therefore regards them as sinners needing
sanctification. The same truth is suggested by the words,
"For whom he did foreknow, he also did predestinate to
be conformed to the image of his Son." Rom. viii. 29.
Here evidently the predestination, including election, did
not find its basis or reason in the conformity of the predestinated to the image of Christ, but the conformity is
the result of the predestination. As to the much-controverted passage in Acts xiii. 48, "And as many as were
ordained to eternal life believed," the only natural interpretation is that they believed because of their ordination
to eternal life. The Arminian view is without foundation
in the word of God ; for election is the source, the only
source, whence spring faith, holiness, and good works.

4. *The purpose of election is irreversible.* This is the only
view of the matter that is worthy of God. Changeable
purposes would detract from his glory as an infinitely
perfect Being. The purpose of election is not arbitrary
is not without reason. God does nothing without reason,
but the reason or reasons of his action he is not always
pleased to reveal. Why he chose some persons to eternal
life in preference to others, we do not know, but if the
reasons of his choice were satisfactory to him when the
choice was made, they will be satisfactory for ever, unless
better reasons should present themselves to his mind—a
supposition which the perfection of his character does not
for a moment tolerate. In short, there can be no philo-
sophic belief that God will reverse his purpose of election, and the Scriptures confirm the teachings of sound
philosophy. Jesus says of his disciples, "And I give
unto them eternal life; and they shall never perish,
neither shall any man pluck them out of my hand. My

Father, which gave them me, is greater than all; and no man is able to pluck them out of my Father's hand." John x. 28, 29. Here the security of believers is strongly asserted ; but whence arises the security? Chiefly from the fact that the Father gave them to the Son in the purpose of election. If, however, the purpose is reversible, there is no security. We are also taught that "God, willing more abundantly to show unto the heirs of promise the immutability of his counsel, confirmed it by an oath : that by two immutable things, in which it was impossible for God to lie, we might have a strong consolation." Heb. vi. 17, 18. The "strong consolation" grows out of the immutability of the divine counsel, which is confirmed by an oath ; and the purpose of election, being included in the divine counsel, is as immutable as the counsel itself. It is not necessary to enlarge. Surely the purpose of election is irreversible.

It is well at this point to answer an objection that is often made to the doctrine of predestination. It is said that while the economy of Nature and grace illustrates the use of means, predestination renders their use unnecessary. Why unnecessary? Because the objector supposes a predestinated end will be accomplished without means. There is nothing, however, to justify such a supposition. We can find nothing in the realm of Nature to countenance it. God said to Noah, "While the earth remaineth, seed-time and harvest, and cold and heat, and summer and winter, and day and night shall not cease." Gen. viii. 22. The object in view requires me to refer only to "harvest" as included among the purposes of God. It will not be denied that God has decreed the production of harvests while the earth remains ; but has he decreed the production of miraculous harvests, that is, harvests without the sowing of seed? Manifestly not. "Seed-time " is mentioned as before ' harvest," and clearly preparatory to it. No harvest is predestinated apart from seed-sowing. The means are appointed equally with the end. Let the nations practically adopt the philosophy of the objection under consideration,—namely, that predestination supersedes the use of means,—and what must follow? Universal starvation. But we need not anticipate this world-wide calamity, for men exercise common sense on every subject except that of religion.

Paul's voyage to Rome is often referred to as illustrative of the connection between means and ends. The apostle had been assured by an angel of God that of the two hundred and seventy-six persons on board the ship not one should be lost; but when he saw that " the shipmen were about to flee out of the ship," he " said to the centurion and to the soldiers, Except these abide in the ship ye cannot be saved." The safe deliverance of all on board the storm-tossed vessel was the predestinated event, but it could not be accomplished unless the " shipmen " remained in their position and performed their duty. Thus in the natural world, on the land and on the sea, we see that means are predestinated as well as ends, and that ends cannot be accomplished without the use of means.

How is it in the realm of grace? The principle is the same, showing the God of Nature to be the God of grace. " Moreover, whom he did predestinate, them he also called: and whom he called, them he also justified: and whom he justified, them he also glorified." Rom. viii. 30. In this verse we have, if I may so call it, a golden chain of four links, and this chain reaches from eternity to eternity. The first link is predestination, and the last glorification, while the two intervening links are calling and justification. The first link has no connection with the last, except through the intermediate links. That is to say

there is no way in which the purpose of God in predestination can reach its end in glorification, if calling and justification do not take place. But calling and justification
are inseparable from "repentance toward God and faith
toward our Lord Jesus Christ." Repentance and faith,
then, not to name other things, are means through which
the purpose of God in election is accomplished. God,
therefore, in predestinating the salvation of his people,
predestinated their repentance, and faith and all other
means necessary to their salvation. If any inquire, as is
sometimes the case, what will become of those elected to
eternal life if they do not repent and believe, it is best to
answer by asking what would have become of the persons in the ship with Paul if the "shipmen" had not remained at their posts of duty. If it is said the "shipmen" did remain, I say, those chosen to salvation will
repent and believe.

The following passages teach the use of means in connection with the purpose of God in election: "God hath
from the beginning chosen you to salvation through sanctification of the Spirit and belief of the truth " (2 Thess.
ii. 13); "Therefore I endure all things for the elect's sake,
that they may also obtain the salvation which is in Christ
Jesus with eternal glory " (2 Tim. ii. 10); "Elect according to the foreknowledge of God the Father, through
sanctification of the Spirit, unto obedience and sprinkling
of the blood of Jesus Christ " (1 Pet. i. 2); "For we are
his workmanship, created in Christ Jesus unto good
works, which God hath before ordained that we should
walk in them." Eph. ii. 10. From the first of these
scriptures we learn that election to salvation is indicated
by " sanctification of the Spirit and belief of the truth ;"
from the second, that Paul's many trials as a minister had
an instrumental connection with the salvation of the elect

from the third, that election is not only through sanctifi
cation of the Spirit, but unto obedience and sprinkling of
the blood of Jesus Christ ; and from the last, that the purpose of election embraces foreordination to good works.
In view of these passages it is plain that the doctrine of
predestination does not supersede the use of means, but
requires them.

Before dismissing this topic it should be said that as
God's purpose of election is "in himself," we can know
nothing about it till it is disclosed in the "calling" already referred to.   Paul, for example, when he preached
in Thessalonica, knew nothing of the election of any of
its citizens to eternal life, but after the grace of God was
displayed in "effectual calling" he did not hesitate to
write, "Knowing, brethren, beloved, your election of
God." 1 Thess. i. 4.   Hence, too, Peter wrote to his brethren, "Give diligence to make your calling and election
sure." 2 Pet. i. 10.   It is observable that he puts calling
before election.   God begins with election, but man cannot.   He must begin with the calling, and when he
makes that sure, the election is sure.   The calling is the
only attainable proof of the election.   It will be seen,
therefore, that the question of election is, in the hands
of a sinner, the most unmanageable of all questions.
The reason is, it is none of his business, and he can do
nothing with it.   The time has been when in some places
sinners, becoming serious on the subject of salvation, instead of repenting and believing in Christ, employed
themselves in efforts equally earnest and fruitless to ascertain whether they were elect or non-elect.   This was,
is, and ever must be, an absurdity.   That which is required of sinners is expressed in the words of Peter:
"Repent ye, therefore and be converted, that your sins
may be blotted out."   **Acts iii. 19.**

In closing this chapter I make a brief reference to what is often called God's purpose of " reprobation," by which, as we have seen, is meant his purpose to leave some to themselves, to give them over " to a reprobate mind." Rom. i. 28. That there is such a purpose is as evident as that God has threatened his incorrigible enemies with everlasting destruction. His threatenings are in pursuance of his purpose, and in the absence of purpose there would be no threatenings That God has purposed to leave to dishonor and the just punishment of their sins any of the human race is a tenet which many regard as both incredible and cruel. This tenet has been often misrepresented, and placed even in an odious light. How many have said with a semblance of holy horror, " Does God make men to damn them? Is he not too good to punish his creatures?" In both of these questions there is a deceptive ellipsis. In the first, the words " for their sins " are omitted ; and in the second the epithet " sinful " should qualify creatures. No intelligent believer in the divine purposes will say that God has made any of the sons of men with a view to their damnation without respect to their sins, or that he is not too good to punish his creatures as creatures. But how is it as to his purpose to damn men *for their sins* and to punish his *sinful* creatures? We must not suppose, because there is a purpose of election uninfluenced by foreseen holiness, that there is therefore a purpose of reprobation which has no connection with the sins of men. There is no such purpose as the latter, for the wages of sin is death. The lost earn the wages paid them—eternal death ; but the saved do not earn eternal life, for it is the gift of God. It is a fact that every mouth is stopped and all the world is guilty before God. All the inhabitants of the world being guilty deserve to be punished ; that is, deserve to suffer the penalty of the law by a violation of which guilt

10 *

has been incurred. God may justly punish the guilty—all the guilty—for their sins. If he chooses to save some of them to the praise of his glorious grace, and to leave the rest to suffer the consequences of sin to the glory of his justice, who shall find fault? Who shall charge God with unrighteousness? But some object to any *purpose* on the part of God to punish sinners. There is nothing valid in the objection. God does punish men for their sins. It is therefore right for him to do so, for he cannot do wrong. If it is right, it cannot be wrong for him to form the purpose to punish, for his purpose is only his intention to do right in vindication of his justice.

Thus does it appear that this purpose of God is in full accord with the soundest principles of reason and righteousness. It is nothing more than his determination to treat those who live and die in impenitence as they deserve to be treated. There will be no departure from these principles in the miseries of hell. No lost sinner will ever feel a pang which he does not deserve to feel. There will be no arbitrary infliction of pain. No groan will be capriciously wrung from the bosom. No tear will be causelessly drawn from the eye. The fires of perdition will glorify the perfect justice of God. The wages of sin is death, and no more wages will be paid than have been earned. Justice will be done, and the sinner will feel that justice has him in custody. What anguish will this fact create! Could the ruined sinner persuade himself that his damnation is his misfortune. and not his fault; that he is unjustly dealt with,—how would his miseries be alleviated! But there will be no such alleviation. The sorrows of hell are unmitigated sorrows. The lost soul will know and feel that it suffers its deserts—no more no less

CHAPTER VIII.

CREATION.

A CONSIDERATION of the work of creation properly follows a discussion of the divine purposes. The reason is obvious, because creation initiates the execution of these purposes. While the purposes of God are as eternal as himself, there could be, so far as we can conceive, no execution of them before the creation of the universe. He must have begun to do, in the exercise of his creative power, what he from eternity had determined to do. It is worthy of God to do "all things after the counsel of his own will;" and this means that he conforms his acts to the plan devised by his infinite wisdom. This plan, if we speak after the manner of men, called for the creation of all things that were brought into existence.

What is creation? is an important question. Some learned men in ancient and in modern times have held the doctrine of the eternity of matter. Those who adopt this view do not believe in creation in the supreme sense of the word. They can only regard it as the disposal and arrangement of materials already existing. The correct theory of creation is the production of something out of nothing. The philosophers of Greece and Rome, as well as the masses of the people, declared this impossible, and accepted as an axiom the proverb, " Out of nothing nothing comes." This is true, so far as finite power is concerned, for it can be exerted only on that which has existence. In other words, it must have something to work upon, and in this sense it is subject to limitations. But this is not the case with infinite power; and therefore that is possible with God which is impossible with men. "In the beginning God created the heaven and the earth." Gen. i. 1. By heaven and earth is no doubt meant what we mean by the term universe, embracing all things; and these things conceived to exist in two classes, things above and things below. When God created heaven and earth he brought into being what had no existence before. There was an absolute production of something out of nothing. We need not ask how this could be, for it is the greatest of wonders and must ever defy finite comprehension. While man in his operations uses materials furnished to his hands, God in creation originated materials themselves. This idea of absolute origination is the central idea in creation.

We are dependent on the Bible for what we know of creation, for the Bible is the book of God. As he was the only being present at creation, it is manifest that the book inspired by him is the only book which can give us an account of the wonderful display of his creative power. "Through faith we understand that the worlds were framed by the word of God, so that things which are seen were not made of things which do appear." Heb. xi. 3. It is worthy of remark that the sacred writer, intending to give illustrations of the power and value of faith, refers first to the creation of the world. No secular history goes oack to creation, and it is therefore useless to search historical records for information concerning the creation of the world. Nor will the speculations of reason and philosophy enable any man to account satisfactorily for the work

of creation. Men have often indulged in such speculations, but they have proved to be vain and unprofitable.
Faith is the only means of attaining satisfactory knowledge of the creation of the universe. "By faith we understand." Faith implies testimony, and the testimony
in this case is to be found in the first chapter of Genesis.
There we learn that the work of creation was performed
by the word of God. In the language of the Psalmist,
"By the word of the Lord were the heavens made; and
all the host of them by the word of his mouth." "For
he spake, and it was done; he commanded, and it stood
fast." Ps. xxxiii. 6, 9. Infinite energy accompanied his
word, and therefore "the worlds were framed by his
word;" and the inspired account of the matter we receive by faith, accepting the testimony only and solely
because it is the testimony of God. How it relieves the
anxious mind and gives rest to the throbbing brain by
faith to understand that the worlds were framed by the
word of God!

But the reasoning of the inspired writer is that if "the
worlds were framed by the word of God," then "things
which are seen were not made of things which do appear." There are two points brought to view here: First,
that things which are seen were made, that is, were
brought into existence; and secondly, that they were not
made out of "things which do appear," that is, out of
pre-existing materials. There was, therefore, in the highest sense of the word, a creation. This was God's work,
for it is his prerogative to "call those things which are
not as though they were."

In contemplating the six days of creation it is well to
refer to the Mosaic account, that we may see what was
done on each day. I therefore quote as follows: "In the
beginning God created the heaven and the earth. And

the earth was without form, and void; and darkness was upon the face of the deep [the abyss]. And the Spirit of God moved upon the face of the waters. And God said, Let there be light: and there was light. And God saw the light that it was good: and God divided the light from the darkness. And God called the light Day, and the darkness he called Night. And the evening and the morning were the first day." Gen. i. 1–5.

Philosophers of ancient times would have prized more highly than thousands of gold and silver this statement, which is sublime in its simplicity and simple in its sublimity. Such information as it affords would have superseded many useless speculations and fruitless inquiries. Of the earth, it is said that it was "without form, and void." What is called "the deep," or the abyss, was covered with darkness. Everything was in a state of chaotic confusion, and "the Spirit of God moved upon [or brooded over] the face of the waters." The imagery employed here is supposed by scholars to be derived from the brooding of fowls over their eggs to communicate life-giving warmth. There was nothing but darkness. Light being necessary in carrying out the divine purposes, God said, "Let there be light: and there was light." The force, the beauty, and the sublimity of these words defy paraphrase. Concerning light many questions may be asked which can receive no answer, but we trace its origin to the first day of creation. It seems at first to have been mingled with darkness, but God divided between the two, calling the light day and the darkness night. When the light making the day was followed by darkness, there was evening; and when the darkness was followed by light, there was morning. The evening and the morning—from the first light until light came again—constituted the first day.

" And God said, Let there be a firmament in the midst
of the waters, and let it divide the waters from the waters. And God made the firmament, and divided the
waters which were under the firmament from the waters
which were above the firmament: and it was so. And
God called the firmament Heaven. And the evening and
the morning were the second day." Gen. i. 6–8.

This language leads us to infer that before the second
day dense vapors and mists enveloped the earth. There
was no firmament, no expanse, and God therefore said, " Let
there be a firmament." The purpose of this firmament
was to effect a division in the waters. The expanse was the
place of division. Below this expanse, or firmament, the
weightier parts of the waters remained in contact with
the earth, spread out on its face, while the lighter vapors
ascended, finding a home in the clouds above the expanse.
This was plainly designed to be a permanent arrangement.
Hence to this day the process of evaporation goes on, sat-
urating the clouds with moisture, which, under suitable
conditions, falls to the earth in the form of rain. This
evaporating process goes on with uninterrupted constancy, and subserves very important purposes.

" And God said, Let the waters under the heaven be
gathered together into one place, and let the dry land
appear: and it was so. And God called the dry land
Earth ; and the gathering together of the waters called he
Seas : and God saw that it was good. And God said, Let
the earth bring forth grass, the herb yielding seed and the
fruit tree yielding fruit after his kind, whose seed is
in itself, upon the earth : and it was so. And the earth
brought forth grass, and herb yielding seed after its kind,
and the tree yielding fruit, whose seed was in itself, after
its kind : and God saw that it was good. And the evening and the morning were the third day." Gen. i. 9–13

Before the occurrences of the third day the world could not be properly called a terraqueous globe. The dry land did not appear. The gathering together of the waters into distinct places involved, of course, the upheaval of certain portions of the earth. This was done by the power of God. The dry land was called Earth, and the waters when they filled the depressions caused by the emergence of the dry land were called Seas. These names are as appropriate now as they were then. The earth was commanded to bring forth grass, the herb yielding seed, and the fruit tree with seed in itself; and, being endowed with vegetative power, the earth obeyed the divine fiat. By these remarkable events was the third day signalized.

"And God said, Let there be lights in the firmament of the heaven to divide the day from the night; and let them be for signs, and for seasons, and for days and years: and let them be for lights in the firmament of the heaven to give light upon the earth: and it was so. And God made two great lights; the greater light to rule the day, and the lesser light to rule the night: he made the stars also. And God set them in the firmament of the heaven, to give light upon the earth, and to rule over the day and over the night, and to divide the light from the darkness: and God saw that it was good. And the evening and the morning were the fourth day." Gen. i. 14-19.

Light, as we have seen, was created on the first day, but on the fourth day the sun and the moon were placed in the heavens as luminaries, or light-bearers. It is worthy of notice that in the sacred narrative the sun and moon, though evidently referred to, are not named, but the sun is described as the "greater" and the moon as the "lesser light." We may suppose that the light created on the first day had been diffusing itself, modifying and relieving chaotic darkness, until the fourth day, when the sun and moon were made its depositories. The sun, however, was the chief depository, for it is well known that the moon shines by light borrowed from the sun and reflected on the earth.

The purpose for which "the two great lights" were established in the heavens was threefold : they were designed to mark a formal division " between the day and the night;" to be "for signs and for seasons, and for days and years ;" and also, so far as this world is concerned, to "give light upon the earth." They have been performing their office for nearly six thousand years. They have divided the day and the night, faithfully answering the purpose of their creation by " affording signs to the mariner to aid his navigation of the ocean ; to the husbandman to guide him with reference to the proper seasons of sowing and reaping ; and to all they serve as the grand regulators, the standard measurers of our time, dividing it into days and months and years." The sun and moon are personified, the former represented as ruling the day, and the latter the night. This has been the case through all the centuries of time.

" And God said, Let the waters bring forth abundantly the moving creature that hath life, and fowl that may fly above the earth in the open firmament of heaven. And God created great whales and every living creature that moveth, which the waters brought forth abundantly after their kind, and every winged fowl after his kind : and God saw that it was good. And God blessed them, saying, Be fruitful and multiply, and fill the waters in the seas, and let fowl multiply in the earth. And the evening and the morning were the fifth day." Gen. i. 20-23.

11

As the third day was the beginning of vegetable life, so the fifth day was distinguished by the creation of animal life. God gave the waters command to bring forth abundantly, even to swarm with living creatures ; and it was so. He created "great whales," or mighty monsters of the sea, and the innumerable little vital forms which are indebted to the microscope for recognition, with all the intermediate grades of animal existence. Jehovah is properly termed in the Sacred Scriptures the living God, for he has life in himself and is the source of life to all creatures. While the waters were commanded also to bring forth fowl, it is to be observed that "God created every winged fowl after its kind," and said, as we read in the margin of our Bibles, " let fowl fly " above the earth. Thus on the fifth day were created inhabitants of the waters and occupants of the earth.

"And God said, Let the earth bring forth the living creature after his kind, cattle, and creeping thing, and beast of the earth after his kind : and it was so. And God made the beast of the earth after his kind, and cattle after their kind, and every thing that creepeth upon the earth after his kind : and God saw that it was good. And God said, Let us make man in our image, after our likeness ; and let them have dominion over the fish of the sea, and over the fowl of the air, and over the cattle, and over all the earth, and over every creeping thing that creepeth upon the earth. So God created man in his own image, in the image of God created he him ; male and female created he them. And God blessed them, and God said unto them, Be fruitful, and multiply, and replenish the earth, and subdue it : and have dominion over the fish of the sea, and over the fowl of the air, and over every living thing that moveth upon the earth. . . . And God saw every thing that he had made, and behold, it was very good. And the evening and the mcrning were the sixth day." Gen. i. 24–31.

"Cattle, and creeping thing, and beast of the earth " are included in the phrase "living creature.' The term " cattle " may be regarded as the representative of all domestic animals; "creeping thing" denotes the various orders of reptiles; while "beasts of the earth " is descrip tive of wild animals that roam over the earth.

Thus it appears that while "the moving creature " and "the fowl " came forth from the waters, "cattle, and creeping thing, and beast " are of the earth, that is, were formed of its substance. Still, it must be remembered that the waters and the earth had no creative power, for it is said that "God created " and that "God made." The creation of living beings as well as of inanimate matter was the work of God.

On the sixth day of creation man was brought into existence. He was made in the image of God after the divine likeness. There is no reference to a bodily image, for God is a Spirit. Man, unlike all other creatures that took the places assigned them on the land and in the sea, was made a rational being, and in this sense he was created in the image of God. The possession of rationality does not, however, by any means exhaust the import of the words "in our image." They are in the highest sense expressive of holiness. We therefore read that "God hath made man upright." Eccl. vii. 29. We learn, too, that regeneration restores fallen man to the image of God, which image consists "in righteousness and true holiness." Eph. iv. 24; Col. iii. 10.

The six days of creation have now passed in rapid review, and it is well to remember that in the giving of the law on Sinai there is incorporated, as a reason for observing the Sabbath day, this language: "For in six days the Lord made heaven and earth, the sea, and all that in them is, and rested on the seventh day." **Ex. xx. 11.**

It is not worth while to encumber these pages with any elaborate reference to the arguments of those who contend very earnestly that the six days of creation were not six natural days, but six periods of indefinite duration, certainly embracing millions of years. They say that the term *day* often denotes an era, as when we say "the day of visitation," "the day of salvation," "the day of judgment." It is true that in these forms of expression twenty-four hours are not meant. But who ever heard it said of one of these indefinite periods that its evening and morning constituted it a day? This, however, is the record in the first chapter of Genesis: " The evening and the morning were the first day ;" "the evening and the morning were the second day." That the half of a period including millions of years should be called the evening of that period, and the other half its morning, is utterly incredible. The statement of this view seems to me its exposure.

The view of Dr. Chalmers is much more plausible. It is substantially this : that the first verse of Genesis is not to be interpreted in immediate connection with the verses that follow ; that the heaven and the earth were created at some period incalculably remote ; and that from that period to the time when God said Let there be light ' the earth was without form and void. Then it is supposed that God began to arrange in order materials which had been created before, and that in six natural days he finished this work of adjustment, making man on the sixth day, and committing to him the lordship of the earth. This view is far less objectionable than the preceding one, and it is perhaps generally held by those who consider geology an established science After all, there is great danger of "darkening counsel by words without knowledge" on a subject so incomprehensible as creation. Surely the creative acts of the Almighty were miracles. He might have performed them all in a moment had he chosen to do so, for who can limit his power? It was his pleasure to employ six days in the work of creation; and because it is a miracle to create, it is easily credible that the six days of Genesis were natural days. At any rate, those who hold this opinion should not be reproached with weakness, for their interpretation is the most natural one, and indeed no other would have been heard of if geology had not suggested it.

Before closing this chapter the teaching of the Bible concerning the purpose of creation will be briefly referred to. The following passage has a manifest bearing on the subject: "Thou art worthy, O Lord, to receive glory and honor and power: for thou hast created all things, and for thy pleasure they are and were created." Rev. iv. 11. The term translated *pleasure* in this verse literally means will, and the best authorities substitute *were* for *are*. Drs. Conant and Noyes therefore translate, "and on account of thy will they were, and were created." The creation of all things is here traced to the will of God. They were brought into existence because it was his will that they should exist; they were created because it was his sovereign pleasure to create them. The will of God, to which creation is ascribed, is inseparable from his glory. That is, God in willing to create the universe designed thereby to promote the glory of his own name. It is needless, and indeed it would be untrue, to say that he had no other object in view; but manifestly his supreme purpose was the glory of his own name. All other pur

11 *

poses are inferior and subordinate to this. For men to seek their own glory is selfish and culpable, because in this case they seek a low and insignificant object; whereas the highest and most important object—namely, the divine glory—should ever be had in view. Hence there is a positive command: "Do all to the glory of God." 1 Cor. x. 31. But how is it with God himself? The divine intellect in the boundless range of its contempla- tions finds no object of such exalted importance as the divine glory, and God is therefore under the blessed necessity of acting with a view to his own glory, and of subordinating everything to its promotion. He had his glory supremely in view in the creation of all things; and as the purpose of creation is executed in providence and redemption, we see that it is one and the same. We therefore learn from the Old Testament that "the Lord Jehovah hath made all things for himself" (Prov. xvi. 4), and that his glory he " will not give to another " (Isa. xlii. 8); while in the New Testament it is said of Christ that "all things were created by him, and for him." Col. i. 16. The statements are in perfect harmony, because the Jehovah of the Old is the Jesus of the New Testament. When the light of eternity shines on us and clarifies our vision, we shall most probably see that the work of crea- tion was performed, in order that there might be a theatre on which should be manifested the glories of redemption by the cross of Christ. Here I cannot resist my inclina- tion to quote from the devout Dr. Edward Payson:[1]

"To the cross of Christ all eternity has looked forward; to the cross of Christ all eternity will look back. The cross of Christ was, if I may so express it, the first object which existed in the divine mind; and with reference to this great object all other objects were created. With

[1] *Works.* vol. ii. p. 50.

reference to the same object they are still preserved.
With reference to the same object every event that takes
place in heaven, earth, and hell is directed and overruled.
Surely, then, this object ought to engage our undivided
attention. We ought to regard this world merely as a
stage on which the cross of Christ was to be erected and
the great drama of the crucifixion acted. We ought to
regard all that it contains as only the scenes and draperies
necessary for its exhibition. We ought to regard the
celestial luminaries merely as lamps, by the light of
which this stupendous spectacle may be beheld. We
ought to view angels, men, and devils as subordinate
actors on the stage, and all the commotions and revolu-
tions of the world as subservient to this one grand design.
Separate any part of this creation, or any event that has
ever taken place, from its relation to Christ, and it dwindles
into insignificancy. No sufficient reason can be assigned
for its existence, and it appears to have been formed in
vain. But when viewed as connected with him every·
thing becomes important; everything then appears to
be a part of one grand, systematic, harmonious whole—a
whole worthy of him that formed it. It was such a view
of things which led the apostle to exclaim, ' God forbid
that I should glory, save in the cross of our Lord Jesus
Christ.' "

This extract contains the seeds of thought, and the fact
that all things were created for Christ requires us to believe that the work of creation had reference to the glory
of God in redemption through the cross. The more we
study the wonders of creation, the more devoutly shall
we say, " Great and marvellous are thy works, Lord God
Almighty." Rev. xv. 3.

CHAPTER IX.

PROVIDENCE.

THAT God created all things by his power and for his glory may be considered an established fact. In doing this he began, as already stated, to execute his purposes and his plans, but there was only a beginning. Many divine works follow, though none precede, creation. What is commonly called Providence, the providence of God, is suggested by creation, and may be inferred from it. For it is natural to suppose that God takes care of that which he was pleased to bring into existence. This is a sufficient answer to the objection urged, from the days of Epicurus till now, against the providence of God; namely, that it is unworthy of God to concern himself about the things, and especially the little things, of this world. It cannot be unworthy of him to care for that which it was not unworthy of him to create. There is nothing in reason to justify the belief that God, having performed the work of creation, retired into the pavilion of his glory, giving himself no concern as to what should become of the workmanship of his hands. Nor is there anything in the Bible to countenance this view. So far from it, the doctrine of providence is taught and illustrated from Genesis to Revelation. Indeed, should we take from the Bible all that it says of providence, the volume would be greatly lessened and would, in truth, become another book.

But it is time to inquire, What is embraced in the providence of God? My answer is threefold:

1. *The preservation of what he has made.* God keeps in being what he was pleased to create. He upholds all things by the word of his power. Creation and preservation are inseparable. It is therefore written as follows in Neh. ix. 6: "Thou, even thou, art Lord alone; thou hast made heaven, the heaven of heavens, with all their host, the earth, and all things that are therein, the seas, and all that is therein, and thou preservest them all." In Job vii. 20 God is recognized as the " Preserver of men," and in Ps. xxxvi. 6 we read, "O Lord, thou preservest man and beast." In preserving his creatures, rational and irrational, God provides for their wants. " These wait all upon thee; that thou mayest give them their meat in due season. That thou givest them they gather: thou openest thine hand, they are filled with good." " The eyes of all wait upon thee, and thou givest them their meat in due season. Thou openest thine hand, and satisfiest the desire of every living thing." " He giveth to the beast his food, and to the young ravens which cry." Ps. civ. 27, 28; cxlv. 15, 16; cxlvii. 9. God's vital power so pervades the universe that " in him we live, and move, and have our being." Acts xvii. 28. I know not how language can express more forcibly the idea of dependence on God than do the words of Paul in his discourse to the Athenians. He teaches that this dependence is so absolute that apart from God there is in us no life, no motion, no existence. Manifestly, this is true. Separation from him would extinguish the mysterious principle called life, would arrest all motion, and put an end to existence. In short, if God's sustaining hand were withdrawn, all his creatures would sink into their original nothingness. His providence keeps them in being. He preserves his rational crea

tures, his friends and his enemies, his irrational creatures, from the huge leviathan to the tiny insect, and
masses of inanimate matter, including the waters of the
ocean and the compacter substances of the solid earth.
Nor is God's work of providential preservation confined
to this world. It extends to all worlds.

2. *The control of what he has made.* This differs from
preservation, though it includes it. God exercises dominion over all his works. Creation gives him the right of
control, and this right he does not transfer. All things
and all creatures are in his hands. He governs the
movements of every planet and the fall of every sparrow
He gives light to the sun in the heavens and to the glow
worm on the earth; for he is "God over all, blessed for
ever."

It may be as well here as anywhere to refer to a matter
about which there has ever been a difference of opinion;
and in doing so I quote from a distinguished author still
living: "There have been disputes among thinking minds
in all ages as to whether the providence of God is general
or particular. Philosophers, so called, have generally
taken the former view, and divines the latter. These two
parties have contended with each other as fiercely as if
there had been a real inconsistency between their views
The general providence of God, properly understood,
reaches to the most particular and minute objects and
events; and the particular providence of God becomes
general by its embracing every particular.

"Those who suppose that there is a general, but that
there cannot be a particular, providence, are limiting
God by ideas derived from human weakness. The greatest of human minds, in contemplating important ends,
are obliged to overlook many minor events falling out incidentally as they proceed with their plans. The legis-

lator, for instance, is sometimes under the necessity of disregarding the temporary misery which the changes introduced by him, and which are advantageous as a whole, may bring along with them. In short, in attending to the general, man must often overlook the particular. But we are not to suppose that an infinite God—infinite in his power, his wisdom, and resources, and present through all his works—is laid under any such inability to attend to particular events because he is also superintending empires and worlds. The pains, if we may so speak, which God has taken to beautify every leaf and flower, nay, every weed that we trample under foot—the new beauties unseen by the naked eye which the microscope discloses in the vegetable kingdom and the beautiful organization of the insect world—all show that the greatness of God is peculiarly seen in the care which he takes of objects the most minute.

" On the other hand, they take a most unworthy view of the divine character who conclude that his attention is exclusively directed to a few favorite objects, in which they themselves possibly feel a special interest. Here, again, we discover the tendency of mankind to measure God by standards derived from human infirmity. It not unfrequently happens that the minute man, who manages with care and kindness his own affairs and those of his family, has no very enlarged views or feelings of general philanthropy. Taking such a model as this, there are piously-disposed minds who would make God ' altogether such an one as themselves,' and conceiving it to be impossible for him, in the attention which he must pay to certain objects, to provide for the wants of all his creatures, they would praise him because, in the exercise of what would truly be a weak favoritism, he is supposed to pass by and disregard the whole world in the extraordinary care which he takes of persons who are the special objects of his regard.

" In the government of this world the individual is not lost in the general on the one hand, nor is the general neglected in the attention to the individual on the other hand. No creature, no object, however insignificant, has been overlooked. The general includes every individual, which finds accordingly its appropriate place. Provision has been made for all and for each in the grand system of the universe." [1]

In view of the subject itself, and of the way in which it is presented in this quotation, it may be safely said that a general and a particular providence so involve each other that the one cannot exist without the other. Generals imply particulars, and particulars are included in generals. I may therefore repeat that God's providence comprehends his control of what he has made. It embraces, too—

3. *The ordering of all events.* Of these events, so far as we are personally concerned, we may notice:

(A.) The time and place of our birth. If we ask why we were not born five thousand years ago or one thousand years ago; why we were not brought into being during the patriarchal age or under the Mosaic economy, but under the Christian dispensation,—the only answer is, The Lord so ordered it. He decided the time of our birth, the period at which we should make our appearance on the theatre of human action to fulfil our appointed destiny. It is obvious that we were not consulted, and that we had no agency in the matter. Everything was in the hands of God and under the control of his providence. If we inquire why we descended from Asiatic or European or African or American ancestors, the same answer must

[1] McCosh, *The Divine Government,* pp. 196–198.

be returned, for the very good reason that no other answer can be given. He who watches the fall of every sparrow determines the birthplace of every human being. If we wish to know why we were born amid the splendors of wealth or the comforts of competency or the privations of poverty, it can only be said that God willed it. If we institute investigations as to differences in color, and other natural distinctions coeval with birth, our researches must end in the belief that there is an overruling providence. It is unquestionable that God, either by his efficient or permissive decree, decided the time, the place, and the circumstances of our birth.

(B.) Occurrences during life. These are more or less numerous in the history of every person. It is estimated that about one-half of the human race die in infancy. This fact, in some of its aspects, is distressing and appalling, yet, all things considered, it is doubtless wisely ordered. If there is anything on earth that agonizes the hearts of loving parents, it is the pale face of a speechless infant tortured by disease, looking imploringly for help, and utterly unable to give an intimation of what would give relief, the weeping parents meanwhile as powerless to aid as if they were a thousand miles away. The multitudinous deaths of infants occur under the mysterious and adorable providence of God. As to persons who reach mature years, how different their conditions! A few are rich, many have a comfortable sufficiency, but the great majority are poor. Some who were poor have become rich, and some who were rich have been plunged into the depths of poverty. Some are always poor and diseased, not knowing, it may be, the luxury of a cradle in infancy, not spending a painless day during life, and indebted to charity for a decent burial.

Some are placed in circumstances which enable them

to acquire education and intelligence. Knowledge opens to them its ample treasures, and they revel amid intellectual delights. Others are uncultivated and ignorant, and scarcely make an effort to rise above their "low estate." Their mental impulses are not strong enough to stimulate them to the pursuit of knowledge. Alas for them! yet in one sense it may be well for them that they do not know the wretched disabilities of their condition.

(C.) The time and place of death. Of the time we may speak with certainty, and yet indefinitely. We know that it will soon come. "As for man, his days are as grass" (Ps. ciii. 15); "It is appointed unto men once to die." Heb. ix. 27. The appointment is inevitable and universal. The stroke of mortality falls on all "born of women." But we cannot tell when it will fall on us. It might gratify our curiosity to know, but it would be of no practical benefit. Whether we shall die at the expiration of a day, a week, a month, a year, or ten years, or twenty years, we cannot tell; so that while death is certain, the time when we shall die is hidden in the mysteries of the future. We are ignorant, too, as to the place where we shall draw our last breath. Though we may wish to die at home and among our kindred, God in his providence may order it otherwise. We may die among strangers, in our own country or in a foreign land, with no familiar face to watch the dying struggle and no hand of kindred to wipe the sweat of death from the pale brow. We might prefer to die on the land, yet we may die on the sea, the pulse beating its last throb amid the majestic roar of ocean waves. It may be our desire to die with some intimation, in the form of disease or other bodily infirmity, that death is at hand; but God's plan may require that we die suddenly and without a moment's warning. Great as our preference may be to die what is called a natural death, we may be hurried into eternity by some unexpected casualty. In short, the time and place and circumstances of our death are as certainly under the providence of God as were those of our birth. To him the time *when* and the place *where* we shall die, and all the surrounding circumstances, are fully known. Everything pertaining to us—birth, death and all intermediate events —is under the direction of God, who " doeth according to his will in the army of heaven and among the inhabitants of the earth." Dan. iv. 35.

Before closing this chapter it is well to notice two additional points :

1. *The doctrine of providence is full of consolation to the saints.* They are assured that the world, that the universe, is not under the dominion of unreasoning Fate or blind Chance. Many of the old philosophers adopted the one or the other of these views. While some of them believed in " gods many and lords many," they at the same time believed these gods and lords to be controlled in all their acts by a fate as irresistible by them as by men. Others ascribed everything to chance. They supposed the world itself to be the result of a fortuitous concourse of atoms, and that everything taking place in it must be as accidental as its formation. There is no comfort in either of these views. Fate and chance are impersonal things. There is neither life nor intelligence in them. We need a personal God on the throne of the universe, infinite in wisdom and goodness and power. Such a God the Bible reveals, and such a God his people worship. He is ever able to help them ; " For the eyes of the Lord run to and fro throughout the whole earth, to shew himself strong in the behalf of them whose heart is perfect toward him." 2 Chron. xvi. 19.

The eyes of the Lord are in every place, and where his eyes are, there is his omnipotent arm to protect. Love

and wisdom control that arm, and its power is exerted in
the interests of his saints ; "For the Lord God is a sun
and shield : the Lord will give grace and glory : no good
thing will he withhold from them that walk uprightly "
(Ps. lxxxiv. 11) ; "And we know that all things work together for good to them that love God, to them who are
the called according to his purpose." Rom. viii. 28.   What
thought can be to the servants of God more replete with
joy than this, that he sits on his throne, wielding a universal sceptre, and with infinite ease making all things
work together for the good of those who love him ?   The
Christian in the profoundest depths of adversity may
ever extract comfort from this precious truth.

2. *There will be a solution of the mysteries of providence.*
Nothing is more true than that now we "know in part."
The present state of being is imperfect, unfinished, and
needs to be supplemented by the future and final state.
When this is done we "shall know even as also we are
known." 1 Cor. xiii. 9.   But now many of the works of
providence are involved in obscurity and darkness.   This
is the doctrine of Scripture : "He holdeth back the face
of his throne, and spreadeth his cloud upon it."   "Thy
way is in the sea, and thy path in the great waters, and
thy footsteps are not known."   "Clouds and darkness are
round about him."   "What I do thou knowest not now,
but thou shalt know hereafter." Job xxvi. 9 ; Ps. lxxvii.
19 ; xcvii. 2 ; John xiii. 7.   Dark providences have often
put the faith of God's people to the severest test.   Jacob
said of his trials, "All these things are against me." Gen
xlii. 36.   The Psalmist was so perplexed by the prosperity
of the wicked that in a moment of despondency he said,
"Verily I have cleansed my heart in vain." Ps. lxxiii. 13
The perplexity of Jeremiah was in substance the same
"Righteous art thou, O Lord, when I plead with thee

yet let me talk with thee of thy judgments: Wherefore do the wicked prosper? Wherefore are all they happy that deal very treacherously?" Jer. xii. 1. Even the pious martyred dead are represented as crying, "How long, O Lord, holy and true, dost thou not judge and avenge our blood on them that dwell on the earth?" Rev. vi. 10.

Jacob in his lifetime saw the mistake he had made— saw that the things were for him which he supposed to be against him—saw that the selling of Joseph by his brothers into slavery would be overruled for the preservation of the chosen race. We may safely say, however, that the solution of most dark providences is transferred and deferred to the future state. But the solution when it comes will be not only a satisfactory, but a triumphant, vindication of the ways of God. It will then be seen that justice and judgment were ever the habitation and the basis of his throne. The trials of the saints, which now often crush their spirits and break their hearts, will then call forth their rapturous hallelujahs. Then will it be seen that their "light affliction, which is but for a moment, worketh for us a far more exceeding and eternal weight of glory." 2 Cor. iv. 17. It will be one of the delightful employments of eternity to contemplate the wonders of God's providence, and see how good was educed from evil, order from confusion, peace from trouble, and glory from gloom. This cannot be seen now, for

> "Blind unbelief is sure to err,
>   And scan his work in vain;
> God is his own interpreter,
>   And he will make it plain."

Yes, so plain that there will reverberate throughout the heavenly mansions evermore the words, "HE HATH DONE ALL THINGS WELL."

12 *

CHAPTER X.

ANGELS.

In preceding chapters there have been incidenta. allu sions to an order of beings called *angels*. They are sub- jects of the divine government, and the part they act in the history of man renders it proper to make special reference to them. Their existence is everywhere taken for granted in the Scriptures; and while they are several times spoken of in the book of Genesis, they are more frequently mentioned in the book of Revelation. To at- tempt to prove, therefore, that angels exist, would be superfluous and uncalled for.

The term *angel*, in its literal import, suggests the idea of office—the office of a messenger, rather than the nature of the messenger. Hence we read in Luke vii. 24, "And when the messengers of John [in the original Greek, the angels of John] were departed." It seems that when the Bible was written it was so common for some superior spiritual being to be divinely sent as messenger to man that such being was in process of time called angel, that is, messenger. It is easy, too, to see that the order of be- ings to which the messenger belonged would likewise be called angels. The term *angel*, being used to designate a spirit bearing a message, would also be employed as de- scriptive of kindred spirits, even though they might not be appointed to bear messages. Thus the heavenly hosts are termed angels, though it may be that comparatively few of their vast numbers are engaged in the delivery of messages. But this is a point on which it is needless to dwell at length.

While the word angels is sometimes used in a specific sense to denote a part of the inhabitants of heaven, as in 1 Pet. iii. 22, I assume that it is usually employed in a general sense as designating all the inhabitants of heaven, with the exception of the redeemed from among men. It will therefore be unnecessary to refer specially to " cherubim," " seraphim," " principalities," " powers," " authorities." Doubtless these terms are significant, but I shall regard them as embraced in the general term angels. This view of the matter makes plain the meaning of Luke xv. 10: " Likewise I say unto you, there is joy in the presence of the angels of God over one sinner that repenteth." No one can suppose that the joy in heaven over a repenting sinner is so confined to angels as to exclude cherubim, seraphim, and others of the heavenly host from participation in it.

Of angels the following observations may be made :

1. *They are immortal spirits.* The term *spirit* may be re garded in general contrast with matter. The two sub stances embrace all the objects to be found in the wide realm of knowledge. There is no substance of which it can be said that it is neither matter nor spirit. The world of matter is all around us. We see it in the earth and its productions, in the sea and its treasures, in the sun and the planets revolving round him. Our senses bring us into contact with the universe of material nature, and we hear, and see, and smell, and touch, and taste. It is manifest, too, that matter is capable of great changes. It may be fashioned into many forms and taken through many processes of refinement. Gold may be purified

seven times—that is, purified to perfection—till every
particle of dross is taken from it; and the diamond by
laborious and persevering effort may be fitted to sparkle
in a monarch's crown; but no operation performed on
matter, and no series of operations, can endow it with
thought, and will, and reflection.   These are peculiarities
of mind or spirit, and where they are found there is
spirit   They are found in angels, and angels are spirits.
They are in perfect contrast with matter, whether in its
grosser or more refined forms.   They are spiritual beings,
and we, burdened with the encumbrances of matter, can
very imperfectly imagine what they are.

While we regard spirit in general contrast with matter,
we may consider it in particular contrast with body.   The
words of Jesus authorize us to do this: "Handle me, and
see; for a spirit hath not flesh and bones, as ye see me
have." Luke xxiv. 39.   This language was addressed to
the disciples when they were in great fear.   To relieve
their minds, excited and alarmed by the supposition that
they were in the presence of a spirit, he said, "Handle
me, and see."   They were by personal examination to
assure themselves that he had "flesh and bones," and this
was to be decisive of the point that he was not a spirit.
A body, we know, has "flesh and bones," for they are so
essential to it that there can be no body without them.
Here, then, the words of Jesus place spirit and body in
most positive contrast.   It follows, therefore, that as angels
are spirits, as we are taught in Heb. i. 7, they are without bodies.   Many suppose that they are capable of assuming bodies or something equivalent at pleasure, and
that this is necessary to the performance of acts ascribed
in the Bible to their agency   Such a supposition, however, may have no other basis than the fact that men are
accustomed to exert their power through their bodily or-

gans and by material mediums. It surely does not follow that the same limitations are placed on angelic power; or, if this is the case, may we not inquire as to the nature of supreme power in God? Who will say that his power cannot be exerted unless a body furnishes the means by which it is done? I refer the reader to the first chapter of this work in proof of the fact that spirit is the original residence of power. Having referred to matter and spirit, it is proper to say that we know nothing as to the essence of either. Our knowledge of the two substances is confined to what can be known of their properties. Acquainted with the properties of matter, we can affirm or deny certain things concerning it; knowing the properties of spirit, we can also affirm or deny. This is all we can do.

Angels are *immortal* spirits. If asked why they are immortal, I can only say that their immortality is to be ascribed to the good pleasure of God. They are not necessarily immortal because they are spirits. Spirits would as certainly die as do bodies, if God should withdraw his sustaining arm. In the absolute and highest sense of the words God " only hath immortality, dwelling in the light which no man can approach unto." 1 Tim. vi. 16. The immortality of angels and men is derived from him and dependent on his will. Angels are immortal, because God has made them so. They will never cease to be, because it is not the divine will that they return to their original acthingness. The words of Jesus shed important light on the immortality of angels. Speaking of the righteous dead at the resurrection, he says, " Neither can they die any more: for they are equal unto the angels; and are the children of God, being the children of the resurrection." Luke xx. 36. It is clear that the equality specially referred to is the impossibility of dying: " Neither can they die any more." For this reason they are equal to the angels, and, like the angels, incapable of death. It is a pleasing thought that angelic spirits will live for ever. They are engaged in the worship and service of God, and he deserves everlasting worship and service. They are students of the wonders of redemption (1 Pet. i. 12), and these wonders invite endless exploration. Angelic research will be prosecuted for ever.

2. *Angels possess great knowledge.* All who believe in their existence accord to them intelligence and wisdom of a high order. The common belief among the Jews in the days of David can no doubt be learned from the fourteenth chapter of the second book of Samuel. Joab, anxious for Absalom's return to Jerusalem, sent "a wise woman of Tekoah " to David, hoping through her agency to accomplish the object. The only thing, however, that has a bearing on the point now under consideration is the following language addressed to David : "For as an angel of God, so is my lord the king to discern good and bad ;" "And my lord is wise, according to the wisdom of an angel of God, to know all things that are in the earth." Here it is assumed that an angel of God is wise and endowed with superior knowledge. Nor is it strange that the history of God's favored people from the days of Abraham encouraged and confirmed this view. There had been frequent angelic interpositions, the natural effect of which was to create the belief that angels excel in wisdom as well as in strength. Their superiority to men is conceded, and the point needs not to be argued. They were, no doubt, created intelligent spirits, their knowledge beginning with their existence. This being the case, we can understand why they, as " sons of God, shouted for joy " when the foundations of the earth were laid, as we are most probably taught in Job xxxviii 7

They, as intelligent creatures, appreciated the power and wisdom of God displayed in the formation of the globe knowing that it would serve as a theatre for the exhibition of the divine glory. Hence their gladness and their shouts of joy. But if the knowledge of angels was coeval with their creation, we may safely conclude that it has been increasing ever since. Their opportunities of observation, and the many experiences they have had in connection, as we may suppose, with direct revelations from God, must have added greatly to the stock of their original intelligence. They are finite beings, and their knowledge is therefore imperfect; and if imperfect, progressive. The knowledge of God cannot be augmented, because he is infinite; the knowledge of angelic spirits is susceptible of increase, because they are finite. If this one part of angelic history—namely, constant improvement in knowledge—could be written, how full of interest would it be! We know full well that angels have never been unconcerned spectators of the works and ways of God; and what centuries of opportunity have they had to learn about divine things! Their knowledge was increased before the Flood, and received new accessions when the human race was, with the exception of one family, exterminated from the earth. They learned much more from Abrahamic and Jewish history, scanned the page of prophecy, and when in fulfilment of prophecy the Saviour was born in Bethlehem of Judea, while one of their number announced the fact to astonished shepherds, a multitude of the heavenly host shouted, "Glory to God in the highest, and on earth peace, good will toward men." Luke ii. 14. From the birth of Christ till now angels have watched and cherished the interests of his religion, learning more and more concerning the achievements of redemption, and looking forward with devout anxiety to the day when the earth shall be filled with truth, righteousness, and salvation. Truly, angels possess great knowledge.

3. *They are very active and powerful.* To give us some faint idea of the rapidity of their movements, the sacred writers represent them as having wings, and as flying on their errands to execute the commands of the Almighty. These forms of expression are not to be understood literally; for wings, and flight by means of wings, pertain to material beings, and we have seen that angels are pure spirits. Of all creatures coming within the range of our vision, those which have wings and fly, exemplify the nighest speed. Angelic activity is, therefore, very impressively taught by the figurative language referred to. There must, however, be a basis and a reason for the use of this figurative language, and they are to be found in the velocity of angelic movement. Here, again, our conceptions fail; for, as physical motion alone comes within the circle of our knowledge, we cannot possibly say what is the nature of the movement by which a spirit goes from one place to another. There is transition from locality to locality, but who can explain it or conceive it? We only know that it must be inexpressibly rapid. In proof of this I may refer to the words of Jesus on the night of his agony and arrest: "Thinkest thou that I cannot now pray to my Father, and he shall presently give me more than twelve legions of angels?" Matt. xxvi. 53. The words were addressed to Peter to show him that his feeble help was not needed in that hour, for more than twelve legions of angels would be sent to his rescue if the divine plans did not forbid their interference. But the thought to be emphasized in the passage is that so many angels, their supposed residence being in heaven, could instantly appear in defence of their Lord. How

these legions of angels could pass with more than telegraphic rapidity from heaven to sad Gethsemane, we know not. We only know that the possibility of the thing indicates an activity truly wonderful.

There is also a passage in the book of Daniel to which reference may be made: "Yea, while I was speaking in prayer, even the man Gabriel, whom I had seen in the vision at the beginning, being caused to fly swiftly, touched me about the time of the evening oblation." Dan. ix. 21. Here there was such velocity of movement as defies conception. The movement of Gabriel was actual, real, whereas the movement of the "more than twelve legions of angels" was potential, possible. The two passages prove beyond doubt the amazing activity of angelic spirits.

Angels, too, are powerful. They are said to "excel in strength." Ps. ciii. 20. We are not to suppose that they possess inherent strength. They do not. They have the power that God gives them, for power in the highest sense of the word belongs to him alone. It has been his pleasure to endow angelic spirits with such power as has often appeared wonderful to men. For example, it seems evident that an angel had control of the pestilence which in the days of David destroyed "seventy thousand men;" for we read, "And when the angel stretched out his hand upon Jerusalem to destroy it, the Lord repented him of the evil, and said to the angel that destroyed the people, It is enough: stay now thine hand." 2 Sam. xxiv. 16. Another striking display of angelic power is recorded in connection with the army of Sennacherib, king of Assyria. The impious monarch threatened the destruction of Jerusalem, but it is said, "And it came to pass that night, that the angel of the Lord went out, and smote in the camp of

13

the Assyrians a hundred four score and five thousand."
2 Kings xix. 35; Isa. xxxvii. 36. This was a fearful
exhibition of the power of an angelic spirit. He smote
with an invisible weapon, and a hundred and eighty-
five thousand warriors fell before him. Having read
these accounts from the Old Testament, we are prepared
for the following in the New: "And after these things
I saw another angel come down from heaven, having
great power; and the earth was lightened with his glory;'
"And a mighty angel took up a stone like a great mill-
stone, and cast it into the sea, saying, Thus with violence
shall that great city Babylon be thrown down, and shall
be found no more at all." Rev. xviii. 1, 21. In view of
such testimony as this we can readily believe that angels
"excel in strength," and that on the last day "the Lord
Jesus will be revealed from heaven with his mighty
angels." 2 Thess. i. 7.

4. *Angelic spirits are sinless and obedient.* If God, as we
are told, made man upright, we may be sure that angels
came from his hand pure, spotless, faultless. We are not
left, however, to conjecture on this point; for the epithet
holy is applied to angels. They are called "holy angels."
Matt. xxv. 31. Their holiness, like the holiness of God, is
not only an exemption from all moral impurity, but an
assemblage of all moral excellences. These excellences,
infinite in the character of God, are of necessity finite in
the character of angels, because they are creatures. They
are objects of God's complacent love. They are just what
he would have them to be. They shine in his moral
image and reflect his glory. They ascribe to him all
conceivable moral perfections, and these perfections they
consider embraced in holiness. They therefore exclaim
with reverential awe, "Holy, holy, holy is the Lord of
hosts: the whole earth is full of his glory." Isa. vi. 3

They have an appreciative sense of the holiness of the divine character; they feel for it an intense admiration, for they are holy beings, and out of their holiness arises love to holiness as exemplified in God. In connection with the purity of angels, it is delightful to think of them as constituting " an innumerable company." Heb. xii. 22. There are countless myriads of them, and they retain their original rectitude. They are resplendent with the beauty of sinless excellence. In short, they are " holy angels," and their obedience is inseparable from their holiness. David calls on them, saying, " Bless the Lord, ye his angels, that excel in strength, that do his commandments, hearkening unto the voice of his word." Ps. ciii. 20. It has ever been characteristic of them to hearken to the voice of the divine word. Thus to hearken is to obey. There is law in heaven, and the will of God is the supreme law. Every angel recognizes this fact, and is practically conformed to the will of God. There is much meaning in the words of Jesus when he teaches us to pray, " Thy will be done in earth, as it is in heaven." Matt. vi. 10. It is taken for granted that the will of God is done in heaven. If so, it is done by angels. They are inhabitants of heaven, and it is their pleasure to do what God requires them to do. It would be a reflection on the completeness of their obedience to intimate that they ask the reason of any command. It is enough for them to know that a command comes from God. The source whence it comes is the reason why it should be obeyed. Angels so understand the matter, and there is, therefore, an alacrity in their obedience highly pleasing to God. Their only question is, What does the Lord Jehovah require? Some one in expressing this thought has said, " If God should send two angels down from heaven, commanding the one to govern an empire, and the other to sweep the streets of a city, they would feel no disposition to exchange employments." Why? Because the will of every angel is perfectly absorbed in the will of God. In such conformity of the will of the creature to the will of the Creator, true happiness is to be found. Angels are therefore happy. Their joy is complete and their bliss unspeakable.

The Ministry of Angels.

Having attempted to show who and what angels are, it is now expedient to refer to what they do. They are doubtless employed, as we have incidentally seen; but what are their employments? How are they occupied? Much might be said of their agency in the administration of God's providential government, but I pass over this topic, or only touch it in its relation to the service they perform for the saints. That there is such a service is plain from these words: " Are they not all ministering spirits, sent forth to minister for them who shall be heirs of salvation?" Heb. i. 14. To minister is to serve. Jesus therefore said, " Even as the Son of man came not to be ministered unto, but to minister, and to give his life a ransom for many." Matt. xx. 28. Christ died for the heirs of salvation ; and angels being in subjection to him, he has appointed them to serve the saints, and the service is most willingly rendered. It is unquestionable that angels take a deep interest in what I may call—

1. *The beginning of saintship.* The greatest of moral changes occurring in this world is that by which a sinner is transformed into a saint, an unbeliever into a believer, a child of the devil into a child of God. This change is inseparably connected with repentance, and repentance is indispensable to salvation. Jesus said in his teaching, "Except ye repent, ye shall all likewise perish ;" and

Peter under divine direction uttered these words: "Repent ye, therefore, and be converted, that your sins may be blotted out." Luke xiii. 3; Acts iii. 19. These scriptures show that repentance has an essential relation to the forgiveness of sins and the salvation of the soul. There is so much involved in repentance, such important consequences result from it, that angels rejoice over the event: "There is joy in the presence of the angels of God over one sinner that repenteth." Luke xv. 10. Such a sinner becomes an heir of salvation, and angels rejoice in anticipation of his ultimate equality with themselves. They at once assume a service which is to them unspeakably delightful, and they serve the Lord Jesus in serving those bought with his blood.

2. *Angels watch and guard the steps of the saints.* It is written, "For he shall give his angels charge over thee, to keep thee in all thy ways. They shall bear thee up in their hands, lest thou dash thy foot against a stone." Ps. xci. 11, 12. The words of Jesus may also be properly quoted here: "Take heed that ye despise not one of these little ones; for I say unto you, That in heaven their angels do always behold the face of my Father which is in heaven." Matt. xviii. 10. Without entering into the controverted question whether every believer has a "guardian angel," it may surely be said that the meaning of this passage is plain: The little ones, according to verse 6, are those who believe in Christ, and the reason assigned why they should not be despised is, that in heaven their angels evermore behold the face of God. Jesus therefore teaches that it is a serious and a perilous thing to treat with contempt the weakest of his followers. To show the estimate he places on them and the honor they enjoy, he refers to "their angels." These words, "their angels," mean something. The little ones who believe in Christ

13 *

can claim these angels as their own—in a sense, it may be, which we cannot fully understand, but still their own, "their angels." I see nothing incredible in the idea that angels are divinely appointed to watch and guard the steps of the saints.

3. *Angels convey the disembodied spirits of the saints to heaven.* If they invisibly accompany Christians through the pilgrimage of life, it is morally certain that they are with them when their pilgrimage ends. But what does Jesus say? Speaking of the rich man and Lazarus the beggar, he used these significant words: "And it came to pass that the beggar died, and was carried by the angels into Abraham's bosom." Luke xvi. 22. No one supposes that the emaciated body of Lazarus was conveyed to Abraham's bosom. It was the immortal spirit of which the angels took charge and which they carried to the heavenly mansions. Nor is the case referred to as peculiar and exceptional, but we are rather led to regard it as a common occurrence; that is to say, the obvious inference is, that angels do for every dying saint what they did for Lazarus—convey his disembodied spirit to the paradise of God. How little we probably know of what takes place in the dying chamber! We see the cold sweat on the pale brow, we hear the death-rattle, we feel the tears as they roll down our cheeks, and we are obliged to listen to the lamentations of bereaved ones. If, however, our eyes could be opened as were those of the young man for whom Elisha prayed (2 Kings vi. 17), we might possibly see an angelic escort waiting to conduct the emancipated spirit to its home in the skies.

4. *Angels will minister to "the heirs of salvation" when Christ comes again.* It is the fundamental fact of the gospel, that Jesus came into the world to save sinners; and a kindred truth is that he will come "the second time with

out sin unto salvation." Heb. ix. 28.   He will come to consummate the salvation of his followers.   His coming will
be grand and glorious, and he has told us that all the
holy angels shall be with him.   They will constitute his
shining retinue.   "And he shall send his angels with a
great sound of a trumpet, and they shall gather together
his elect from the four winds, from one end of heaven to
the other."   Matt. xxiv. 31.   The Saviour in his explanation of the parable of the "tares and wheat" said, "The
reapers are the angels," and added, "The Son of man
shall send forth his angels, and they shall gather out of
his kingdom all things that offend, and them that do iniquity."   Matt. xiii. 41.

We may form some feeble conception of the interest
angels will feel in gathering the saints together, for these
saints will be the same persons over whose repentance, as
sinners, they rejoiced.   Having ministered to them through
their earthly life, having been present with them in death,
having conveyed their separate spirits to the realms of
bliss, they continue their kind offices at the resurrection.
How will they exult when they see the bodies of the
saints, at the bidding of their Lord, come up out of the
grave radiant with glory and clothed with immortality!
When the redeemed hosts are invited to "inherit the
kingdom" of God, they will doubtless take possession of
their inheritance amid angelic congratulations.   Through
everlasting ages saints and angels will live in blessed
companionship.

SINFUL ANGELS.

Having referred to the character and ministry of holy
angels, it is proper in the close of this chapter to direct
attention to sinful angels.   I designate them thus, because
Peter describes them as "the angels that sinned," and

Jude denominates them "the angels that kept not their first estate, but left their own habitation." 2 Pet. ii. 4; Jude 6. It is plain that they had a "first estate," and a "habitation" peculiarly their own. Why they kept not "their first estate, but left their own habitation," we cannot tell, for the reason has not been given. True, one passage (1 Tim. iii. 6) contains an intimation that the sin of the devil was "pride," but as to the cause of his pride we know nothing; nor are we under obligation to adopt the theory of Milton or of any other great man. The fact that some of the angels sinned is the thing which concerns us, and we are concerned in it, because their sin had a disastrous connection with the destiny of man. There is much less of mystery in the sin of Eve in the garden of Eden than in the origin of sin among the angels. Eve was influenced by an artful and plausible temptation presented by another being, but this could not be the case with the first angel that sinned. There was no external influence or temptation leading to sin. Sin must have been the result of internal thought and purpose; but how the thought arose and how the purpose was formed in a holy being we shall not know till the judgment of the great day discloses all the circumstances connected with the angelic revolt.

It is evident that no federal headship was recognized among angels, but that they acted in their individual capacity. On this account some, in the exercise of their free agency, sinned, and others maintained their allegiance to God. All the probabilities are that sin originated with Satan, and that he had some kind of superiority, which enabled him to propagate his influence successfully among his fellow-spirits. Unless we regard him in this light—namely, as the head and prime mover of the angelic insurrection—it will be difficult to say why Jesus speaks of "the devil and his angels." Sinful angels are not his by any creative tie, for he has no creative power; but they must be his, because he is their leader and they act in subordination to him. He is, therefore, everywhere referred to in the Scriptures as pre-eminent among apostate spirits, and is called "the prince of this world" and "the god of this world." In the common version of the Bible we have the term *devil* very frequently, both in the singular and in the plural number. It is not so in the original Greek. The term translated "devil," in its application to Satan, is always used in the singular number. There are two other terms sometimes translated "devil" in the singular, but more frequently "devils" in the plural, but the best scholars tell us, that in every instance the translation should be *demon* and *demons*. The teaching of Scripture, therefore, is, that there are among fallen angels many demons, but only one devil, who presides over the demons.

This view seems to be sustained by Eph. vi. 11, 12. There we have reference to "the wiles of the devil," and we are told that our contest is not against human foes alone, but "against principalities, against powers, against the rulers of the darkness of this world, against spiritual wickedness in high places." Doddridge's paraphrase of the twelfth verse is so forcible that I will not resist my inclination to quote it. The reader will remember that the words in *italic* letters are Doddridge's translation, while the other words are explanatory: " *For* in the warfare we are carrying on, *our struggle* and contention *is not with flesh and blood* alone; not merely with human adversaries, however powerful, subtle, and cruel; not only with the remaining corruptions of animal nature, which often give us such painful exercise; *but* we are called to wrestle and contend *with* sagacious and mighty spirits, once

ranked among celestial *principalities*, though now degraded by their apostasy to be chiefs in hell, and *with powers*
that employ their utmost strength to ruin us, and that
still keep their regular subordination, that their efforts
of mischief may be more effectual; we contend *with* those
who are *the rulers of the darkness of this* age and *world*, who
have long usurped a dominion over it, and who in the
present age hold men in the chains of hereditary super-
stition and destructive errors, which have been delivered
down to them through many succeeding generations, and
with spirits who became authors and abettors *of wickedness*
even while they abode *in heavenly* [*places*], where they re-
belled against the God of heaven, and drew in multitudes,
who were before holy and happy spirits, to take part with
them in their ungrateful and impious revolt. With these
are we struggling for that great celestial prize which they
had for ever lost; and their nature, experience, and situation give them most formidable advantages against the
weak children of men, surrounded with so many examples of evil and with such powerful temptations to it." [1]

That the influence of the devil, which includes the influence of all the fallen angels, is very great, appears from
the effects ascribed to his agency. He is said to " take
away the word of God out of their hearts, lest they
should believe and be saved " (Luke viii. 12); to " blind
the minds of them which believe not " (2 Cor. iv. 4); and
sinners are said to be " taken captive by him at his will."
2 Tim. ii. 26. Christians, too, are the objects of his implacable hatred. He has " devices " against them, and
seeks their ruin. He is fertile in expedients to lead
them astray, and even transforms himself " into an angel
of light " to accomplish his evil purposes. He is the
chief adversary of God, and with unwearied constancy at

Family Expositor, p. 698.

tempts to defeat the divine purposes. His malignant depravity has shown itself in all ages, and the lapse of many centuries has not diminished its power. There is one fact which, perhaps above every other, indicates the greatness and the extent of Satan's influence. It is this The most effectual restraints are to be placed on this influence before the day of millennial glory can come. When in the strong, figurative language of Scripture the devil is "bound . . . and cast into the bottomless pit," then, and not till then, will "earth keep jubilee a thousand years."

While, however, we ascribe to Satan and his accomplices great influence for evil, we must not suppose that they possess compulsory power. They do not, and the fact of temptation proves it. Why should the devil tempt and allure men to sin, why present inducements to sin, if he could coerce them to commit sin? The process of coercion, so far as we can see, would be much more simple than the process of temptation. As Satan possesses no power of compulsion, men are culpable and guilty when they yield to his temptations. Whenever assailed by temptation they should, in imitation of the example of Jesus, say, "Get thee hence, Satan."

Speculation with regard to the future of fallen angels would be unjustifiable, but something can be said that does not belong to the realm of speculation. They are evidently in custody now, reserved to the judgment of the great day. I quote again from Peter and Jude: "For if God spared not the angels that sinned, but cast them down to hell, and delivered them into chains of darkness, to be reserved unto judgment," etc.; "And the angels that kept not their first estate, but left their own habitation, he hath reserved in everlasting chains under darkness unto the judgment of the great day." 2 Pet. ii. 4; Jude 6

Other scriptures prove abundantly that men will be judged on the great day, but these passages teach the same thing concerning the angels that sinned. They are "reserved unto judgment." All the facts having a bearing on their sin will be brought to light, their inexcusable guilt will be shown, and the divine procedure in their case will be fully vindicated. Truly, "the day of the Lord" will be a great day—great in publicly fixing the destinies of angels and men.

Wretched as are fallen spirits now, there is reason to believe that there will be decided increase of their wretchedness after sentence is pronounced on them at the judgment. In proof of the correctness of this view, I refer to Matt. viii. 28, 29: "And when he was come to the other side, into the country of the Gergesenes, there met him two possessed with demons, coming out of the tombs, exceeding fierce, so that no man might pass by that way. And behold, they cried out, saying, What have we to do with thee, Jesus, thou Son of God? Art thou come hither to torment us before the time?"

The demons, having effectual control of the unfortunate men, spoke through them. There was no denial, but rather a recognition, of their future doom. They seem, however, to have regarded that doom as distant, and they were anxious to know whether Jesus was so anticipating it as to torment them before the time. We may regard these demons as representing the whole confederacy of fallen angels; and if so, it follows that there is a universal belief of a fixed period when their torment will be greatly augmented. The basis of that belief, we may reasonably suppose, is to be found in some intimation given them when they learned that they were to be "reserved to the judgment of the great day."

CHAPTER XI.

MAN.

ANGELS and men, so far as we know, constitute the two orders of intelligent beings that God has made. It would be rash and foolish to assert that he has created no more than these two orders. There may be rational creatures in many worlds immeasurably distant from this—worlds the existence of which the telescope has not yet revealed to the astronomer. But, on a point like this, wisdom is silence. Having in the preceding chapter called attention to angels good and evil—to their ministry of righteousness and to their work of destruction—the claims of the human Race to consideration are next in order.

THE FIRST STATE OF MAN.

We have already seen that when the work of creation was finished it was "very good." In this work was included the formation of man, as to his body, out of "the dust of the ground," while God "breathed into his nostrils the breath of life; and man became a living soul." Gen. ii. 7. This language suggests the superiority of man to the various orders of animals, but his superiority is more clearly indicated in these words: "And God said, Let us make man in our image, after our likeness: and let them have dominion over the fish of the sea, and over the fowl of the air, and over the cattle, and over all the earth, and

14   157

over every creeping thing that creepeth upon the earth." Gen i. 26. Language could not more forcibly express the idea of universal dominion. Man was to be pre-eminent on earth, the lord of the lower creation. This is so plain that some have supposed it to be all that is meant by man's being made in the image of God. While dissenting from this view, I freely admit, and indeed insist, that man was, under God, to have supreme authority and control over the land and over the sea. This of course embraced dominion over the inhabitants of the land and those of the sea.

But it is time to inquire more particularly what is meant by the words, "And God said, Let us make man in our image, after our likeness." There can be no reference to a bodily image, for God has no body, but is a pure spirit. A physical resemblance is out of the question, because impossible. There have been useless attempts made to point out a difference in the meaning of "image" and "likeness" in the passage under consideration. I only refer to the matter to express the opinion that there is no difference. The image of God is his likeness, and his likeness is his image. In what sense was man made in the image of God?

1. *He was made a rational being.* In this he differed from all inferior animals. Of many of them it may be said that they excel man in sagacious instinct. What is instinct? Dr. Paley has said, "An *instinct* is a propensity prior to experience and independent of instruction." It is a blind, unreasoning impulse, that prompts animals to do certain things without knowing why or caring to improve the manner of doing them. Hence the instincts of animals act with unchangeable uniformity, and there is no improvement. Migratory birds perform their migrations just as birds did a thousand years ago; the beaver

constructs its habitation as it was made in other centuries; and the bee builds its cell as in the days of antiquity. Of all inferior animals it has to be said that they are irrational. The difference between them and man is as wide as the poles, for man is rational. He is endowed with mental faculties which are capable of indefinite improvement. He can, therefore, rise higher and higher in the scale of intellectual excellence. Man was originally made a rational creature; and, though we may suppose that his rationality did not escape the effects of the Fall, he is still rational. To this fact the apostle James no doubt refers when he speaks of men as "made after the similitude of God." Jas. iii. 9. They are now made after the image of God as rational, intellectual beings. This is evident, because they are proper subjects of moral government, and without a rational nature they could not be accountable. Human governments recognize this view of the matter, for they do not hold idiots and lunatics responsible. The reason is that in idiots the rational powers have never been sufficiently unfolded to furnish a basis for moral accountability ; and in the case of lunatics the intellect, though once developed, has been so impaired as to nullify moral obligation.

It is quite manifest that of all the numerous orders of earthly creatures man alone was made in his rational nature after the image of God. This was his glory—not his chief glory, as we shall see, but his glory. To be made like God, what a distinction! To possess a rational, spiritual principle, which is in a peculiar sense an emanation from the "Father of Spirits," what an honor! For it is very worthy of remark that while God is referred to as the Maker and Former of bodies, he is never called the Father of bodies, but "the Father of spirits." The idea seems to be that there is something in spirit which allies it specially to God—allies it in a sense in which no object composed of matter can be allied to him. Man, as possessed of rationality, intellect, spirit, was made after the image of God.

2. *He was made after the moral image of God.* This means that he was created a holy being, and this was the chief glory with which he was crowned. It was great glory to be made like God in his intellectual excellences, but it was the greatest glory to be made like him in his moral perfections. We are told that "God hath made man upright." Eccles. vii. 29. Our first parents came from the hand of God as spotless as the angels in heaven. There was no stain upon them, no taint of imperfection in their character. They were in their finite nature holy as God is holy. The beauty of holiness was symbolized by the oeauty of Eden, and all the surroundings of the first pair were in delightful harmony with the sinlessness of their nature and the purity of their emotions.

The character of God is the standard of moral right and moral perfection. Therefore, whatever comes up to this standard is morally right and perfect. Man in his original state was fully conformed to this standard. The disposition of his heart was right, his affections were placed supremely on God, his will was in blessed unison with the divine will, his understanding was full of light, and nothing came within the cognizance of conscience without securing its approval. The stamp of holiness was on the first man, the ancestor of the race. There is an indirect proof of the original rectitude of man which should not be overlooked. It is found in two passages in Paul's Epistles: "Put on the new man, which after God is created in righteousness and true holiness" (Eph. iv. 24); "And have put on the new man, which is renewed in knowledge after the image of him that created him.'

Col. iii. 10. The doctrine taught in these passages seems to be that regeneration is the restoration of man to the image of God, which image consists in "righteousness and true holiness." This being the case, it follows that the righteousness and holiness restored in regeneration were lost by the Fall; and, if lost then, must have existed before that great disaster. Man's original state was a state of innocence, integrity, uprightness, and purity. The approving smile of God was upon him.

Were we disposed to do so, it would be difficult to restrain our thoughts from going out in contemplation of the happy condition of the primeval pair. They walked in the unclouded light of the divine countenance. Their souls were filled with love and peace and joy. Every desire was gratified, every want was supplied. They lifted up their hearts with their voices to God in thanksgiving and praise for the blessings bestowed upon them in richest profusion. There was no need of prayer, and therefore ampler opportunity for praise. God was pleased to have worship on earth as well as in heaven.

How beautiful must have been the garden which "the Lord God planted eastward in Eden"! In it was to be found "every tree pleasant to the sight," whose "fruit was good for food." We may imagine that on every hand were flowers of thornless beauty and sweetest perfume, birds of brilliant plumage and richest voice, while the river which "went out of Eden to water the garden" sent forth its limpid stream bright by day and musical by night. The sun shone in cloudless splendor in the heavens, but beneficent only were his rays; while the moon threw a milder charm on all surrounding objects, leaving the happy pair in blessed perplexity whether to give preference to the sun and the day or to the moon and the night. How lovely was Paradise ere sin shed its curse and its blight

14 *

on the earth! What a suitable abode for man in his
original state! Alas! his original state was not permanent.

THE FALL OF MAN.

"And the Lord God took the man, and put him into
the garden of Eden to dress it and to keep it. And the
Lord God commanded the man, saying, Of every tree of
the garden thou mayest freely eat: but of the tree of the
knowledge of good and evil, thou shalt not eat of it: for
in the day that thou eatest thereof thou shalt surely
die." Gen. ii. 15–17.

These words seem to have been addressed to Adam before Eve was made, but it is evident from the subsequent
part of the narrative that she considered them as equally
applicable to herself. How long our first parents remained in a sinless state—in other words, how long they retained the moral image of God, in which they were made
—it is impossible to say. The matter comes not within
the horizon of human knowledge. Some have supposed
that man's state of innocence continued about a century,
and others have thought that it was of only a few days
duration. Conjecture is useless and vain. It is enough
for us to know that it continued until the fact was proved
that man was capable of obedience. This fact being
proved, it follows that his obedience might have been
permanent. That is to say, as there was nothing to make
his obedience impracticable while he rendered it, so there
was no reason why that obedience might not have been
perpetual. What was done for a day or a year might
have been done for an indefinite number of days or
years, and would have been done, but for man's voluntary decision to disobey. Alas for that decision!

Before proceeding farther it will be well to give the
scriptural account of the Fall.

" Now the serpent was more subtile than any beast of the field which the Lord God had made. And he said unto the woman, Yea, hath God said, Ye shall not eat of every tree of the garden? And the woman said unto the serpent, We may eat of the fruit of the trees of the garden: but of the fruit of the tree which is in the midst of the garden, God hath said, Ye shall not eat of it, neither shall ye touch it, lest ye die. And the serpent said unto the woman, Ye shall not surely die for God doth know that in the day ye eat thereof, then your eyes shall be opened, and ye shall be as gods, knowing good and evil. And when the woman saw that the tree was good for food, and that it was pleasant to the eyes, and a tree to be desired to make one wise, she took of the fruit thereof, and did eat, and gave also to her husband with her; and he did eat." Gen. iii. 1–6.

With regard to the serpent, it may be said that though the animal is not to be identified with Satan, yet Satan so evidently acted through it, that in Scripture *serpent* has become one of his names. This will appear from the following passages: " And the great dragon was cast out, that old serpent, called the Devil and Satan, which deceiveth the whole world ;" " And he laid hold on the dragon, that old serpent, which is the Devil and Satan, and bound him a thousand years." Rev. xii. 9; xx. 2. It is manifest that Satan is called serpent because he availed himself of a serpent in tempting Eve, and is called " that old serpent " because he began his work of deception and ruin in the world's infancy. It is difficult to divest ourselves of associations that have clung to us from our earliest years; and as there is in the serpent something very repulsive, we are apt to think it strange that our mother Eve was successfully approached by such an animal. We must remember that the serpent is not now what it was before the fall of man. The curse pronounced on it was heavy, and was expressed in part in these words: "Upon thy belly shalt thou go, and dust shalt thou eat all the days of thy life." Gen. iii. 14. It may be inferred from this language that the serpent before receiving its doom was erect, and most probably there was no animal so beautiful and graceful. Certainly, Satan, to accomplish his purpose, selected the most suitable instrument.

Some have thought it unworthy of God to make results so grave and so fearful contingent on eating the fruit of a certain tree. How could it be unworthy of him? He designed to test the obedience of the two rational beings he had placed in the garden. Obedience can be tested as well by a little thing as by a great thing, and possibly better. In doing a great thing, a man may be influenced more by the magnitude of the thing than by the authority enjoining its performance; whereas, in doing a little thing, so called, he is much more likely to act out of reverence for the authority of God. This is the very essence of true obedience. There is no genuine obedience without it. If any one of a thousand considerations possible should prompt one to the performance of an act that God requires, it would not be an act of obedience unless it were performed because required by him.

In the case of Adam and Eve the temptation to disobedience was by no means strong. They were permitted to eat the fruit of all the trees in the garden except one. Only one prohibition was laid upon them. They were told that, if they violated this prohibition, a terrible evil, death, would come upon them. So far as we can judge, there was no reason in favor of eating the forbidden fruit, and a reason of tremendous strength in favor of abstaining from it. The serpent, however, beguiled Eve and she ate the fatal fruit, giving it to her husband, who also ate. Paul tells us that "Adam was not deceived, but the woman being deceived was in the transgression." 1 Tim. ii. 14. This is in perfect accordance with the account we have in the third chapter of Genesis. Eve was beguiled and sinned under deception, but Adam sinned, as we say, with his eyes open. He knew what he was doing, and with purpose linked his destiny with that of his wife, while he cast the blame of his act on God, saying, "The woman whom thou gavest to be with me, she gave me of the tree, and I did eat." Gen. iii. 12.[1]

Eve, though acting under a mistake and a delusion, was by no means excusable, but Adam was far more inexcusable than she, for he acted intelligently as well as voluntarily. There was, in his case, not a single circumstance of palliation. He knew what he was doing. It is to be remembered, too, that the sin of Adam had a far more important connection with the human race than the sin of Eve. The man, and not the woman, was to be the head and representative of the race. We are therefore told that "by one man sin entered into the world," and that "in Adam all die." Rom. v. 12 ; 1 Cor. xv. 22. Men in contemplating the disastrous results of Adam's sin have asked many questions: They have wished to know whether his sin could not have been prevented—

---

[1] It is strange that so many persons believe that Adam blamed Eve for his act. He blamed God. "The woman whom thou gavest to be with me." As if he had said, Thou gavest me this woman to be with me as my wife; and how could the purposes of our conjugal companionship be carried out unless, by copying her example, I made her character and destiny mine?

whether he could not have been made incapable of sinning, etc. No doubt, if God had chosen so to exert his power, he could have prevented sin; but he did not choose thus to prevent its introduction into the world. He could have made man incapable of sinning. In how many ways he could have done this, we know not; but we are sure he could have done it by making man a piece of mere machinery, irresponsible, because not a free agent. That there are mysteries connected with the existence of sin, no one will deny; but it is certainly unreasonable to complain that Adam was made a free agent. What is free agency? As an agent is an actor, so the central essence of free agency is the power of acting as the agent pleases. This power was given to Adam. He had the capacity to love and serve God, in proof of which he did for a time love and serve him. In doing so he exercised powers that God had given him, and acted in accordance with his inclination. In sinning also he acted in accordance with his inclination, and illustrated the doctrine of free agency, for there was a perfect absence of all compulsory influence. Adam sinned because he chose to sin; he chose to sin in the exercise of his free agency; and he was capable of sinning, because he was a man and not an irrational creature.

Sometimes it is curiously inquired whether Adam and Eve did not sin in their hearts before they sinned in eating the forbidden fruit. No doubt they did. The sin of Eve had its beginning in unbelief. In giving credence to what the tempter said she called in question the truth of what God had said, and the unbelief of her heart led to the outward act of eating the fruit. As Adam was "not deceived," his consent to disobey God—and consent is of the heart—must have preceded the external act of disobedience. It seems plain, therefore, that the sin of our first parents had its origin in their hearts.

The threatened penalty claims attention. It is in these words: "In the day that thou eatest thereof thou shalt surely die." Most persons, perhaps, in reading this language, receive the impression that natural death is referred to. No doubt it is, but the death of the body by no means exhausts the reference. The bodies of Adam and Eve did not die *actually* on the day of trangression, but they died *virtually*. They were at once placed under the law of mortality—sin put them there—and the seeds of death were planted in them. There was, in consequence of sin, subjection to disease, infirmity, and dissolution; and the physical death of the guilty pair became just as certain when they sinned as if it had occurred while yet they were eating the fatal fruit. Not only did the natural death of Adam result from his sin, but the natural death of all his posterity results from the same cause. This fact, as it seems to me, is utterly destructive of the theory that the body of Adam would have died even if he had not sinned. The Bible knows nothing of death where sin is not.

I have intimated that something more than the death of the body is meant by the threatening, "Thou shalt surely die." Spiritual death is evidently referred to; and it is far more fearful than bodily death. The latter takes place when the spirit leaves the body; the former takes place when God leaves the spirit. By how much the soul is worth more than the body, by so much is spiritual worse than natural death. The cessation of union, communion, and fellowship with God is so great a calamity that death is its fittest designation. The spirit cut off from God as the source of blessedness feels a wretchedness which language is powerless to define. It may wander to the outermost limits of space in quest of something to satisfy its large desires, but that something is not found. It has never been found, and it never will be found. The life of the soul is in its union with the blessed God; the death of the soul, not its annihilation, consists in its separation from God. The consummation of spiritual death is death eternal. This consummation is sure to come, unless spiritual death is abolished by the impartation of spiritual life Now, Jesus, looking on eternal death, the culmination of spiritual death, as the greatest conceivable evil, seems not to have thought the death of the body worthy of mention. He therefore said, "If a man keep my saying, he shall never see death." John viii. 51. "He shall not see death for ever," is the more accurate translation of the last clause. He who keeps Christ's word will of course die a natural death, but, being saved from spiritual death, will not die for ever—will never see death in the most appalling sense of the term. Adam and Eve died a spiritual death the very day they sinned against God. They were cut off from him as the source of their happiness and joy. No longer did they live in the light of his countenance, with his complacent smile resting upon them; but they walked in darkness, and trembled under the frown of the Almighty. The garden of Eden was no longer their home, for they had sacrificed its delights and forfeited its pleasures. They learned by painful experience the lesson which their posterity have been learning from that sad day till now—namely, that it is an evil and bitter thing to forsake God. Jer. ii. 19. It is written of the apostate head of our race, "Therefore the Lord God sent him forth from the garden of Eden to till the ground from whence he was taken. So he drove out the man: and he placed at the east of the garden of Eden cherubim, and a flaming sword which turned every way, to keep the way of the tree of life." Gen. iii. 23, 24.

THE PRESENT STATE OF MAN.

We cannot suppress the sigh and the tear that the original state of man was followed by his fall, and it intensifies our sadness to know that his fall was the fall of all his descendants, and therefore our fall. Julius Cæsar fell in the senate-chamber at Rome, and the great poet of nature centuries after attributed certain words to Mark Antony while pronouncing the funeral oration. Taking the term "countrymen" in its widest sense to embrace all the inhabitants of the world, every man may say of the day of Adam's disobedience,

> "Oh what a fall was there, my countrymen!
> Then you, and I, and all of us fell down."

The truth is as resistless as an axiom, that the effects of Adam's sin were not restricted to himself, but have been transmitted to his posterity. By his posterity I mean every human being—beginning with Cain and Abel—that has lived or is now living on the face of the earth. In expressing myself thus definitely I only adopt the words of Paul in Athens when he says, that God " hath made of one blood all nations of men to dwell on all the face of the earth, and hath determined the times before appointed, and the bounds of their habitation." Acts xvii. 26. The unity of the human race has been denied by philosophers, so called, because they were unable to reconcile with such unity the discordant peculiarities of different nations. When the Bible speaks, let the philosophy of this world keep silence. The passage just quoted asserts most positively that " God made of one blood all nations of men." A perfectly literal translation would be, " God made out

15

of one blood every nation of men." This, of course, means that every nation, and all the individuals composing every nation, have descended from a common stock. There have not been many bloods; the Bible recognizes only " one blood." How could the unity of the human race be more distinctly taught? Then, too, the divine purpose is declared to be that " all nations of men should dwell on all the face of the earth." If all the face of the earth is to be occupied by a population descended from one blood, where will a place be found for any other population? The Spirit of God in the significant passage under review must have designed to meet and refute, through all time, every argument in favor of a plurality of races propagated from different ancestral heads. The doctrine of the unity of the human race is vastly important, for the Scriptures teach that ruin comes through " the first Adam," and salvation through " the last Adam," the Lord from heaven. But if any of the inhabitants of the earth sustain no relation to the first Adam, how can they be brought into union with Christ, " the last Adam "? There can be no connection with Calvary, if there is no connection with Eden. He who cannot trace his natural lineage to Adam will never trace his spiritual lineage to Christ.

In illustration of the unity of the race, it may be said that all men are sinners, for sin is everywhere and has been in all generations. It has never been confined to the white or the black or the red or the copper-colored peoples of the earth. It has prevailed with disastrous uniformity among all peoples. The highest mountains are not barriers to its progress, nor do the widest oceans stop its march of ruin and desolation.

All the inhabitants of the world, too, are the subjects of sorrow. All men, however descended, have been " born unto trouble as the sparks fly upward." Job v. 7.

Tears, the exponents of the sorrows of broken hearts, have flowed, and are now flowing, from human eyes in every clime.

All men are liable to disease and death. Physical suffering is universal. There is no escape from it. Men of every hue feel it. The name of the maladies to which flesh is heir is legion. Death has swayed a universal sceptre. His ravages have not been circumscribed by the limits of kingdoms and empires and continents, but have been world-wide. The stroke of mortality has fallen indiscriminately on all the nations, "from the rising of the sun to the going down of the same."

Surely, such sad similarities as these would not have been illustrated in all lands and in all centuries if the nations, though differing in circumstances, had not been substantially one.

The indivisible unity of the human race being a settled point, it follows that Adam was the head of the race. He was its natural head, and it was before the Fall that the first pair received the command, " Be fruitful, and multiply, and replenish the earth, and subdue it." Gen. i. 28. Their descendants were, according to the divine arrangement, to fill the earth. There is, outside of the Bible, no plausible account of the peopling of the world. We are dependent on sacred history for all satisfactory information, and it is from the word of God alone that we learn of Adam in connection with the natural headship of his race. We regard him as the ancestral source of human existence, whence every human being has lineally descended.

Adam was the representative of his race. I am aware that the Scriptures do not say in so many words that he was the federal head of his posterity, but they say that which can be explained on no other supposition. Hence,

after the Fall, God said to Adam that which was as true in his representative as in his personal capacity. For example: " In the sweat of thy face shalt thou eat bread, till thou return unto the ground ; for out of it wast thou taken : for dust thou art, and unto dust shalt thou return." Gen. iii. 19. Eating bread in the sweat of the face has been the universal law of humanity from the day of the expulsion from Eden to this day. There is an established connection between eating bread and the sweat of the face. He who eats bread does it in the sweat of his own face or the sweat of another's face. Adam, after he sinned, was obliged to extort from the unwilling soil the means of living, and his descendants are now doing the same thing. The toiling millions of earth's inhabitants are a monumental proof of the truth of the words, " In the sweat of thy face shalt thou eat bread." Many an infidel, while he neglects the Bible, is, in wiping the sweat from his brow, a living illustration of one of the truths of the Bible. When God said to Adam, " Dust thou art, and unto dust shalt thou return," he spoke to him representatively as well as personally. His return to dust was assured, and also that of his posterity. The fearful sentence has been in course of fulfilment to this hour. Nothing is going on more constantly in this world, than are the pulverizing processes of the grave. It is as true now as when Solomon wrote, that at death " shall the dust return to the earth as it was." Eccles. xii. 7.

Now, if it be asked, why Adam's descendants suffer such disabilities and receive from him so sad an inheritance, I can only say, Because he was by divine appointment constituted the covenant head of his race. I use the term in this connection as denoting that arrangement, that order, that constitution of things, under which Adam was made and placed in the garden of Eden. His position as rep resentative of his race was such that if he had retained his integrity he would thereby have secured the holiness of his descendants; but as he swerved from his integrity and sinned against God, he by so doing, not only ruined himself, but involved all his posterity in his sin and in its penal effects.

No one is more fully convinced than the writer of these lines that it is very easy to ask unanswerable questions concerning Adam's sin and its effects on his posterity; and it is well to remember our liability to "darken counsel by words without knowledge." It may be safely said, however, that from the fifth chapter of the Epistle to the Romans we may learn some very important truths. We are there taught that "by one man sin entered into the world, and death by sin; and so death passed upon all men, for that all have sinned." v. 12. We learn also that Adam, through whose transgression ruin came on his race, was a figure, a type, of Christ; that is, there was a resemblance between the two, which is seen in the fact that they both acted in a representative capacity. The resemblance is seen in nothing else. Moreover, it was "by the offence of the one" that "the many died," and it was "by one offence" that "judgment came upon all men to condemnation." It is very observable that the one man, Adam, is not only said to have brought ruin and death on his race, but to have done this by one offence; for I assume that in the latter part of verse 16 the "many offences unto justification" are in contrast with the "one [offence] to condemnation." We may suppose, without a doubt, that the sins of Adam after his fall affected his posterity no more than the sins of another man. His one specific, fatal offence was eating the forbidden fruit. According to the appointment of God, abstaining from or eating that fruit was to

15 *

decide the happy or wretched destiny of his race. The one offence

"Brought death into the world, and all our woe."

The fatal deed of Adam, designated "sin," "transgression," "offence," is in verse 19 termed "disobedience;" and it is said that "by one man's disobedience many were made sinners." They were so united to him, that they stood in him while he stood, and fell in him when he fell. Thus were they constituted sinners.

Adam's apostate children have often blamed their apostate ancestor for his disobedience, but they practically endorse it as soon as they are able to discern between good and evil. They invariably choose the evil and reject the good. Their depraved nature shows its depravity in their preference of the ways of sin. They love darkness rather than light. All the teachings of history confirm the truth of what the Bible says about the present state of man, and show that some great disaster has spread itself over the whole area of humanity. The condition of fallen man is clearly described in the Sacred Scriptures. When the apostle speaks of the condition in which the Ephesian believers once were, he describes the natural state of every one of Adam's fallen race: "Who were dead in trespasses and sins; wherein in times past ye walked according to the course of this world, according to the prince of the power of the air, the spirit that now worketh in the children of disobedience; among whom also we all had our conversation in times past in the lusts of our flesh, fulfilling the desires of the flesh and of the mind; and were by nature the children of wrath, even as others." Eph. ii. 1-3. This represents man in a condition of guilt and utter helplessness. He is guilty in his helplessness, and helpless in his guilt. He is the subject of depravity and condemnation, equally impotent to counteract the former or to remove the latter. The apostasy of the race is universal, and the proof of it is found everywhere from the equator to the poles. "The Lord looked down from heaven upon the children of men, to see if there were any that did understand, and seek God. They are all gone aside, they are all together become filthy: there is none that doeth good, no, not one." Ps. xiv. 2, 3.

CHAPTER XII.

MAN NEEDS A SAVIOUR.

THIS conclusion is irresistible. It follows the sad truth that man is a sinner; and this truth has been made evident in the preceding chapter. For, as we have seen, Adam, though created holy, did not remain in that state, but by voluntary transgression fell therefrom, bringing ruin on himself and his posterity. His sinful nature is propagated by ordinary generation; and the propagation had an early beginning, for it is said of Adam that he 'begat a son in his own likeness, after his image." Gen. v. 3. This declaration is specially worthy of notice in view of the fact that "God created man in his own image." Gen. i. 27. Had Adam remained in his state of innocence, no doubt his children would have been born as he was created, namely, in the moral image of God. But he sinned, and humanity, becoming poisoned in its source, has transmitted poisonous streams only through all generations. Paul, assuming as true the universal corruption of human nature, refers to "the children of disobedience," and says, as we have seen, that himself and the members of the church of Ephesus had formerly a place among them: "Among whom also we all had our conversation in times past in the lusts of our flesh, fulfilling the desires of the flesh and of the mind; and

were by nature the children of wrath, even as others."
Eph. ii. 3.

Children of wrath are children of sin, and if we are by
nature children of wrath, we are by nature children of
sin. Man's wretched condition as a sinner, and his consequent need of a Saviour, are also clearly taught in the
following portion of Scripture: " For we have before
proved both Jews and Gentiles, that they are all under
sin; as it is written, There is none righteous, no, not one:
there is none that understandeth, there is none that
seeketh after God. They are all gone out of the way,
they are together become unprofitable: there is none
that doeth good, no, not one. Their throat is an open
sepulchre; with their tongues they have used deceit; the
poison of asps is under their lips: whose mouth is full
of cursing and bitterness. Their feet are swift to shed
blood. Destruction and misery are in their ways: and
the way of peace have they not known. There is no
fear of God before their eyes. Now we know that what
things soever the law saith, it saith to them who are
under the law: that every mouth may be stopped, and
all the world may become guilty before God." Rom. iii.
9–19.

This is a very severe indictment of the human race,
for it includes Jews and Gentiles, the two divisions of
the race, and declares all guilty before God. Every
mouth is stopped in view of the just sentence of condemnation pronounced by the law. This is what is usually
called the moral law, the only law whose jurisdiction extends to " all the world." It is manifest that the foregoing
scripture teaches man's condemnation and his depravity
He is condemned because he has transgressed the law of
God, and the justice of the sentence of condemnation is
so undeniable that his " mouth is stopped;" that is, he

can give no reason why the sentence should not be executed.

As to man's depravity, it is clearly seen in his not seeking after God. He does not seek after God, because he does not love him; and not to love God is the essence of depravity. When the throat is declared to be an open sepulchre the repulsive corruption of the heart is indicated. An open sepulchre sends forth from a putrefying corpse the most offensive effluvia. What, then, must be the state of man's heart when his throat, which gives vent to what is in his heart, is "an open sepulchre"? When the tongue uses deceit, it is because the heart is deceitful; when the poison of asps is under the lips, there is always poison in the heart; when the mouth is full of cursing and bitterness, the cursing and bitterness are first in the heart; and when the feet are swift to shed blood, it is the heart whose murderous impulses give swiftness to the movements of the feet. The heart is the seat of depravity What says Jesus the great Teacher?—" For from within, out of the heart of men, proceed evil thoughts, adulteries, fornications, murders, thefts, covetousness, wickedness, deceit, lasciviousness, an evil eye, blasphemy, pride, foolishness: all these evil things come from within, and defile the man." Mark vii. 21–23. What a corrupt, polluted thing the natural heart is! How imperative the necessity of a new heart if man is to be saved! Salvation must have an indispensable connection with a change of heart.

Now, to show that man needs a Saviour, it is only necessary to show that he cannot by anything he can do remove the obstacles out of the way of his salvation. These obstacles may be termed *legal* and *moral*. The former are embraced in condemnation, and the latter are comprehended in depravity. These topics require distinct and earnest discussion:

1. *Condemnation.* I use this term to denote man's just exposure to the curse of the divine law. The wrath of God abides on him. The curse of the law is a righteous curse, and the wrath of God is righteous wrath. This will be seen if we consider that "the law is holy, and the commandment holy, and just, and good." Rom. vii. 12. It must, then, be a transcript of the moral excellence of the divine character. All that is meant by holiness, justice, and goodness belongs to the law, and it is therefore a perfect law. It is scarcely necessary to say that it has a penalty, for this is characteristic of all law. Divested of penalty, law would become mere advice, which might be taken or rejected at pleasure. If penalty belongs to law the better the law, the severer should its penalty be. The reason is, the better the law, the stronger the motives to obedience and the greater the guilt of disobedience. It follows, therefore, that the very perfection of God's law requires that there shall be embodied in its penalty a righteous severity, of which all our conceptions are probably very inadequate. If penalty as well as precept is a part of God's law, then both are "holy, and just, and good." That is, we are not at liberty to apply these epithets to the precept and withhold them from the penalty. They are as applicable to the one as to the other. If the "holy, and just, and good" precepts of the law are transgressed, the transgressor exposes himself to the "holy, and just, and good" penalty of the law. The penalty, being a righteous one, should be executed, unless something can be done to render its remission consistent with righteousness. Can man do this? If so, it must be accomplished by what he does or by what he suffers, or by a combination of doing and suffering. As to doing, it is clear that nothing can be done by man in the way of atoning for his sins. unless he is able to do more than the

divine law requires, so that the superfluous obedience of the present and the future may make up for the failures of the past. But is superfluous obedience a possible thing? Obviously not; for "the first and great commandment" of the law says, "Thou shalt love the Lord thy God with all thy heart, and with all thy soul, and with all thy mind, and with all thy strength." Mark xii. 30. If all the strength that man possesses is to be expended in the love and service of God, it is manifest that he can do no more than this. All *is* all. His obedience must be continuous, filling up the measure of every moment. If for the present moment and every future moment of his life his obedience is perfect, he only meets the obligations of duty—does nothing more; and what does Jesus say?—"So likewise ye, when ye shall have done all those things which are commanded you, say, We are unprofitable servants: we have done that which was our duty to do." Luke xvii. 10. This passage at once and for ever explodes the idea of a sinner saving himself by nis own merit. There can be no merit on the part of a sinful man, unless he can do more than his duty, which is impossible. Suppose man, however, to do all his duty from this hour to his dying hour, still the government of God holds him justly chargeable with all the sins of his past life. What is to be done with them? What disposal is to be made of them? Man cannot dispose of them at all, for he can do nothing with them. He cannot change the past, nor can he bring God under obligation to change it. He is under the penalty of the divine law, and can do nothing that will so honor the law as to justify the remission of its penalty. Release from condemnation by man's works is plainly impossible. "By the deeds of the law there shall no flesh be justified in his sight." Rom. iii. 20.

What, then, is to be said of suffering? If man cannot save himself by doing, can he save himself by suffering? It is needless to speak of the sufferings of this world, for they are a very small part of the penalty of the law. Eternal death is the truly awful part of the penalty. This we have seen in what was said of the fearful words, " In the day that thou eatest thereof thou shalt surely die." Gen. ii. 17. The same truth is taught in Rom. vi. 23: " For the wages of sin is death; but the gift of God is eternal life through Jesus Christ our Lord." There can. be no consistent interpretation of this passage which does not make the life and the death equal in duration, for the death is in direct contrast with the eternal life. Now, if the penalty of the law involves the eternal death of the sinner, and if eternal death involves eternal suffering, then it is clearly true that man by suffering cannot release himself from the condemnation which rests on him. The suffering will be commensurate with eternity, and we can form no idea of anything which outreaches eternity. How, then, can the suffering of a creature make it either proper or possible to remit the penalty of the law when the exhaustion of the penalty requires eternal suffering?

We may surely conclude that man, neither by doing nor suffering, can save himself from condemnation. If the doing by itself is insufficient, and if the suffering by itself is insufficient, it needs no argument to show that the doing and the suffering combined are insufficient. It follows that the legal obstacles in the way of man's salvation cannot be removed by man. He rests under the condemnation of the law, and there he must remain for ever if there is for him no deliverance but self-deliverance. How sad is man's state! He is justly condemned, and utterly helpless in his condemnation. The thunders of the divine law roll over his head and strike terror to his soul, but he can do nothing to silence those thunders. He must hear them for ever, unless salvation shall come from a source outside of himself. This is the only ground of hope.

2. *Depravity*. It has been said that in depravity are comprehended the *moral* obstacles in the way of man's salvation. Man, in his natural state, is the enemy of God. I use the term in its widest sense, as embracing the whole human race. We have seen that, according to the inspired utterances of Paul, Jews and Gentiles were involved in the miseries of a common apostasy. His argument is that the Gentiles, though less favored than the Jews, had sufficient knowledge of God and of their relation to him to leave them without excuse for their idolatry. More than this: their idolatry was not the cause, but the effect, of their depravity. For the sake of illustration, it may be said that depravity was the moral disease under which they were laboring, while idolatry was but a symptom of the disease. To the Jews, with their superior advantages, Jesus said, " Ye are of your father the devil," and " I know you, that ye have not the love of God in you." John viii. 44; vi. 42. In all ages and in all climes the carnal mind has been " enmity against God."

Whether man is totally depraved has often been the subject of theological discussion. In discussing any question, the first thing to be done is to ascertain the precise meaning of the terms in which it is expressed. If by " total depravity " it is meant that man is as bad as he can be, the doctrine receives no human illustration; for the Bible represents wicked men as becoming " worse and worse." Nor can we suppose that fallen angels, and the chief of them, Satan himself, are as bad as they can be. They are, doubtless, in a state of progressive moral deterioration—growing worse and worse as in character they become less and less like God. " Total depravity " in this sense of the phrase has no exemplification on earth or in hell.

The correct meaning of " total depravity " is entire destitution of holiness. Man is totally depraved in the sense that there is in his heart no love to God. We see in many unregenerate persons an exhibition of amiable qualities and social virtues which renders them desirable neighbors and useful citizens, but there is in them no spark of holiness. The influence of many things that they say and do may be beneficial to society, and even to the world at large, but they do nothing with a view to the glory of God. They are not prompted by the high and holy motive which the Bible recognizes and approves. The reason is they do not love God, and therefore care not for his glory. Who can ask for a stronger argument to prove man's total depravity, than the fact that he is totally destitute of love to God, and, consequently, totally destitute of holiness ? The depravity of man shows itself everywhere on the face of the wide earth. In civilized and in savage climes—where intelligence triumphs and where ignorance reigns—where despotism forges its fetters and where all men are free—" from the rising of the sun to the going down of the same "—man is a depraved creature. He may leave the land of his birth, sail across the sea, and wander over foreign realms, but wherever he goes or wherever he stays he has within him a sinful and a corrupt heart.

Now, the question is as to the counteraction and the removal of this depravity, which has alienated man from God. Will man himself start some counteracting process ? He does not wish his depravity counteracted. He will make no effort to remove his moral corruption, for he does not desire its removal. He is satisfied with the state of his heart, and lives according to its inclinations He is the voluntary slave of sin, and is therefore pleased with the slavery. Here, too, we may see that if man could save himself from condemnation—a thing, as we have seen, impossible—he would, under the impulses of his depravity, sin again and fall once more into condem- nation. In short, if he could remove the *legal* barriers out of the way of his salvation, the existence of *moral* barriers would render certain the creation of other legal barriers.

Such is the powerful dominion of depravity over the heart of man, that it can never be broken by influences originating within the heart itself. They must come from without if they come at all. Man, being not only a sinner, but in love with sin, does not wish to be holy. He cannot desire holiness while he takes pleasure in sin ; and even if he had all the "ability" that has ever been claimed for him, it is morally certain that he would not exercise it. It is as unreasonable as it is unscriptural to expect sinful creatures to act in opposition to the pre- vailing inclinations of their hearts. Hence I argue that man cannot remove the *moral* obstacles out of the way of his salvation. They are as incapable of removal by hu- man agency as are the *legal* obstacles already considered. Truly, man is in a state of ruin, from which he is utterly powerless to save himself. Self-help is impossible. We know what self-ruin means, but we shall never know what self-salvation is.

In view of the considerations now presented, it is as clear as the sun in heaven that man needs a Saviour. This is his great need. All other necessities are trivial as compared with the necessity of salvation. Man needs a Saviour to do for him what he cannot do for himself He is in moral darkness, and needs spiritual illumina

tion; he is in a condemned state, and needs justification; he is the captive of Satan, and needs deliverance;
he has a depraved heart, and needs regeneration.

The heading of this chapter—" Man Needs a Saviour—"
would only torment him before the time if there were no
Saviour. Indeed, it would be the refinement of cruelty
to remind man of his urgent, perishing need, without telling him how that need can be supplied. There is a Saviour. "This is a faithful saying, and worthy of all acceptation, that Christ Jesus came into the world to save sinners." 1 Tim. i. 15. It will be my business in future
chapters to call attention to the person and work of the
Lord Jesus, thus showing that he is the very Saviour that
man needs, the "only-begotten Son," whom God gave
" that whosoever believeth in him should not perish, but
have everlasting life." John iii. 16.

16 *

CHAPTER XIII.

THE PROMISED SAVIOUR.

IF, as has been shown, man needs a Saviour, it is a matter of the greatest importance to know whether a Saviour has been provided. On this point we get no information from the light of Nature or the teachings of human philosophy; because the science of salvation is above Nature, and comes not within the realm of man's philosophy. We must turn to the Bible if we would know what salvation is, and who is the Saviour.

It is an interesting fact that the first intimation of mercy to our race was given in the garden of Eden, immediately after the Fall and just before the expulsion of Adam and Eve. It is found in connection with the curse pronounced on the serpent. The words are God's, and they are these: "And I will put enmity between thee and the woman, and between thy seed and her seed; it shall bruise thy head, and thou shalt bruise his heel." Gen. iii. 15. It is quite worthy of notice that the seed of the woman, and not of the man, is referred to. The language seems to be prophetic of the miraculous birth of Jesus of Nazareth. His body was not produced by ordinary generation, but by the supernatural agency of the Holy Spirit. He therefore escaped the depravity transmitted by Adam to all his lineal descendants. Paul expresses the same idea more definitely as follows: "But

186

when the fulness of the time was come, God sent forth his Son, <u>made of a woman,</u> made under the law." Gal iv. 4. The words "made of a woman" suggest a peculiar relation to the female sex—a relation not sustained to the other sex—a relation created by the miraculous formation of the body of Jesus in the womb of the Virgin Mary. The promised Saviour was to be "the seed of the woman."

Centuries rolled away, and there was a renewal of the promise concerning the Christ. After the expiration of two thousand years, Abraham was called to leave his country and to go to a land which the Lord would show him. At this time, God said to Abraham, "In thee shall all families of the earth be blessed." Gen. xii. 3. Subsequently, just before the destruction of Sodom, the Lord said of Abraham, "All the nations of the earth shall be blessed in him." Gen. xviii. 18. After the offering of Isaac on the altar, Jehovah said to Abraham, "And in thy seed shall all the nations of the earth be blessed." Gen. xxii. 18. The nations were of course to be blessed in Abraham's seed, but the fact was not stated in so many words till after the offering of Isaac. As to the seed of Abraham we may learn much from Paul, who says, "Now to Abraham and his seed were the promises made. He saith not, And to seeds, as of many; but as of one, And to thy seed, which is Christ." Gal. iii. 16. The apostle under inspiration seized hold of the important fact that the seed of Abraham is Christ, in whom all nations are to be blessed. Thus the promised Saviour was known to Abraham, of whom Jesus said to the Jews, "Your father Abraham rejoiced to see my day: and he saw it, and was glad." John viii. 56.

There are in the Old Testament so many references to the promised Saviour, that they cannot be referred to in detail. His coming is predicted by the prophets, **and it** is assumed by them that he would come to suffer **and to** die. That they did not fully understand their predictions is manifest from the words of Peter: "Of which salvation the prophets have inquired and searched diligently, who prophesied of the grace that should come unto you: searching what, or what manner of time the Spirit of Christ which was in them did signify, when it testified beforehand the sufferings of Christ and the glory that should follow." 1 Pet. i. 10, 11.

It may have been that the prophets themselves were in some degree influenced by the Jewish opinion that the Messiah would come to live and reign, and not to suffer and die. We may be sure that it is next to impossible for us to imagine how difficult it was for Jews of Old Testament times to unite the two ideas of humiliation and exaltation in the person of the Christ. No man, so far as we know, was competent to the task till the rich effusions of the Holy Spirit were granted on the day of Pentecost. Till then the apostles, though they had enjoyed the personal instructions of Jesus, were in comparative darkness.

"What think ye of Christ?" is a question of infinite importance. Is he the promised Saviour, whose coming was foretold by the prophets? Do the Old Testament Scriptures refer to him? Of these very writings Jesus of Nazareth said, "They are they which testify of me." John v. 39. On the day of his resurrection we are told of his interview with two disciples as they "went into the country," and it is said that, "beginning at Moses and all the prophets, he expounded unto them in all the Scriptures the things concerning himself." Luke xxiv. 27. There are, then, in the Scriptures things concerning Jesus Christ, and these things, having reference to the

Old Testament, are chiefly prophetic. Without attempting an exhaustive reference to the prophecies relating to the Messiah, I shall mention certain classes of predictions, with a view of showing that they have been fulfilled in Jesus of Nazareth. Ay, more—that if they have not been fulfilled in him, they can never be fulfilled at all. May God enable me to present the matter in such a light as to show that the promised Deliverer of the Old Testament is the Jehovah-Jesus of the New Testament!

The classes of predictions alluded to are such as the following: Those that refer to—

1. *The tribe and family to which he belongs.* As to the tribe, we have definite information in the following words: " The sceptre shall not depart from Judah, nor a lawgiver from between his feet, until Shiloh come; and unto him shall the gathering of the people be." Gen. xlix. 10. From 1 Chron. v. 1, 2 we learn that " Reuben, the first-born of Israel," by an atrocious crime forfeited "the birthright" which "was given unto the sons of Joseph." The sacred historian tells us, however, that " the genealogy is not to be reckoned after the birthright;" and the explanation is that " Judah prevailed above his brethren, and of him came the chief ruler."

In exposition of the words of Jacob already quoted I make the following extract from the " Annotated Paragraph Bible:" " Having announced the sovereignty of Judah, the patriarch goes on to declare that it should have no end until one should come bearing the name of 'Shiloh,' whose sway both Israel and all mankind should acknowledge. The subsequent history presents the fulfilment of this prediction. In the journeyings of the Israelites through the wilderness, and under the theocracy in the Promised Land, this tribe took the precedence; after the return from Babylon it absorbed the others and gave its name to the whole nation; and even under the dominion of the Romans it retained a measure of authority. But on the appearance of Christ all this quickly passed away, to make room for the spiritual and universal reign of the Prince of Peace."

It is needless to say more of the tribe from which the promised Saviour was to come, and in the New Testament we read, "It is evident that our Lord sprang out of Judah." Heb. vii. 14. If the prediction of the dying Jacob has not been fulfilled in Jesus Christ, it can never be fulfilled. The conditions of its fulfilment once existed, but they can never exist again.

As to the family honored by its connection with the promised Saviour, it is without doubt the family of David. God said to him, "Of the fruit of thy body will I set upon thy throne." Ps. cxxxii. 11. The universal expectation of the Jews was that the Messiah would be the descendant of David. When, therefore, Jesus asked the Pharisees, "What think ye of Christ? whose son is he? they say unto him, The Son of David." Matt. xxii. 42. The multitudes also at his triumphant entry into Jerusalem cried, "Hosanna to the Son of David!" Matt. xxi. 9. Paul says of Christ that he "was made of the seed of David according to the flesh" (Rom. i. 3), and Jesus himself says, "I am the root and the offspring of David." Rev. xxii. 16. We have no need of additional testimony. It is not historically possible to show that any one except Jesus of Nazareth is, in the sense of these passages, the "Son," the "seed," the "offspring," of David.

2. *The time of his coming.* Of this there is all the certainty that can be desired. An important prophecy reads thus: "Know therefore and understand, that from the going forth of the commandment to restore and to build Jerusalem, unto the Messiah the Prince. shall be seven

weeks, and threescore and two weeks: the street shall be built again, and the wall, even in troublous times. And after threescore and two weeks shall Messiah be cut off. but not for himself." Dan. ix. 25, 26.

I take it for granted that in the "weeks" here mentioned every day represents a year. With this understanding we see that the periods of time designated must have expired about the year of the world 4000. It is perhaps not possible to make a perfectly accurate statement on account of the difficulty of knowing what "commandment" is referred to. There were more commandments than one. Hence we read, "And they builded, and finished it, according to the commandment of the God of Israel, and according to the commandment of Cyrus, and Darius, and Artaxerxes, king of Persia." Ez. vi. 14. The general opinion is that from the last of these kings Ezra the scribe received all needful help, and with a large company of exiles returned from Babylon to Jerusalem about the year 457 before Christ. This of course was some years after "the commandment of Cyrus;" but we can see with sufficient certainty at what time the promised Saviour was to come.

From the prophecy of Haggai we learn that the second temple was to be superior to the first. The superiority, however, was not to be in splendor and beauty of architecture, but in the personal presence of "the Desire of all nations:" "And the Desire of all nations shall come: and I will fill this house with glory, saith the Lord of hosts. The silver is mine, and the gold is mine, saith the Lord of hosts. The glory of this latter house shall be greater than of the former, saith the Lord of hosts." Hag. ii. 7-9.

The Messiah is "the Desire of all nations," and his presence rendered the second temple more illustrious than the first. The words of God through the prophet were verified when Jesus of Nazareth appeared in the temple at Jerusalem and taught the lessons of salvation. We learn from the prophecy that the promised Saviour was to come during the existence of the second temple, and therefore at some period between the commandment to rebuild Jerusalem and the destruction of the city in the year of our Lord 70. Jesus of Nazareth came at the time when God by the prophet said "the Desire of all nations" would come. Is he not, therefore, "the Desire of all nations"? No man of sane mind will say that during the centuries referred to the second temple was made more glorious than the first by the personal presence and teaching of any one except Jesus of Nazareth. I may say, then, that the prophecy has been fulfilled in him. If this is denied, the denial is a virtual declaration that the prophecy is unfulfilled; and if so, its fulfilment is impossible, for the second temple was destroyed eighteen hundred years ago, and can never exist again.

3. *The place of his birth.* The most striking prediction bearing on this point is the following: "But thou, Bethlehem Ephratah, though thou be little among the thousands of Judah, yet out of thee shall he come forth unto me that is to be ruler in Israel; whose goings forth have been from of old, from everlasting." Mic. v. 2.

That the birth of the Messiah, when he came, would take place at Bethlehem of Judea, was the opinion of all the Jews. When, therefore, Herod inquired of "the chief priests and scribes of the people" where "Christ should be born," they said, "In Bethlehem of Judea." During the Saviour's ministry "the chief priests and Pharisees" once attempted to discredit his claim to be a prophet by assuming that he was born in Galilee; and then they said, "Out of Galilee ariseth no prophet." John vii. 52. Humanly speaking, the birth of Jesus in Bethlehem was very remarkable. His mother was a resident of Nazareth, as we see from these words : "And in the sixth month the angel Gabriel was sent from God, unto a city of Galilee, named Nazareth, to a virgin espoused to a man whose name was Joseph, of the house of David; and the virgin's name was Mary." Luke i. 26, 27. Joseph, the reputed father of Jesus, lived at Nazareth, and most probably died there. Why he did not live at Bethlehem, as he "was of the house and lineage of David" (Luke ii. 4), we do not know; we only know that in obedience to the edict of Augustus, the Roman emperor, he went to Bethlehem to be taxed—or rather enrolled—because of his connection with the family of David. Bethlehem was some distance from Nazareth. Why was it not sufficient for Joseph to go alone? Why was it necessary for Mary to perform the laborious journey? I do not know that we can answer these questions, but we may reasonably believe that it was not sufficient for Joseph to go alone, and that it was necessary for Mary to make the journey. However this may have been, the decree of Augustus was the means of making Bethlehem the birthplace of Jesus Christ. Nothing was further from the design of the emperor, but the God of heaven over-ruled the imperial decree for the accomplishment of a great prophecy. Thus was the angel of the Lord author-ized to say to the trembling shepherds, "Fear not ; for, behold, I bring you good tidings of great joy, which shall be to all people. For unto you is born this day, in the city of David, a Saviour, who is Christ the Lord." Luke ii. 10, 11 The promised Saviour was born in Bethlehem, and that Saviour is the Lord of glory. No birth but his has conferred earthly immortality on Bethlehem.

4. *The treatment he was to receive.* Isaiah had prophesied (chapter 53) that he would be "despised and rejected of men," and that for very shame they would hide their faces from him. The prophets had expressed all the reproach and contempt of men in saying, "He shall be called a Nazarene." Matt. ii. 23. It is worthy of notice that no one prophet is named. The language is, "that it might be fulfilled which was spoken by the prophets." The idea clearly is that, according to the predictions of the prophets, the Messiah would be the object of contemptuous reproach. For Nazareth was in bad repute. Indeed, there seems to have been a sort of interrogative proverb in circulation among the people—"Can there any good thing come out of Nazareth?" John i. 46. Even Nathanael, a guileless Israelite, was prejudiced against the place.

The contemptuous treatment which the prophets said the promised Saviour would receive was received by Jesus of Nazareth. His name was cast out as evil. His enemies said, "Behold, a man gluttonous, and a winebibber, a friend of publicans and sinners." Matt. xi. 19. They meant, not only that he was the associate of "publicans and sinners," but that he was as bad as they. When his expulsion of demons was too manifest to be denied, the Pharisees said, "This *fellow* doth not cast out demons, but by Beelzebub the prince of the demons." Matt xii. 24. Thus they charged that Jesus acted in concert with Satan himself. There could not be an imputation of greater wickedness than this. When his enemies determined to secure the condemnation and death of Christ, they presented two counts in the indictment against him—blasphemy and sedition. There was a malicious shrewdness in this, for it was designed that the charge of blasphemy should influence the Jewish council, and that the charge of sedition should render certain a sentence of death from Pilate the Roman governor. Thus was Jesus the object of reproach, and thus he endured the " contradiction of sinners against himself." Heb. xii. 3.

5 *The manner of his death.* It was predicted that the promised Saviour would die, but not an ordinary death. It was to be a death by violence, for he was to be " cut off out of the land of the living." He was to die in the place of others, giving an example of substitution such as had never been given before. Of all this the fifty-third chapter of Isaiah contains abundant proof. It teaches also that the wonderful Sufferer was to be " stricken, smitten of God, and afflicted," while he was to be " led as a lamb to the slaughter." The death of the cross is no doubt alluded to in the words, " They pierced my hands and my feet." Ps. xxii. 16. It is scarcely conceivable that the piercing of the hands and feet would have been required by any other form of death; yet crucifixion was not a Jewish punishment. The remarkable Personage referred to is represented as saying, " I may tell all my bones: they look and stare upon me. They part my garments among them, and cast lots upon my vesture." These words are found in the same psalm, as also the exclamatory question, " My God, my God, why hast thou forsaken me?" This appeal to God indicates that the Sufferer's usual state had been one of intimacy and fellowship with God, and that the suspension of this blessed communion was regarded as the greatest of calamities. To be forsaken of God was the climax of the grief the promised Saviour was to be called to endure.

We may now direct our attention to the death of Christ, and see if it does not correspond to the death just referred to, and so strikingly portrayed in the Old Testament

Certainly, the death of Jesus was not an ordinary, but a violent, death. It was described in the words of the apostles to the Jewish council: "Whom ye slew and hanged on a tree." Acts v. 30. He died as a substitute, "the just for the unjust" (1 Pet. iii. 18), "giving his life a ransom for many." Matt. xx. 28. His hands and his feet were pierced, and his garments were divided by lot. Matt. xxvii. 35.

Such a death as that of Jesus on Calvary never occurred before, and will never occur again. The event stands alone, clothed with all the glory of majestic isolation. It may be said, too, that, if the prophecies concerning the death of the Messiah were not accomplished in the death of Christ, they can never be accomplished. All the conditions requisite to their fulfilment existed when Jesus died, never existed before, have not existed since, and cannot exist in the future. That the death of Christ was infinitely remarkable appears in view of such facts as these—facts which I merely present without dwelling on them: It was instigated by Satan, facilitated by a professed disciple, demanded by Jewish clamor, sanctioned by Roman authority; it took place in pursuance of the purpose of God, was inflicted by him as the Lawgiver and Executive of the moral universe, and it was, on the part of Christ, a voluntary death. The victim went willingly to the altar of sacrifice. What strange things are these! Satan, Judas, Jews, and Romans acted most freely, yet God through them executed a decree equally irresistible and eternal, while Jesus died of his own accord, verifying his own words: "No man taketh my life from me, but I lay it down of myself. I have power to lay it down, and I have power to take it again." John x. 18.

In view of the preceding considerations, which might

be expanded into a volume, I claim that the promised Saviour is Jesus Christ. He was promised in the sure word of prophecy, for "to him give all the prophets witness, that through his name whosoever believeth in him shall receive remission of sins." Acts x. 43. It may be said, too, that every sacrificial altar of patriarchal and Jewish times was a promise of the coming of him whose one offering of himself would be the consummation of the whole system of sacrifices. The blood of slain animals typified for forty centuries the blood of Calvary, the blood which "cleanseth us from all sin." 1 John i. 8.

17 *

CHAPTER XIV

THE PERSON OF CHRIST.

A REFERENCE to this topic properly follows the preceding subject, for if there is a promised Saviour, his person
claims attention. Who is he? is a question of the greatest importance. Manifestly, salvation depends on what
he is, as well as on what he does; for what he is able to
do depends on what he is.

This chapter needs not to be a long one, as I have written at some length on the Deity of Christ.[1] There will
be no repetition of arguments already adduced to prove
the Lord Jesus divine. Believing those arguments valid,
I regard the point as settled. We are accustomed to say
that Christ is God, and that Christ is man; and what we
mean is true; but neither statement is perfectly accurate.
The second person of the Godhead, apart from his assumption of human nature, is not the Christ; nor is the
Son of man, apart from his union with the divine nature,
the Christ. The only-begotten Son of God dwelt in the
bosom of the Father from eternity, but he was not the
Christ, till by his incarnation he became the Son of man.
A union of divinity and humanity was essential to the
constitution of the person of the Christ. It follows,
therefore, that the Christ is God-man. Divinity and
humanity are united in him, but they are not blended.

[1] See Chapter V

Humanity is not deified, and divinity is not humanized. This is plainly impossible. Divinity cannot take into its essence anything finite, and the human is finite. Humanity cannot be so absorbed in Deity as to become part of it. The two natures must ever remain distinct, while the person of Christ formed by their union will ever be one and indivisible. That he has two natures in one person is true, and must ever be true, of the Messiah. The union of the two natures is confessedly mysterious, but the doctrine is not, on this account, to be rejected. Its rejection, for this reason, would be strangely inconsistent in men who cannot understand the union of matter and spirit in their own persons. So far as we know, there are no two things more diverse than matter and spirit. The point of contact between the two is not only invisible, but the manner of contact defies comprehension. The fact however, of the union between soul and body in the person of every man, is unquestionable. To doubt it would awaken a suspicion of lunacy. While, then, we can neither deny nor comprehend the complexity of men's persons, we must accept as true what the Scriptures teach concerning the person of Christ. Divine and human elements belong to it. The explanation of this fact is given when we are told that the Word, who in the beginning "was with God," and who "was God," "was made flesh and dwelt among" men. There was on his part a voluntary incarnation, for the incarnation pertained to the second person of the Godhead, and not to the first or the third. It is not, therefore, strictly proper to say, without qualification, that the divine nature became incarnate, for this would imply the incarnation of all the persons of the Godhead. It is better to say that the divine nature in the second person of the Trinity—or, better still, that the second person himself—became incarnate. The act of incarnation was his, and the result of the act was the manifestation of God in the flesh. I do not mean by this language that the incarnation was not approved by the Father and the Holy Spirit—far from it—but that it was the personal act of the only-begotten Son of God. He it was who "though he was rich, yet for our sakes became poor" (2 Cor. viii. 9), and "made himself of no reputation." Phil. ii. 7.

There have been various false views of the humanity of Christ. To only two of these views will I refer: It was supposed by some at an early day, perhaps in the latter part of the apostolic age, that Christ was not in reality a man, but that he only assumed the appearance of a man. Whether this opinion grew out of the difficulty of believing that a Divine Being assumed human nature, or out of an unwillingness to believe that Jesus really suffered and died, it is useless to inquire. It seems almost certain that John intended to meet and refute this heresy when he wrote as follows: "That which was from the beginning, which we have heard, which we have seen with our eyes, which we have looked upon, and our hands have handled of the Word of life." 1 John i. 1. There seems to be a striking gradation in the proofs given of the possession of a human body. First, we have hearing; then seeing, as more convincing than hearing; next, looking upon, intently contemplating, as more satisfactory than seeing; and lastly, handling, as rendering the proof complete. Jesus was really a man. He called himself a man when he said to the Jews, "But now ye seek to kill me, a man that hath told you the truth which I have heard of God." John viii. 40. There is additional proof of his humanity in these words: "Forasmuch then as the children are partakers of flesh and blood, he also himself likewise took part of the same." Heb. ii. 14. We could not be taught more clearly than in this verse that the Son of God assumed the nature of those he came to redeem. He partook of their "flesh and blood."

The other false view, which also deserves most decided condemnation, is, that Christ had no human soul. It is supposed by the advocates of this theory that the Word in becoming flesh took a human body only into union with himself. The necessity of a human soul is denied, and is thought to be superseded by what is called a "divine soul." Hence, in passages in which the soul of Jesus is referred to, it is said that his "divine soul" is meant. It would perhaps be difficult for them to say just what they mean by a "divine soul." Whether they make a distinction between this "divine soul" and Christ's proper divinity, I will not undertake to say. If they do, they seem to attribute to the person of Christ an element not strictly divine or human. If they do not, it is needless to use the words at all, for the term "divinity" or the phrase "divine nature" would answer every purpose. I imagine that some obscurity rests on the views of those who refer to Christ's "divine soul," and they would perhaps find it impossible to dispel the obscurity. It is surely not our business to attempt it.

To prove that Jesus had a human soul it is only necessary to prove him a man. This surely is not difficult, for he was pleased to call himself "Son of man." If the phrase "Son of God" indicates that Jesus was divine, the phrase "Son of man" indicates that he was human. Isaiah prophesied of him as "a man of sorrows," and God by the mouth of Zechariah said, "Awake, O sword, against my Shepherd, and against the man that is my fellow, saith the Lord of hosts." Zech. xiii. 7. I have shown already, by reference to John viii. 40, that Jesus called himself a man. Paul says: "The first man is of the earth, earthy: the second man is the Lord from heaven " (1 Cor. xv. 47); " For there is one God, and one Mediator between God and men, the man Christ Jesus." 1 Tim. ii. 5. Language cannot more plainly declare that Christ is a man.

But the advocates of the theory I am opposing will admit this. They say without hesitation that Christ is a man. They suppose that his assumption of a human body made him a man. This I deny, and to present the matter in a clear light it is proper to ascertain what man is, what the term " man " means. We cannot do better than to go back to the first use of the word: " And God said, Let us make man in our image, after our likeness. . . . So God created man in his own image, in the image of God created he him." Gen. i. 26, 27. This language cannot refer to a bodily image, for God is a Spirit. The reference must be to man's rational, spiritual nature. The formation of man's body is described as follows: " And the Lord God formed man of the dust of the ground." Gen. ii. 7. In view of these passages of the divine word it is evident that spirit and matter both enter into the constitution of the person of man. The union of the two elements is so essential, that without it there cannot be a man. That is, a rational spirit or soul is not of itself a man, and no form of matter is of itself a man. In proof of this I need only say that when a man is dying we call him a man till he is dead—not after he is dead. We then speak of the disembodied spirit, but we do not apply to it the term " man." We talk about the corpse, but we call it " body," not " man.' Why these forms of expression? They grow out of the universal belief that the union of soul and body is so essential to a man, that when it is dissolved the term " man " cannot be properly applied to either of the severed parts.

Now, the bearing of all this on the point under consideration is obvious. For if Jesus Christ did not possess a soul as well as a body, he was not a man. The union of a body with his divine nature would not make him a man. In such a union the more important element of humanity would be absent, for there would be no human soul. There must be the union of a human body and a human soul to constitute Jesus a man, and then there must be the union of his humanity with his divinity to constitute him the Christ. Nor are we for a moment to suppose that he has two personalities. He has two natures, but one person.

The view now presented supplies the only basis for a rational interpretation of certain passages of Scripture. For example, it is said, " And Jesus increased in wisdom and stature, and in favor with God and man." Luke ii. 52. It is evident that increase of wisdom referred to his soul, while increase of stature had reference to his body. The term "wisdom" cannot be applied to the material part of man. Shall I ask whether the divine nature in Christ was capable of degrees in wisdom? He who answers affirmatively must have low views of divinity, but those whose theory I deny must answer affirmatively or not at all. They are shut up to affirmation or silence, and if they preserve silence, it is because it is too startling to affirm.

In the garden of Gethsemane Jesus said, " My soul is exceeding sorrowful, even unto death." Matt. xxvi. 38 No words could more fully express the fact that the emotional nature of Jesus was excited to the highest degree of intensity. It was his soul that was sorrowful, and it was his human soul, because he was a man.

That the soul of Christ, like the souls of men, was capable of separation from his body, appears from these words: " He hath poured out his soul unto death." Isa. liii. 12. Should it be said that "soul" here means life, the import of the passage would not be materially changed For when the life is poured forth death occurs, because the soul leaves the body. The soul of Jesus left his body at death, as does the soul of every man in the dying hour; and therefore the only reasonable view of the matter is that the soul of Jesus was a human soul.

The Deity of Christ having been proved in another place, his humanity is, if I mistake not, demonstrated in this chapter. Jesus is both the Son of God and the Son of Mary. The statement of this fact suggests that, by virtue of the constitution of his person, he possesses all needful mediatorial qualifications.

"Great is the mystery of godliness;" and to many it seems a mystery that we can say of Christ's one person what is true, but which is not true of both of his natures. His one person is more frequently referred to than his two natures. Whatever is true of his person is true of one of his natures. If this were not so, the element of truth would be wanting entirely. To illustrate what I mean: We learn from the Scriptures that Christ hungered, thirsted, slept, and wept. This is true of his person, and true of his human nature. He hungered as a man, thirsted as a man, slept as a man, and wept as a man. But these things cannot be affirmed of his divine nature. We dare not say that he hungered, thirsted, slept, and wept as God. This would not be true. On the other hand, it is true of the person of Christ and true of his divine nature that he withered the fruitless fig tree, gave sight to the blind, hearing to the deaf, cast out demons, and raised Lazarus from the dead. These things, however, if affirmed of his human nature, would not be true. Does any one question the accuracy of these statements? To make the matter plainer, if possible, I may say that the same principle is illustrated in men every day Should it be said of a man, that he is tall, or corpulent, or sick, every one would know that the body was meant. The declaration would be accepted as true of the man in his physical nature, but not in his mental nature. Should it be said of a man, that he is wise or ignorant, sad or joyful. the truth of the statement would be granted in its relation to man's mental constitution, but its truth would be denied in its application to the body, because the body is not wise, ignorant, sad, or joyful. It may be said of every man that he is mortal, and also that he is immortal. Two expressions cannot be more contradictory than these, but they are both true. How? Both true in relation to man—the one in relation to his body, the other in relation to his soul.

Thus it is concerning Christ. All that the Scriptures say of him is true as to his person, but it does not follow that it is true of both his natures. Nor should we anxiously concern ourselves about the matter. It is safe for us to believe that what the Scriptures say of Christ as to his person is true, even though we may be utterly unable in many things to discriminate between the emotions and operations of his divinity and his humanity. We read, for example, as follows: "For unto us a Child is born, unto us a Son is given: and the government shall be upon his shoulder: and his name shall be called Wonderful, Counsellor, the mighty God, the everlasting Father, the Prince of Peace." Isa. ix. 6. In pondering these sublime words we know that the being described is the God-man, the Christ, and we know from other scriptures that Christ was born, that he died, that he was buried, that he rose from the dead, that he ascended to heaven, and that he is making intercession for us at the right hand of God. Infinite value must attach to all the acts and sufferings of such a being in the room of guilty men.

18

I close this chapter by quoting the following from a very able theologian now living, and who, I trust, will live for many years to come:[1]

"Thus have we seen, in the review of the Scripture teachings as to the doctrine of the suffering Christ, that in the possession of an unchanged and proper divine nature, and a complete human nature, Christ suffered on our behalf. The Sufferer was God and was man. Yet it was not God that suffered, but he that is God, being also man, suffered in his human nature. As the same person, however, was united with both natures, and as that person was the Son of God, so we may say that the Son of God suffered. This, however, is the suffering of a divine person, not of the divine nature, and of that person, otherwise incapable of suffering, through the assumption of human nature. If, therefore, called upon to give expression to the Scripture statement upon this whole subject, we may express it thus: There is one God in three persons, distinct in personality, but undividedly and unchangeably the same in essence and nature. We may speak of a divine person, but not of a divine nature; we must say *the* divine nature. A divine person may therefore become incarnate, and yet the incarnation be not of the whole Godhead, for the persons are distinct; but the divine nature cannot, because, as common to all, its incarnation would be that of the whole Godhead. It was a person of this Godhead, the Son, the Word, who so united to himself human nature as to become in that nature a man. In this union he assumed all that constitutes a man. The fact that he had no other personality than such as had always subsisted in the divine nature does not make him an impersonal man. It only forbids the idea of an addi-

[1] Rev. Dr. James P. Boyce, who so worthily fills the office of President of the Southern Baptist Theological Seminary, Louisville, Ky

tional personality exclusively in the human nature.
This human nature was assumed, because necessary to
the work of salvation, it being impossible that a being
only divine could undergo the experience necessary to
redeem man. In its assumption the divine nature of
Christ was wholly unchanged, and the human nature
still remained purely human. The nature of personality,
however, allows a most vital union of the two natures in
his own person. Thus uniting in himself God and man,
Christ suffered. There was here, therefore, no participation of the divine nature in the suffering. Such participation would involve actual suffering of that nature.
But there *was* this connection of God, even of the undivided divine essence, that he who thus suffered subsists
eternally and essentially in that essence, and is God
Yet, intimate as is the connection of the two natures, they
are not merged in each other, nor does either of them
lose its separate conscious existence or the possession
of those peculiarities which make the one divine and the
other human. It is one person, truly God and truly
man—as much God as though not man, as much man
as though not God. The human can add nothing to the
divine, except that it gives to the person that is divine
the means of suffering for, and sympathizing with, us.
The divine adds to the human only that it gives to him
that is thus man that dignity and glory and power which
enables him to perform the work of salvation, and to
give to that work inestimable value." [1]

[1] *Baptist Quarterly*, vol. iv. pp. 409–411.

CHAPTER XV.

THE MEDIATORIAL OFFICE OF CHRIST.

A MEDIATOR, as the word is commonly used, is a person who interposes between two parties; and the need of interposition arises from the fact that the parties are at variance. In view of what has been said in preceding chapters, it is without doubt true that God and man are at variance. God is holy, and man is sinful. There cannot be more direct antagonism than that between holiness and sin.

If the person of Christ has been properly described—that is, if he is the God-man—he is perfectly qualified to assume the office of mediator. The reason is, that he combines in his person the nature of God and the nature of man. In matters of mere human mediation it is sufficient for men to intercede between men. In every such case the mediator possesses the nature of each party. When God and man are the parties at variance, the mediator must have that relation to both which is exemplified only in the person of Christ. He alone possesses the two-fold constitution in which divine and human elements unite. There is no being like Christ; and while we cannot comprehend his mysterious person, we can see the necessity of it. It was requisite that he should possess the nature of God, in order that the rights of the divine government might be suitably cared for and vindicated. It was indispensable for him to have the nature of man that he might be capable of human sympathies, human sufferings, and a human death. Paul says, that "there is one Mediator between God and men, the man Christ Jesus" (1 Tim. ii. 5); and while we accept the statement as true in its literal import, it is also true in the sense that this one Mediator alone possesses necessary mediatorial qualifications. He only, as "daysman," can lay one hand on the throne of God to protect its majesty inviolate, while with the other he reaches down to man to raise him from his wretchedness and ruin. There is no mediator but Christ. By a blessed necessity the work of mediation is confined to him alone.

The personal holiness of Christ was essential to his mediatorship. We are therefore told that "such an high priest became us, who is holy, harmless, undefiled, separate from sinners." Heb. vii. 26. It is too plain to require argument that a sinful being could not mediate between a holy God and sinful men. In case of such a thing there would be a complicity with evil that would vitiate all attempts at mediation. The purity of Christ's character was put to the severest test. He was artfully and violently assailed by temptation. Satan, no doubt, exerted all his tempting power, and Christ was "in all points tempted like as we are, yet without sin." Heb. iv. 15. He retained his sinless integrity to the last, saying to his enemies, "Which of you convicteth me of sin?" John viii. 46. When he died he suffered, "the just for the unjust." 1 Pet. iii. 18. His personal holiness shone bright, even amid the darkness that gathered around his cross.

There is another qualification of a mediator between God and men. I cannot do better than to call it the right of self-disposal. Here we see at once how essential to effective mediation is the divine element in the person

18 *

of Christ. In the absence of this element the right of self-disposal cannot exist. What creature is at liberty to dispose of himself? His supreme obligation is to God. All that he can do is, on his own personal account, due to God—a fact which makes it impossible for one creature to act in the room of another. But there was substitution in the mediation of Christ. He came into the world to save sinners; and to save them, he must take their place in law and die in their stead. It is therefore said, that he was "made under the law, to redeem them that were under the law." Gal. iv. 4, 5. The language implies that he was originally above law. He was never under it till made under it; and how was it possible for him to be made under it? The answer is, That it was possible, because he had the right of self-disposal. There was no coercion in the matter. To compel the innocent to suffer for the guilty would violate every principle of propriety and justice, but Jesus suffered voluntarily. He did so in the exercise of his right of self-disposal—a right vital to his mediatorial work.

There is still a mediatorial qualification to be considered. It is the mediator's capability of death. He must be able to die, and must, therefore, have a nature capable of death. The Son of God before his incarnation had not such a nature. He must, for this reason, assume a nature that could die. As human redemption was his purpose, he assumed human nature—the nature of those to be redeemed by his blood. He became "the man Christ Jesus," but we must remember that never as a man did he exist apart from the divine nature. He became incarnate in order to die. Hence we read: "And for this cause he is the Mediator of the New Testament, that by means of death, for the redemption of the transgressions that were under the first testament, they which are called might receive the promise of eternal inheritance. For where a testament is, there must also of necessity be the death of the testator. For a testament is of force after men are dead: otherwise it is of no strength at all while the testator liveth." Heb. ix. 15-17. Here we learn the necessity of the Mediator's death, and the fact is set forth prominently that it was necessary to the pardon of sins committed under the first covenant. If so, it is necessary to the forgiveness of sins in all ages. Dr. Ripley well remarks: "The death of Christ being, by anticipation, efficacious for the pardon and salvation of men during the Mosaic age, its efficacy extended back, beyond doubt, to the very commencement of human transgressions; and thus, it appears, it was designed to cover the whole period of the human race."[1]

Unquestionably, all the people of God, from the da of Abel to the coming of Christ, were saved by virtue of the prospective death of the Mediator, even as all saved since that great event have been saved by the blood shed on Calvary. Through all the centuries of the world's history there has been but one Mediator between God and men, and there will be no other while the world stands. The matter, however, claiming special attention in this connection is the necessity of the Mediator's death. This necessity made it imperative that the Son of God should assume human nature, in order to perform the work of mediation. In other words, he must have a nature capable of death, and he must actually die. Such a nature the second person in the Godhead took into union with his divine nature, and that Christ died is the central fact of history. In view of the foregoing considerations, it is not only manifest that Christ fills the mediatorial office, but that he is the only being in the universe by whom it can be filled. There is but one Jesus Christ.

[1] *Notes on the Epistle to the Hebrews*, pp. 112, 113.

The general office of Mediator includes the three subordinate offices of Prophet, Priest, and King. There are
many passages of Scripture which teach that Christ performs the functions of these offices.

1. *He is Prophet.* " For Moses truly said unto the fathers,
A prophet shall the Lord your God raise up unto you of
your brethren, like unto me; him shall ye hear in all
things whatsoever he shall say unto you." Acts iii. 22. I
may say, in passing, that for the phrase " like unto me '
Dr. Noyes in his translation substitutes the words " as
he raised up me," which clearly convey the idea of the
original Greek. The point now in hand, however, is the
fact that a prophet was to be raised up in fulfilment of
the prediction of Moses. The expectation was general
among the Jews that such a prophet would come. When,
therefore, " the Jews sent priests and Levites " to ask John
the Baptist who he was, they inquired, " Art thou Elias?
And he saith, I am not. Art thou that prophet? And
he answered, No." John i. 21. They evidently meant the
prophet of whom Moses spoke, and for whom they were
looking. When Jesus came and entered on his ministry,
he was recognized as the great prophet, not only by his
disciples, but by the people. It is therefore said, " And
when he was come into Jerusalem, all the city was moved,
saying, Who is this? And the multitude said, This is Jesus
the prophet of Nazareth of Galilee." Matt. xxi. 10, 11.

It is a very common opinion, if I mistake not, that the
chief, if not the exclusive, function of a prophet was prediction—telling beforehand what should come to pass.
That the ancient prophets, and the New Testament
prophets also, predicted coming events is true, but they
did much more than this. They revealed and interpreted
the will of God to men, for he spoke to the fathers by the
prophets. If we were to trace the term " prophet " to its

origin, we should probably find that it was used at first to denote a messenger speaking *in front of* a monarch or king, and occupying this position because speaking *for* the monarch or king. While, therefore, the primary meaning of the Greek preposition *pro* is *in front of*, we can easily see that its secondary meaning, *in place of* that is, *for*, was inevitable.

In ancient times " holy men of God spake as they were moved by the Holy Ghost." 2 Pet. i. 21. They spoke for God because God spoke through them. Jesus the great Teacher is in the highest sense the prophet of God. All other prophets were subordinate to him, and indebted to him for their official positions. For this reason it is said, " No man hath seen God at any time: the only-begotten Son, which is in the bosom of the Father, he hath declared him." John i. 18. We may therefore say that to Christ as prophet the world is indebted for all that it knows of God. As words are used to express ideas, it is probable that the second person of the Trinity was called the Word, because through him divine revelations have been made to men. There were gradual disclosures of the will of God from the fall of Adam to the end of the book of Revelation, but they were all under the superintendence of Jehovah-Jesus, the great Prophet. Indeed, it is written in the last chapter of the Bible, " I Jesus have sent mine angel to testify unto you these things in the churches." Rev xxii. 16. During the personal ministry of Christ on earth Moses and Elijah rendered to him their devout homage. They appeared with him on the Mount of Transfiguration. Out of all the Old Testament saints there were no two who could more fitly recognize the Prophet of heaven. Their recognition, however, was feeble as compared with the higher recognition expressed in the words that came from the excellent glory: " This is my beloved Son, in whom I am well pleased; hear ye him." Matt. xvii. 5. Christ as Prophet has the seal of the Father's approval He is the object of the Father's complacent love, and in the audience of the world the Father says, "Hear ye him." Well may we hear him, for "never man spake like this man." John vii. 46. No man ever spake like him in the authoritative manner of his teaching; in the adaptation of what he said to the common people; in his revelation of the character of God; in his delineation of human nature; in his development of the way of salvation; in the light he poured on the doctrine of the soul's immortality, the resurrection of the body, the bliss of heaven, and the miseries of hell. Who ever spoke like him among sages, philosophers, patriarchs, or prophets? He stands forth in the majesty of approachless superiority, extorting from his enemies the reluctant eulogy, "Never man spake like this man." John vii. 46.

Truly we may say there is no teacher, no prophet, like Christ. Happy, thrice happy, are those who reverently hearken to his teachings! They not only find rest to their souls in this life, but will in the life to come be exalted to the enjoyment of eternal glory in heaven. Awful will be the doom of those who turn away from the teachings of Christ. He who hears not this Prophet shall be destroyed. So Moses wrote. Alas! who can tell how much is implied in the destruction which comes on those who refuse to learn the lessons of salvation as taught by Christ? Good, indeed, were it for them had they never been born!

2. *Christ is Priest.* The chief functions of his priestly office are atonement and intercession. Nothing is said on these topics here, as they are treated elsewhere.[1]

---

[1] See Chapters XVI. and XVII. The intelligent reader will know why these topics have a distinct presentation.

3. *Christ is King.* When he stood before Pilate and made what Paul terms "the good confession," he said, "My kingdom is not of this world : if my kingdom were of this world, then would my servants fight, that I should not be delivered to the Jews: but now is my kingdom not from hence. Pilate therefore said unto him, Art thou a king then? Jesus answered, Thou sayest that I am a king. To this end was I born, and for this cause came I into the world, that I should bear witness unto the truth. Every one that is of the truth heareth my voice." John xviii. 36, 37.

In reading these words we are reminded of what the Saviour said on another occasion : "Judge not according to the appearance." John vii. 24. Judgment based on the appearance of things when Jesus was arraigned as an evil-doer would have been fatal to his kingly claims. There was no royal banner around which devoted subjects were rallying and shouting, "O King, live for ever!" The marks of royalty were conspicuously absent. The "despised Galilean" was insulted by his enemies and forsaken by his friends. Where was his kingdom? In the worldly sense of the term there was none. He, however, referred to a kingdom not of this world, and claimed it as his own. He said, "My kingdom." A kingdom implies subjects, and the loyal subjects of Jesus are those who are " of the truth." This utterance by the illustrious prisoner at Pilate's bar was enough to relieve the suspicious Roman emperor Tiberius of all apprehension. The subjects of Cæsar were not required to be " of the truth."

Christ is King. I refer not now to the dominion which he, as one of the persons of the Godhead, exercised before his incarnation. There must have been such dominion, for as he made all things he must have ruled all things. I refer to Christ's mediatorial kingdom. As the God-man, all authority is committed to him. This authority he is represented as receiving from the Father. For this reason it is said, "The Father loveth the Son, and hath given all things into his hand." John iii. 35. The Son was appointed to his mediatorial kingship by the Father, and is therefore inferior to the Father in office, though equal in nature. The official subordination of Christ to the Father makes plain such scriptures as the following: 'Yet have I set my King upon my holy hill of Zion" (Ps. ii. 6); "Therefore let all the house of Israel know assuredly, that God hath made that same Jesus, whom ye have crucified, both Lord and Christ" (Acts ii. 36); "Wherefore God also hath highly exalted him, and given him a name which is above every name: that at the name of Jesus every knee should bow, of things in heaven and things in earth, and things under the earth; and that every tongue should confess that Jesus Christ is Lord, to the glory of God the Father." Phil. ii. 9–11.

It will be seen from these passages that Christ, as mediatorial Lord and King, has been exalted to universal dominion. "He must reign till he hath put all enemies under his feet." "Then cometh the end," and, according to the teaching of Paul, it seems that Christ is to deliver up his mediatorial kingdom to God the Father, from whom he received it, that God, in his threefold unity, may be all in all. See 1 Cor. xv. 24–28. I of course admit that there is some obscurity resting on this passage, which I am incompetent to remove.

The phrases "kingdom of Christ," "kingdom of heaven," and "kingdom of God" are used in the Scriptures with some diversity of meaning. Many of the parables of Christ were designed to teach and illustrate important truths concerning his kingdom, but they were not all de-

signed to teach and illustrate the same truths. Sometimes one peculiarity of the kingdom is presented, and
sometimes another. One parable, it may be, refers to the
kingdom as embracing Christ's rule over the righteous
and wicked; and in another, his dominion over his saints
may be specially referred to. A notable instance of his
dominion over the good and the bad is seen in the parable of the " Tares and Wheat." In his explanation of
this parable Jesus said, " The Son of man shall send forth
his angels, and they shall gather out of his kingdom all
things that offend, and them which do iniquity." Matt.
xiii. 41. There is a sense, then, in which "things that
offend " and persons who " do iniquity " are in the kingdom of heaven, but they are to be gathered out by angels
on the last day. When, however, Paul refers to deliverance from the power of darkness and translation into the
kingdom of God's dear Son (Col. i. 13), it is plain that regenerate persons are meant. They alone have been the
subjects of such a deliverance and such a translation.
When James mentions the heirs of the kingdom which
God "hath promised to them who love him " (chap. ii. 5),
there seems to be special reference to the kingdom of
glory. When the kingdom of God is said to be " right
eousness, and peace, and joy in the Holy Ghost " (Rom
xiv. 17), the blessed effects of the reign of God in the
soul are signified.

But my purpose does not permit me to enlarge on
matters like these. I wish to make prominent the fact
that Jesus claims the right to exercise kingly authority
over his churches. Such right is implied in the first use
of the term " church " in the New Testament: " Upon this
rock I will build my church, and the gates of hell shall
not prevail against it." Matt. xvi. 18.[1] It will be observed

---

[1] It does not accord with my plan to enter into a critical examination

that Christ says, "my church." It was to be his property, belonging to him in a sense that justified him in claiming it as his own. This is true of the term "church" in the two prominent acceptations in which it is used by Christ and the apostles. It is employed to denote the aggregate body of the redeemed, the "glorious church" which Christ is to present to himself, "not having spot or wrinkle, or any such thing," as we are taught in Eph. v 27. In almost numberless cases in the New Testament the word *church* is used to describe a local congregation of Christ's baptized disciples, united in the belief of what he has said, and covenanting to do what he has commanded In the former sense the church of course belongs to Christ, having been bought with his blood. He is her King, and she cheerfully and gladly yields to his authority, rejoicing to own him as Lord. Through endless ages the church, "the sacramental host of God's elect," will recognize Christ as the Author of redemption, and be animated by the spirit of loyal submission and loving obedience to him.

As to local assemblies, so often called churches in the New Testament, their very organization implies an acknowledgment of Christ's kingly authority. Their right to existence depends on his authority. Those who can rightfully enter into them as members must first be called out of the world. This calling out from the world must ever precede scriptural church membership; and they are called out who obey Christ's command and experience the truth of his promise, "Come unto me, all ye that labor and are heavy laden, and I will give you rest."

of passages. I do not, therefore, examine this controverted verse. My opinion is that the "Rock" is Christ the Son of the living God. This was the great truth confessed by Peter, which the Father had revealed to him.

Matt. xi. 28. This, however, is not all that "the called out" are required to do. Their King and their Lord says, "Take my yoke upon you." v. 29. The yoke is the symbol of subjection. Christ requires unconditional subjection, and this is professed in the ordinance of baptism, which formally draws the line of demarcation between the churches of Christ and the world of the ungodly. This ordinance, of open, public consecration, he himself appointed, for it was he who said to his apostles, "Go ye, therefore, and teach [disciple] all nations, baptizing them in the name of the Father, and of the Son, and of the Holy Ghost: teaching them to observe all things whatsoever I have commanded you: and, lo, I am with you alway, even unto the end of the world. Amen." Matt. xxviii. 19, 20.

Baptism is administered and received upon the authority of Christ. The subjects of baptism are baptized into Christ; and having professed their faith in his name, are to be instructed to do all that he has commanded. The language is very specific: "Teaching them to observe all things whatsoever I have commanded you." The great commission was to be executed first among Jews, who had an almost idolatrous reverence for what Moses had commanded; but Jesus, the King of his churches, said, "teaching them to observe," not what Moses commanded, but "all things whatsoever I have commanded.' The apostles had no discretionary authority, but were strictly required to teach the baptized disciples of Christ to observe all his commands.

The exclusive authority of Christ as King was recognized in the formation of churches, and hence Paul uses the phrase "churches of Christ" (Rom. xvi. 16), and takes it for granted that "the church is subject to Christ." Eph. v. 24. The nature of a church, its membership, its offices.

its doctrines, its government, its discipline, its work of evangelization, all were determined by Christ. Every church should regard itself as an executive democracy solemnly appointed to carry into effect the laws of Christ. He is the Lawgiver. The legislation in his kingdom is all his own. He is " Head over all things to the church."

CHAPTER XVI.

THE ATONEMENT OF CHRIST.

As already stated, the two chief functions of the priestly office of Christ are atonement and intercession. The former of these topics claims attention in this chapter, and will be discussed in the following order:

I. THE NATURE OF THE ATONEMENT.

The term *atonement* is used but once in the New Testament. It is found in Rom. v. 11: "We also joy in God through our Lord Jesus Christ, by whom we have now received the atonement." This passage, according to the present meaning of the word "atonement," does not correctly express the sense of the original. We—that is, believers—are represented as receiving the atonement. But, strictly speaking, we receive only the benefits of the atonement, while the Lawgiver receives or accepts the atonement itself. The original word means "reconciliation," and "atonement" was often used in that sense at the time when our translation was made. Shakespeare, who died five years after the common version of the Bible was published, uses the word "atonement" where we should now employ "reconciliation," as in the following lines:

> "He seeks to make atonement
> Between the duke of Glo'ster and your brothers."

It is probable that the translators employed the word in the same sense in Rom. v. 11. At the same time, it should be noticed that they also used it in the sense to which it is now confined, to express the idea of "expiation," as in the subjoined passages : "And Aaron shall bring the bullock of the sin-offering, which is for himself, and shall make an atonement for himself and for his house" (Lev. vi. 11) ; "And Moses said unto Aaron, Take a censer, and put fire therein from off the altar, and put on incense, and go quickly unto the congregation, and make an atonement for them : for there is wrath gone out from the Lord; the plague is begun. And Aaron took as Moses commanded, and ran into the midst of the congregation ; and, behold, the plague was begun among the people : and he put on incense, and made an atonement for the people. And he stood between the dead and the living ; and the plague was stayed." Num. xvi. 46-48.

In these and in similar forms of expression the idea seems to be that an atonement, an expiatory measure, was resorted to as the means of effecting reconciliation. In the passage last quoted we are informed that wrath had gone out from the Lord. This wrath was excited by the sins of the people, and before God could be consistently propitious, an atonement—in that case a ceremonial one—must be made to justify the cessation of wrath and the exercise of mercy.

Though the word "atonement" was sometimes used, perhaps generally, two or three hundred years ago, to signify reconciliation, this meaning has been obsolete for at least a century, and it now denotes expiation, satisfaction, reparation of injury. In proof of this I refer to the following among standard authors : "Junius," in his inimitable *Letters*, says, "The ministry not *atoning for* their former conduct by any wise or popular measure." Pope

says. "The murderer fell, and blood *atoned for* blood."
Other extracts might be given from other authors, but it
is needless. It is evident that an atonement is that which
repairs an injury, gives satisfaction, makes amends. With
this view of the import of the term let us consider the
atonement of Christ. What is it? It is the expiation of
sin by the satisfaction rendered to the law and justice of
God through the obedience and death of Christ. I know
of no better definition than this.

It should be remembered that the atonement of Christ,
though intended to satisfy the claims of the divine law, is
a measure above law. I will not say contrary to it, but
obviously above it. The law of God contemplated no
atonement, and anticipated no reparation of its dishon-
or, apart from the punishment of personal transgressors.
This must have been the case; for if the law had held
out the idea that something would be substituted for the
personal punishment of the guilty, instead of deterring
from sin it would probably have encouraged its commission. The hope of escaping the consequences of sin
would have been presented to every one tempted to trans-
gress. Such a hope in many cases would have been
almost a bribe to sin. The law of God, being "holy, and
just, and good," could neither directly nor indirectly countenance the commission of sin; for this would have been
equivalent to a defeat of the object of its own enactment.
In view of these and kindred considerations it is manifest that the atonement of Christ is a measure above
law.

Man's ruin was brought on him by a violation of the
divine law, and his recovery from that ruin, if effected at
all, must take place in a manner consistent with the law.
God, therefore, "when the fulness of the time was come
sent forth his Son, made of a woman, made under the law

to redeem them that were under the law." Gal. iv. **4, 5**. Christ was made under the law that he might render the obedience and suffer the death already referred to. Man in sinning had treated the law with indignity and dishonor. He had cast contempt on it. He had virtually and practically said that it was not a good law, and that he would not obey it nor be governed by it. When Jesus came in the flesh, then did he truly "magnify the law and make it honorable." Isa. xlii. 21. By his obedience and death he removed the dishonor, the indignity, the contempt which rested on the law, and showed to the universe that it is a perfect law. He clothed it with a moral grandeur more sublime than it had before its violation. He exalted it to a dignity as glorious as a full vindication of its claims could give it. He honored the law by being born under it, honored it more by obeying it, and honored it in the highest degree by suffering its death-penalty.

That the atonement of Christ is an expiation of sin is clear from the following scriptures: " He was wounded for our transgressions, he was bruised for our iniquities : the chastisement of our peace was upon him ; and with his stripes we are healed. All we like sheep have gone astray ; we have turned every one to his own way ; and the Lord hath laid on him the iniquity of us all " (Isa. liii. 5, 6) ; " Behold the Lamb of God, that taketh away the sin of the world " (John i. 29) ; " Whom God hath set forth to be a propitiation through faith in his blood, to declare his righteousness for the remission of sins that are past, through the forbearance of God; to declare, I say, at this time his righteousness: that he might be just and the justifier of him that believeth in Jesus " (Rom. iii. 25, 26); "Once in the end of the world hath he appeared to put away sin by the sacrifice of himself" (Heb. ix 26): " Who his own self bare our sins in his own body on the tree " (1 Pet. ii. 24); " Herein is love, not that we loved God, but that he loved us, and sent his Son to be the propitiation for our sins." 1 John iv. 10.

These are a specimen of the passages of Scripture that teach the doctrine of atonement. Christ assumed the legal responsibilities of those he came to save. Hence his obedience and death on their account. "To bear his iniquity " is a phrase of frequent occurrence in the Old Testament. It means, to suffer the consequences of his iniquity. This can be seen by a reference to Lev. v. 1: " And if a soul sin, and hear the voice of swearing, and is a witness, whether he hath seen or known of it; if he do not utter it, then he shall bear his iniquity." The supposition here is, that the witness may refuse to tell what he knows about the matter in question. His concealment of his knowledge would defeat the purposes of justice, and would therefore be a sin. It is called iniquity, and was to be borne in the sense of endurance of the penalty attached, in such cases, by the Mosaic statute. The unfaithful witness, in bearing his iniquity, suffered the consequences of his iniquity. This was an instance of the bearing of iniquity in the personal punishment of the sinner.

We are now prepared to understand, in their application to Christ, such scriptures as the following : " He shall bear their iniquities;" " Christ was once offered to bear the sins of many;" " who his own self bore our sins in his own body on the tree." Isa. liii. 11; Heb. ix. 28; 1 Pet. ii. 24. They mean that when our iniquities were laid on Christ he suffered the consequences of our iniquities. He bore our sins in the sense of bearing the penalty of the law, which law we had violated. He was not personally guilty. The epithet *guilty*, in its present acceptation, can with no propriety be applied to Christ. Some centuries ago the term *guilt* was used to denote "liability to punishment," but this is not now its meaning. In our current literature it suggests the idea of personal criminality, and consequent desert of punishment. This is the understanding of everybody when the jury brings in the verdict of *guilty*. How, then, can it be affirmed that Christ was *guilty?* It is impossible, for when he died there was no personal criminality, but personal innocence in its most attractive form.

But while Christ was not guilty—that is, was not personally blameworthy—there was exemplified in him what Dr. J. Pye Smith and others have termed "legal answerableness." In assuming the place of sinners, Christ of necessity incurred their legal responsibilities. This was indispensable to atonement. Without it, the sufferings of Christ might have been calamitous, but in no sense expiatory. They could not have satisfied the claims of the law, for there would have been in them no element of satisfaction. The idea of "legal answerableness" makes the matter plain. Christ having voluntarily taken the place of sinners, there was a sacred propriety in his being held answerable for them. It was proper, right, just for him to suffer, because he was legally responsible for those in whose behalf he suffered. "Ought not Christ to have suffered these things?" Luke xxiv. 26. This question he himself asked the two disciples on their way to Emmaus after his resurrection; and it indicates the fitness, the propriety, as well as the necessity, of his sufferings. The Jews thought salvation through a suffering Christ unworthy of God, but the Scriptures say, "It became him for whom are all things, and by whom are all things, in bringing many sons to glory, to make the Captain of their salvation perfect through sufferings." Heb. ii. 10. It was worthy of God to do this.

Instead of detracting from his glory, it exhibits his character in new aspects of loveliness, and will call forth the sweetest hallelujahs of heaven.

Jesus was "made perfect through sufferings." There is no reference to moral, but to official or mediatorial, perfection. That is to say, his sufferings, which resulted in death and accomplished the work of atonement, perfectly qualified him to act as the Saviour of sinners. It is therefore said, "And being made perfect, he became the author of eternal salvation unto all them that obey him." Heb. v. 9. His becoming the Author of salvation was the consequence of his being made perfect; and as there could be no salvation without expiatory sufferings, he was made perfect through sufferings.

The doctrine of atonement involves the kindred doctrine of substitution. We are therefore told that Christ "died for us" (1 Thess. v. 10), "gave himself for us" (Tit. ii. 14), "gave himself a ransom for all." 1 Tim. ii. 6. It is true that these forms of expression teach that Jesus died for our benefit, but they teach much more. The Socinian of England and the Unitarian of America say, that Jesus died for our benefit as "a martyr to the truth," but they carefully exclude from his death the idea of expiation. Paul died as "a martyr to the truth," and in this respect died for our benefit, but there is an exclusive sense in which Jesus died for us. He died as our substitute. He placed himself in our legal relation to the divine government, and incurred all the responsibilities of such a position. This Paul could not do— this an angel could not do—this no creature could do. Christ died for our benefit, because he died in our stead. We are benefited by *his* death, because it was substituted for *our* death. There could be no saving benefit without this substitution; and it is to be feared that the words

"for our benefit" delude many to their eternal ruin
They vainly suppose that they will be benefited by the
death of Christ, whereas they divest it of the very peculiarity which enables it to confer benefit. The Redeemer's
death possesses saving power for men, because he died
for men, in the room of men; but it possesses no such
power for fallen angels, because he did not die for fallen
angels. It cannot be insisted on too earnestly that the
only reason why we are savingly benefited by the death
of Christ is that he died in our place. He suffered in
our stead and " put away sin by the sacrifice of himself."
Heb. ix. 26. His obedience and death sustained the
dignity of the divine throne, vindicated the rectitude of
the divine administration, honored the preceptive and
penal claims of the divine law, and opened a channel
for the consistent exercise of mercy to guilty sinners.
In short, the atonement of Christ exerts so important an
influence on the throne of God, as to make its occupant
"just and the justifier of him which believeth in Jesus."
Rom. iii. 26. What words the atonement puts together
—*just and the justifier!* Blessed collocation of terms!
Without the atonement we should have heard of God as
just and the condemner—with it we hear of him as "just
and the justifier." He justifies through the atonement
the very persons whom, had there been no atonement,
he would have righteously condemned for ever. This
is one of the sublime wonders of the cross.

II. The Necessity of the Atonement.

On this point I am not to be understood as intimating
that God was under obligation to provide an atonement,
or that there was an *absolute* necessity for guilty men to
be saved. There was a perfect exemption from obligation on the part of God, as is seen in the fact that *grace*

reigned in providing the atoning sacrifice. The necessity of salvation was not absolute; for men, like fallen angels might have been left to the consequences of their rebellion. Had they been so left, the eternal Throne would have remained bright with the awful glory of its rectitude, and no suspicion of injustice would have attached to the divine administration.

By the necessity of atonement is meant this: That it was indispensable to a consistent exercise of mercy toward condemned sinners, and therefore without it there could have been no salvation for them. It is proper, however, to say that the atonement of Christ was not necessary to excite the love of God to man, for it is the *effect*, and not the *cause*, of God's love. Jesus therefore said to Nicodemus, "God so loved the world that he gave his only-begotten Son, that whosoever believeth in him should not perish, but have everlasting life." John iii. 16. It is plain from this superlative summary of the gospel that the love of God was the originating cause of atonement. There was antecedent love in the divine bosom—there was compassion for lost men. But without an atonement that love could not, consistently with law and justice, express itself in the salvation of sinners; that compassion could have no development. It is incorrect, therefore, to say that the atonement of Christ rendered God propitious to sinners, and stop there; but it is strictly true to say that it rendered him propitious to sinners *according to law and justice*. It follows, then, that the necessity of atonement originated in the obstacles interposed by the law and the justice of God to the salvation of sinners. The law, having been transgressed, demanded the execution of its penalty, and justice concurred in the demand. The law being " noly, and just, and good," holiness, and justice, and goodness all com-

20

bined and required the infliction of its curse. Here, then, we see that the law, having been violated, rose up in its terrible majesty, restrained the exercise of divine mercy in man's salvation, and called for the execution of its penalty. At this point the necessity of an atonement clearly appears. In order to the salvation of sinners an expiatory measure must be introduced into the divine government to meet the claims of the law, by preserving its honor and vindicating its penal sanctions. Justice required the introduction of such a measure or the execution of the penalty of the law on personal transgressors. The atonement of Christ was the measure introduced. It rendered satisfaction to the law and the justice of God, and removed the restraints which they had placed on the exercise of mercy. It harmonized the divine perfections in the salvation of sinners. This is the glory of redemption through the blood of the cross.

There is a cordial co-operation of the divine attributes in the salvation of the guilty. Mercy triumphs in all its glory; justice shines forth in all its majesty; holiness appears in all its beauty; while wisdom, in devising the wondrous plan, exhibits itself to infinite advantage. In treating of the necessity of Christ's atonement it is generally deemed sufficient to refer to it as satisfying the law and the justice of God. When this is done the interests of truth are not likely to suffer. Sometimes, however, it is well to go more thoroughly into the matter of necessity, and trace it *to the ill-desert of sin*, and thence *to the nature of God*. The logical and the theological exigences of the case require this. For it may be asked why the law of God, when violated, needs satisfaction. This is a legitimate question, and finds its only answer in the nature of sin and the nature of God.

There is intrinsic demerit in sin, which renders it deserving of punishment. It is better to present the matter concretely than abstractly. I say, then, that a sinner, because he is a sinner, deserves punishment. He is a rebel against the government of God, and justice requires that he shall pay the penalty of rebellion. He is guilty of high treason against the Majesty of heaven, and every principle of righteousness demands that he shall suffer the consequences of his capital crime.

It is to be regretted that the philosophy of punishment is by many imperfectly understood, and is not therefore presented in its most important aspect. They regard punishment as exemplary; that is, they suppose that criminals are punished to deter others from committing crimes. This is only the secondary reason for punishment; the primary reason is that the punishment is deserved. It may be classed almost among the intuitive beliefs of the human mind that criminals ought to be punished because they personally deserve to be punished. The benefit which society receives from their punishment is incidental and collateral; and this benefit would be precluded if personal ill-desert was not regarded as the true ground of punishment. For how could suffering inflicted on the innocent—that is, inflicted without regard to personal criminality—promote the welfare of society? How could its influence be suppressive of vice and conducive to virtue? Would not the question arise in the mind of many a citizen, " Why should I specially concern myself about obeying the laws when the innocent are made to suffer as well as the guilty?" Thus does it appear that a government, by disregarding the primary object of punishment and keeping in view the secondary object alone, would more effectually defeat the secondary than if the primary object was regarded. These considerations are deemed sufficient to show that the design in the execution of the penalty of law is to punish the transgressor according to the demerit of his offence, and not merely to present him as an example to deter others from crime. But, to make the position I maintain still stronger. I need only ask, What would have been the state of things if it had been the pleasure of God to bring into existence but one rational creature? Suppose this one creature to rebel against him. Would not justice call for the penalty of rebellion, although, on the supposition, there would be no other creature to be affected by the execution of the penalty? In other words, Would not the personal guilt of such a creature render it proper for him to bear the curse of the law, though in a state of perfect isolation? How could the non-existence of other creatures affect his ill-desert? To say that it could is, in effect, to say that the relations of creatures to creatures are more important than the relation of a creature to God. This is of course an absurdity, because the creature's relation to God is the first and supreme relation, from which all subordinate relations spring.

If any inquire what this reference to the philosophy of punishment has to do with the necessity of atonement, the answer is, To trace its necessity to the demerit of sin. Sin against God is a great evil, and deserves punishment. This punishment is due to the transgressor on account of his personal demerit, and the law of God calls for its infliction. This demand made by the law implies the intrinsic evil and ill-desert of sin. There could be no such demand were it not for the sinner's personal blameworthiness. Hence it follows that there is something in the nature of sin which requires the execution of the penalty of God's violated law. This penalty must fall either on the transgressor himself or on his substitute. It *must fall somewhere.* The ill-desert of sin makes this inevitable. If the sinner is punished in person, both the spirit and the letter of the law are carried into effect; if his iniquity is laid upon a voluntary substitute, though the letter of the law is dispensed with, its spirit is fully preserved. If the transgressor bears his own iniquity, there is of course no pardon; if the substitute bears it, the transgressor may be pardoned and go free. The iniquity must be borne. The necessity of atonement, therefore, arises from the fact that while the pardon of sin is indispensable to salvation, sin is so great an evil, and so justly deserving of punishment, as to be for ever unpardonable without an expiatory sacrifice.

But the necessity of atonement is traceable from the nature of sin to the nature of God. It can be traced no further. All reasoning on the subject is destined to culminate at this point, and here to exhibit its supreme strength. For if we ask why the law of God is what it is, the answer is, Because the nature of God is what it is. If we ask why sin is such an evil as to deserve punishment, the answer is, Because it is antagonistic to the nature of God. Here, therefore—in the divine nature— is the field on which is to be decided the contest *for* or *against* the necessity of atonement. All theories which teach that the aspects of Christ's atonement are *manward* and not *Godward* virtually deny the justice and holiness of God. The correct view is that the atonement has reference both to God and man. Its saving influences reach man, because its propitiatory merit first reaches the throne of God. It is idle, therefore, to talk of what the atonement can do for man, unless it does something for the government of God. This is so obvious, that those who say that the death of Christ does not affect the divine administration toward men, but only affects men toward the divine administration, usually deny that his death was, in any proper sense of the words, a vicarious sacrifice. Not believing that the God of justice needed to be propitiated so as to turn away his holy wrath from the guilty, they cannot believe that Jesus died as an atoning substitute for sinners. If they use at all such words as propitiation, expiation, substitution, it is to be feared that many of them do so to " deceive the simple." To say that no influences emanate from the cross Godward is equivalent to a denial of all expiatory value in the sufferings of Christ. They may possess other and inferior values, but if their atoning quality is abstracted, to what saving purpose can those values be applied? But this may be called philosophizing; and it may be asked, What do the Scriptures teach? To the Scriptures, then, we go.

The Bible teaches that there is something in the nature of God to which sin is so offensive, so infinitely hateful, as to excite his holy wrath. It may be said, too, that sin is the only thing in the universe that has ever excited the wrath of God. That moral quality of the divine nature which causes hatred of sin excites wrath against sin, and therefore makes necessary an atonement, in order that sin may be pardoned. If sin originates wrath in God, it is morally certain that *that* wrath can never be turned away, unless some provision is made for the forgiveness of the sin that originates it. What do the Scriptures say in regard to the wrath of God?—" He that believeth on the Son hath everlasting life; and he that believeth not the Son shall not see life; but the wrath of God abideth on him " (John iii. 36); " The wrath of God is revealed from heaven against all ungodliness and unrighteousness of men " (Rom. i. 18); "The wrath of God cometh on the children of disobedience " (Eph. v. 6); " Which delivered us from the wrath to come." 1 Thess. i. 10. Here are several passages of Scripture which speak of wrath, nor can it be doubted what wrath is meant. It is expressly termed "*the wrath of God.*" We are not to suppose that wrath in God is something like excited passion in man. It is not. God's wrath is his holy and just indignation against sin. We are not left to conjecture whether this wrath exists, for it is revealed from heaven. It comes on the children of disobedience, abides on unbelievers, and believers are saved from it through Jesus Christ. Wrath against sin and love for sinners are perfectly consistent. The feelings of every good man may be appealed to in proof of this fact, but the fact itself receives its highest exemplification in God. He so loved sinners and so hated their sins as to send his Son from heaven "to put away sin by the sacrifice of himself" (Heb. ix. 26), that he might gratify the impulses of his love in saving sinners. In the cross, God shows himself to the universe as the sinner's friend and the uncompromising and eternal enemy of sin

Some think that it detracts from the perfection of his character to speak of the wrath of God. Their view of wrath is that it is a vindictive, resentful passion. Such a passion is, they think—and properly, too—unworthy of God. But there is a vast difference between *vindictive* and *vindicative;* and while the wrath of God is not vindictive, it is vindicative of his justice, his law, his government. This is seen in the agony of Gethsemane and in the tragedy of Calvary.

To understand many passages of Scripture we must consider God the Father as Lawgiver and as the guardian of the rights of the divine government. He presided over the awful transaction of Calvary. Whatever Jesus suffered, the Father required him to suffer as the voluntary Substitute for sinners Hence the Saviour, when his death was at hand, said, "The cup which my Father

hath given me, shall I not drink it?" John xviii. 11. It
was an inconceivably bitter cup, but the Father gave it.
As the preserver of the authority of his law and the pro-
tector of the interests of his moral empire, he was obliged
to give that cup. Jesus, with the legal responsibilities of
sinners resting upon him, was obliged to drink it. This
was determined in Godhead council before the worlds
were made. We therefore read on the prophetic page,
"It pleased the Lord to bruise him; he hath put him to
grief" (Isa. liii. 10); "Awake, O sword, against my Shepherd, and against the man that is my fellow, saith the
Lord of hosts: smite the shepherd and the sheep shall be
scattered." Zech. xiii. 7. How much was implied in the
bruising and *smiting* no finite mind will ever know. They
were inflicted by the omnipotent Hand. They were worthy
of a God terrible in his majesty and inflexible in his pur
pose to vindicate the rectitude of his throne. We are not
to suppose that the Father in smiting the Son inflicted
sufferings merely physical. The bodily sufferings of
Christ seem to have made on him scarcely any impression. When the crown of thorns was put on his head;
when he was buffeted, scourged, nailed to the cross, there
was not a word of complaint. But when the lowering
cloud of Heaven's wrath poured out its awful contents
on his soul; when he tasted the bitterness of that wrath;
when angels looked on aghast and impotent to help;
when communion with heaven was suspended; when
the Father, as the Executive of the divine government,
abandoned him to the responsibilities he had assumed,
leaving him alone to feel all the anguish of excruciating
solitude, all the horrors of unmitigated desolation,— then
did his agony reach its climax and extort the exclamatory question, "My God, my God, why hast thou forsaken
me?" Matt. xxvii. 46. He was forsaken by his Father.

l ecause he was in the place of sinners, their iniquities were laid upon him and sin was condemned in the flesh — that is, in the nature that had sinned. The Father must show his displeasure against sin and his judgment of its ill-desert, even when charged to his beloved Son, not personally, but by imputation. It really seems that hatred of sin is, if possible, a stronger feeling in the bosom of the Father than love for his Son. What mighty emotions stirred that bosom when Calvary was bathed in blood! According to human conception there must have been a sublime antagonism between those emotions. Never did the Father love the Son more intensely than then. Never was he more inflexibly attached to the principles of justice embodied in his law. Never was his abhorrence of sin more implacable, and never so fully shown. The divine displeasure against sin indicates the divine estimate of sin, and this estimate grows out of the divine nature and is inseparable from it. It follows, therefore, that the supreme argument in proof of the necessity of atonement is supplied by that moral quality in the nature of God to which sin in its intrinsic demerit is so odious as to be pardonable only through an atoning sacrifice of infinite worth.

What wonders are involved in the preceptive obedience and penal sufferings of Jesus the Nazarene! Had there been no sin, there would have been no atonement. Had there been no atonement, we should know far less of every divine attribute than we know now, and, consequently, much less of the divine character. Thus it appears that the existence of sin, the abominable thing that God hates, has been so overruled as to give the universe sublimer and more comprehensive views of the perfections of God. This is the wonder of wonders.

III. The Value of the Atonement.

On this point I shall not write at length, for the limits prescribed to this chapter require that the remaining portion of it be abridged. Nor is it necessary to elaborate the arguments which prove the worth of Christ's atoning sacrifice. It will be sufficient to present briefly a few of these arguments, and leave them to make their proper impression. I refer to the following:

The value of Christ's atoning sacrifice is seen from the following considerations:

1. *It was the antitype and the consummation of all sacrifices.* I assume that the sacrificial rite was divinely appointed immediately after the fall of man. Abel, we are told, offered to God a more excellent sacrifice than Cain. He laid on the sacrificial altar one of the firstlings of his flock. He approached God by means of blood. Abraham offered sacrifices, and Job did the same thing. At Mount Sinai there was an enlargement of the sacrificial system. Many additions were appended to it, and provision was made for greater regularity and solemnity in its offerings. Now, all the sacrifices of the patriarchal and the Jewish ages prefigured the one Sacrifice of the cross. Every altar sent its blood and smoke in the direction of Calvary. The many victims pointed to *one victim.* The many oblations called attention to the *one oblation* to be offered in "the end of the world." Heb. ix. 26. The rivers of animal blood typified Immanuel's blood. There must have been this anticipatory reference to the atoning death of Christ, for otherwise all sacrificial regulations would have been unmeaning. With this reference there was in them an expressive significance. The Epistle to the Hebrews is a sufficient justification of this view of the matter. I argue, then, the value of Christ's atone-

ment because for four thousand years God in his wisdom caused typical atonements to be made by animal sacrifices, and thus directed attention to the death of his Son. It cannot be supposed that preparation so elaborate, and continued for forty centuries, was made for an unimportant transaction, and therefore the atonement of Christ possesses unspeakable worth. When Jesus died the type yielded to the antitype and the shadow to the substance. It follows that the atoning sacrifice of Christ was the consummation of all sacrifices.

2. *The appointment of God* furnishes a further proof of the value of Christ's atonement. While it would not be true to affirm that its value arises chiefly from divine appointment, it is true that such appointment conduces materially to its worth. The reason is manifest, and it is this: No expiatory offering could be admitted, in the administration of the divine government, to possess the requisite value, unless it were sanctioned by divine approval. Christ's atonement was divinely appointed. In proof of this I refer to two out of many passages of Scripture: " Behold the Lamb of God which taketh away the sin of the world;" " Him hath God the Father sealed." John i. 29; vi. 27. In the former of these passages Christ is referred to in his sacrificial character, and is called the Lamb of God—that is, the Lamb that God provided. The latter passage probably refers to a custom observed among certain nations of antiquity. That custom was to place a seal on every animal selected for sacrifice. Wherever the seal was seen it was known that the animal was destined to the sacrificial altar. God the Father sealed his Son, designated him as the Messiah, the Mediator, and set him forth as a propitiation. See Rom. iii. 25. It is plain, therefore, that the atonement of Christ possesses whatever value divine appointment can confer. In relying on this

atonement we rely on God's constituted and approved medium of salvation.

3. *The dignity of his person.* This supplies the strongest argument in proof of the value of Christ's atonement. Every sacrifice is, according to the logic of Scripture, materially affected by the character of its victim. This is the reasoning in the Epistle to the Hebrews: "It is not possible that the blood of bulls and of goats should take away sins." x. 4. Why? Such sacrifices were divinely appointed. We see, therefore, that divine appointment does not *of itself* give requisite value to a sacrifice. But why could not animal sacrifices take away sins? There was a want of dignity and worth in the victims sacrificed, and for this reason their blood was inefficacious. This blood could make, and did make, ceremonial atonements, but was entirely incompetent to make a real atonement for sin. But behold the Victim slain once for all. Let the intelligent universe contemplate him. Who is he? This question is answered in the chapter on the Person of Christ. The Sufferer of Calvary is the God-man, the Christ. All the majestic glories of Supreme Deity and all the excellences of sinless humanity belong to him. It was the union of divinity and humanity in the person of Christ that gave atoning merit to the blood he shed on the cross. While suffering and death are to be restricted to the human nature of Christ, we may well rejoice in the belief that his divinity imparted infinite worth to the sufferings and blood and death of his humanity. Thus the atonement was made. Nor is there anything to forbid the belief that the atoning agonies of Jesus possess as great value as if his divinity had been capable of suffering and had really suffered. The merits of his death grow out of the divine element in the twofold constitution of his person. Were this ele-

ment abstracted, his death would be nothing more than a
martyr's death, whereas the Scriptures represent it as an
atoning death. In this aspect it is unlike all other deaths,
it is unique, and clothed with a glory all its own. Now, if
the worth of Christ's sacrifice arises chiefly from the dignity of his person, while the dignity of his person grows
out of his divinity, and is inseparable from it, who can set
limits to the value of his atonement when divinity is the
chief factor in the creation of that value? Must it not
be, by a sublime logical necessity, infinite? Must not its
merits be exhaustless? It cannot be too earnestly insisted on that the strongest proof of the value of Christ's
atonement is furnished by the dignity of his person as
the God-man; and this suggests, by contrast, the worth-
lessness of those schemes of theology, so called, which
deny the Deity of Christ. A denial of this fundamental
truth leads to a denial of the doctrine of atonement.
For if Christ is not divine, he could not become the Substitute for sinners, and substitution is indispensable to
atonement. To reject the divinity of Jesus is a virtual
rejection of every truth pertaining to a sinner's salvation.
It makes the obedience of his life of no avail, and takes
from his death its redemptive significance. I do not see
how salvation is possible to those who deny the divinity
of Christ. For them I see no comfort in the gospel of the
grace of God. But there is precious consolation for all
who receive Christ as the gospel reveals him, and who,
in the fulness of their hearts, adopt the words of
Thomas, "*My Lord and my God!*" John xx. 28.

IV. The Extent of the Atonement

This topic, if considered in all its amplitude, would em
brace the atonement in its relations to the universe. That
it sustains such relations is entirely credible, but we are

specially concerned with its relation to God and men. In this view the subject is one of deep personal interest to all the human race. As to the sufficiency of the provisions of the atonement for the salvation of the world, there can be no doubt and there need be no controversy. If, as has been shown, the value of the atonement arises chiefly from the dignity of Christ's person, and if his dignity results by a sublime necessity from his divinity, it is a grand impertinence to attempt to limit its sufficiency. So far as the claims of law and justice are concerned, the atonement has obviated every difficulty in the way of any sinner's salvation. In supplying a basis for the exercise of mercy in one instance it supplies a basis for the exercise of mercy in innumerable instances. It places the world, to use the language of Robert Hall, "in a salvable state." It makes salvation an attainable object. That is, all men, in consequence of the atonement, occupy a position where saving influences can reach them. There is no natural impossibility in the way of their salvation. If it be asked why all men are not saved, I reply, The answer is not to be sought in the atonement, but in the culpable unwillingness of sinners to be saved. Here the question is to be left, and here it ought always to have been left.

The sufficiency of the provisions of the atonement for the world's salvation, is the only basis on which can consistently rest the universal invitations of the gospel. On this point I cannot express my views so well as Andrew Fuller has done in the following language:

"It is a fact that the Scriptures rest the general invitations of the gospel upon the atonement of Christ. But if there were not a sufficiency in the atonement for the salvation of sinners without distinction, how could the ambassadors of Christ beseech them to be reconciled to

God, and that from the consideration of his having been made sin for us who knew no sin, that we might be made the righteousness of God in him? What would you think of the fallen angels being invited to be reconciled to God from the consideration of an atonement having been made for fallen *men?* You would say, It is inviting them to partake of a benefit which *has no existence*, the obtaining of which, therefore, is *naturally impossible.* Upon the supposition of the atonement being insufficent for the salvation of any more than are actually saved, the non-elect, however, with respect to a being reconciled to God through it, are in the same state as the fallen angels; that is, the thing is not only morally, but *naturally impossible.* But if there be an objective fulness in the atonement of Christ, sufficient for any number of sinners, were they to believe in him, there is no other impossibility in the way of any man's salvation, to whom the gospel comes at least, than what arises from the state of his own mind. The intention of God not to remove this impossibility, and so not to save him, is a purpose to withhold not only that which he was not obliged to bestow, but that which is never represented in the Scriptures as necessary to the consistency of exhortations or invitations.

"I do not deny that there is *difficulty* in these statements, but it belongs to the general subject of reconciling the purposes of God with the agency of man; whereas in the other case God is represented as inviting sinners to partake of what has no existence, and which, therefore, is physically impossible. The one, while it ascribes the salvation of the believer in every stage of it to mere grace, renders the unbeliever inexcusable; which the other, I conceive, does not. In short, we must either acknowledge an objective fulness in Christ's atonement for the salvation of the whole world, were the whole world to believe in him, or, in opposition to Scripture and common sense, confine our invitations to believe to such persons as have believed already."[1]

This extract from the writings of Mr. Fuller is commended to candid and earnest consideration, especially that part of it which presents the absurdity of offering salvation to fallen angels because an atonement has been made for fallen men. The absurdity arises from the fact that the atonement has no reference to fallen angels; and if there are sinners of Adam's race to whom it has no more reference than to fallen angels, the offer of salvation to those sinners would be a repetition of the absurdity.

The sufficiency of the provisions of the atonement for the salvation of all the world is the only doctrine which harmonizes with the commission of Christ to the apostles: "Go ye into all the world, and preach the gospel to every creature: he that believeth and is baptized shall be saved; but he that believeth not shall be damned." Mark xvi. 15, 16. According to this commission, salvation is to be offered to the whole human family. Language could be neither more general nor more specific—"into all the world," "to every creature." But the fearful intimation is that some will not believe, and through unbelief will incur damnation. It must then be the duty of all to believe. Believe what? The gospel. And what is it to believe the gospel? It is so to credit its facts and its truths as to trust in Christ for salvation. Faith is said to be "in his blood;" that is, it involves reliance on the atonement made by his blood. If, then, it is the duty of all men to believe, and if faith implies reliance on the atonement, and if the atonement was made for a part of the

[1] *Works,* vol. ii p 691, 692, American Baptist Publication Society's edition.

race only, it follows that it is the duty of those for whom no atonement was made to rely on that which has no existence. This is an absurdity. The more the point is considered, the more evident it will appear that the duty of all men to believe the gospel is inseparable from the "objective fulness" of the provisions of the atonement for the salvation of all men.

Again, in believing in Christ we not only believe, primarily, that he died for sinners, but, secondarily, that he died for us as included among sinners. The latter belief is by no means to be made so prominent as the former, but it is essential to a joyous appropriation of the blessings of salvation. Now, if Christ did not die for all, and if it is the duty of all to believe in him, it is the duty of some—those for whom he did not die—to believe an untruth. This also reduces the matter to an absurdity for it cannot be the duty of any one to believe what is not true. We must either give up the position that it is the duty of all men to believe the gospel, or admit that the atonement of Christ has reference to all men.

Much more might be said on this point, but there is not room for more in the narrow limits of a compendium of theology. Such is the extent of the atonement, that salvation is offered to all men; nor dare we question God's sincerity in making the offer. While the atoning merit of the blood of Christ is infinite, its saving efficacy is restricted to its application. We may therefore say of the atonement that it is so general that all are saved who "come to God" by Christ, and so limited that none are saved who do not "come to God" through the Mediator, "the man Christ Jesus, who gave himself a ransom for all." 1 Tim. ii. 5, 6.

21 *

CHAPTER XVII.

THE INTERCESSION OF CHRIST.

Atonement by sacrifice, being the first branch of the priestly office of Christ, is appropriately followed by Intercession, which is the second part of the same office. As the literal meaning of intercession is "going between," 't will be seen that in this sense it might be used as synonymous with mediation, since Christ in the whole of his mediatorial work occupies a position *between* God and men. The Scriptures, however, employ the term in a more limited sense, not as including the atonement, but as related to it and founded on it. This is the import of the word in theological writings. In treating of the intercession of Christ it will be well to consider the following points:

1. *The fact of his intercession.* Proof of this fact is found in such passages as these: "It is Christ that died, yea, rather, that is risen again, who is even at the right hand of God, who also maketh intercession for us" (Rom. viii. 34); "Wherefore he is able also to save them to the uttermost that come unto God by him, seeing he ever liveth to make intercession for them" (Heb. vii. 25); "My little children, these things write I unto you, that ye sin not. And if any man sin, we have an advocate with the Father, Jesus Christ the righteous." 1 John ii. 1.

In the first two of these passages it is affirmed that

Christ makes intercession. We are not left to infer that he intercedes, but the assertion is positive that he does. In the last passage he is termed " an Advocate with the Father." His advocacy is his intercession. Let us accept with gratitude the blessed fact that Christ intercedes, and notice—

2. *Where he intercedes.* The place is heaven. I do not mean that his prayer as recorded in the Gospel of John (chap. xvii.) is not properly termed his intercessory prayer, but that heaven is emphatically the place in which he makes intercession. " For Christ is not entered into the holy places made with hands, which are the figures of the true; but into heaven itself, now to appear in the presence of God for us." Heb. ix. 24. There is here reference to the entrance of the Jewish high priest every year into the holy place, or rather the most holy place, of the tabernacle or temple. As the high priest was a type of Christ, so the most holy place was a type of heaven. The high priest entered within the veil by the blood of a slain animal, but of Christ it is said by his own blood " he entered in once into the holy place, having obtained eternal redemption for us." Heb. ix. 12. Peter says of Jesus, " Who is gone into heaven, and is on the right hand of God." 1 Pet. iii. 22. Heaven is the place in which Christ ever lives to intercede, "a high priest for ever after the order of Melchisedec.' Heb. vi. 20.

3. *The basis of his intercession.* This is manifestly his own atoning death. The plea which he urges in the presence of God for us cannot rest on our merit, for we have no merit. It cannot recognize our worthiness, for there is no worthiness in us. Nor does our helpless wretchedness furnish the reason which our Intercessor urges in our favor. This wretchedness, brought on us by our own sin, rather suggests that we be left to ourselves. There are no

considerations personal to ourselves which our great **High Priest** can plead in our behalf. His atoning death on Calvary is his plea. He died, and therefore pleads that those for whom he died may live. All the reasons connected with their salvation sustain a vital relation to his death. He intercedes in heaven, because he died on earth The heavenly intercession was preceded by the earthly sacrifice, and the value of the sacrifice makes the inter cession efficacious. It is said that " Christ also hath loved us, and hath given himself for us an offering and a sacri fice to God for a sweet-smelling savor." Eph. v. 2. This language denotes that the sacrifice is acceptable to the Father, and for this reason the intercession of the Son is also acceptable. The words heard more than once from the excellent glory, "This is my beloved Son, in whom I am well pleased," are full of meaning. They are suggestive of the idea that, as God is well pleased with his Son, he is well pleased with his atonement, and therefore well pleased to grant, through the atonement, the requests presented by his interceding Son. Hence, when we are told that " we have an advocate with the Father, Jesus Christ the righteous," we are told also that "he is the propitiation for our sins." 1 John ii. 1, 2. Thus the advocacy of Christ is inseparable from his atonement, for his inter cession is the outgrowth of his sacrificial death.

4. *His qualifications as Intercessor.* Of these I shall refer only to the more prominent:

(a) He has authority to intercede. In referring to the Jewish priesthood the writer of the Epistle to the He brews says: "And no man taketh this honor unto himself, but he that is called of God, as was Aaron. So also Christ glorified not himself to be made an high priest: but he [glorified him] that said unto him, Thou art my Son, to-day have I begotten thee." Heb. v. 4, 5. It is true that this language is as applicable to Christ in his work of sacrifice as in that of intercession; but the latter topic is now under consideration. Christ has the right to intercede, and his intercession is therefore authoritative. He does not appear as an intruder in the court of heaven. He has rightfully entered within the veil, for his own atoning blood has given him the right of entrance. He "appears in the presence of God for us," and he does so in pursuance of the provisions of the covenant of redemption. As already said in substance, he bases his intercessory pleas on his atonement, made by appointment and approval of the Father, and therefore his presence as Intercessor in heaven is in accordance with the Father's good pleasure. Christ intercedes with rightful authority.

(b) The righteousness of his character. This differs from rightful authority. A king may have rightful authority, his occupancy of the throne may be constitutional, yet he may be an unrighteous man. Historical illustrations of this truth are without number. The character of Christ is perfect. It is the bright focus in which all the rays of glory meet. Eulogy is exhausted when it is said of him that he is "holy, harmless, undefiled, separate from sinners." Heb. vii. 26. In the same connection we are told that "such an high priest became us"— that is, was suitable for us. This truth we are obliged to accept, for it is self-evident that an intercessor of unrighteous character could not be permitted to plead our cause in the presence of a God whose name is *The Holy One.* He who mediates between a righteous God and sinful men must himself be righteous. Any defect of character would be a fatal disqualification. Sin has so disgraced and degraded us that it cannot comport with his majesty for God to permit us in person to approach him.

We dare not personally draw near to him. **Every at** tempt to do so would be repelled. We must approach him in the name of an Advocate. We must appear before him by Attorney. Jesus is our Attorney, and in connection with his advocacy he is termed "*the righteous.*" It is certain, therefore, that in his intercessions there is an inflexible adherence to the principles of righteousness. There is no connivance at sin, but a decided condemnation of it, and at the same time a plea for its pardon through the blood of the cross. It is a most encouraging fact that our Advocate in the court of heaven is Jesus Christ the righteous.

(*c*) He is full of sympathy. This qualification may be properly considered in connection with the preceding. While the righteous element in the character of our Intercessor makes it certain that he will properly respect and guard the interests of the divine government, his sympathy for the subjects of his intercession leads him to pity them and to make all necessary allowances for them.

What says an inspired writer on this important point? —"Seeing, then, that we have a great high priest, that is passed into the heavens [rather, *through the heavens*, as Jewish high priests passed through the veil], Jesus, the Son of God, let us hold fast our profession. For we have not an high priest which cannot be touched with the feeling of our infirmities, but was in all points tempted like as we are yet without sin. Let us therefore come boldly unto the throne of grace, that we may obtain mercy, and find grace to help in time of need." Heb. iv. 14–16. Some in apostolic times may have been tempted to believe that the exaltation of the Son of God to the throne of glory precluded sympathy for men. But the sacred writer gives assurance of Christ's sympathy, and gives the best reason for its exercise: "For we have not an high priest who cannot be touched with the feeling of our infirmities." This double negative is equivalent to an affirmative, and the truth taught is that our High Priest is touched with the feeling of our infirmities. It is worthy of remark that in the Greek we have the word from which we derive our word "sympathize," and the literal rendering would be "to sympathize with our infirmities;" but who can give up the strong phrase, "touched with the feeling of"? Christ is a sympathizing Intercessor. His heart is full of compassion—as full of compassion now as when it throbbed and bled with anguish on the cross.

But why is Christ touched with the feeling of our infirmities? The reason assigned is that he "was in all points tempted like as we are." During his humiliation on earth he experienced temptation in all its power and in all its variety. We may not be able to understand how he could be tempted in every respect as we are, but we have the inspired words, "in all points tempted like as we are." The scriptural teaching is that by personal experience of temptation he acquired the habit of sympathizing with his followers in their temptations, and that having "suffered, being tempted, he is able to succor those that are tempted." Heb. ii. 18.

In view, therefore, of the sympathy of Christ and of the reason for its exercise, there is abundant encouragement to come to the throne of grace. The intercession of a compassionate Saviour in heaven may well call forth the earnest prayers of the saints on earth. There is no fact better adapted to excite the spirit of prayer and supplication.

5. *For whom does Christ intercede?* I shall not take it on myself to affirm that there is not a sense in which Christ may be said to intercede for those who will not be finally

saved, even as he offers them salvation in the gospel. Be this as it may, all will admit that Christ intercedes specially for his people, those given him by the Father. If we wish to know what blessings he asks in behalf of his disciples, we need only refer to his intercessory prayer as recorded by the evangelist John, chap. xvii. There is nothing to forbid the belief that this prayer was a specimen and an anticipation of his intercession in heaven. He says of his disciples, "I pray for them," and his prayer expanded itself into four prominent petitions, as follows:

(*a*) Their preservation from evil. He said, "I pray not that thou shouldest take them out of the world, but that thou shouldest keep them from the evil." John xvii. 15. Some suppose that "the evil" here referred to means the evil one—that is, Satan—but the more satisfactory view is that evil in general, evil in its connection with the world, is meant. It must be admitted, however, that Satan has much to do with evil in all its forms. Paul speaks of "this present evil world." Gal. i. 4. The world is full of evil. We see evil everywhere and in all circumstances. It is to be found in unsanctified prosperity and in unsanctified adversity. It is to be seen in boasting wealth and in complaining poverty, nor is a competency a shield from it. No situation in life protects from the incursions of evil. The world is a foe to grace, and this truth Christians learn to their sorrow. They are in danger from its fascinating smiles, from its disparaging ridicule, and from its intimidating frowns. Can they in their own strength preserve themselves from the evil to which they are exposed? As well may we ask whether the chaff of the threshing-floor can resist the victorious progress of the storm. There is absolutely no hope for the preservation of Christians from evil, unless they are "kept by the

power of God through faith unto salvation." 1 Pet. i. 5
That they may be thus kept is one of the purposes which
Christ has in view in his intercession. He intercedes for
his disciples, and asks of the Father that they may be
preserved from the evil which surrounds them. The
words of Jesus to Peter are very suggestive: "Simon,
Simon, behold, Satan hath desired to have you, that he
may sift you as wheat: but I have prayed for thee, that
thy faith fail not." Luke xxii. 31, 32. We may well con-
sole ourselves with the thought that our Intercessor in
heaven prays for all his followers that their faith fail not,
and that through their faith they may be preserved from
all the phases of worldly evil. Christians themselves
pray for the accomplishment of these objects, and their
prayers have a blessed connection with the incense of
Christ's intercession, as we are probably taught in Rev.
viii. 3.

(*b*) Their sanctification through the truth. Jesus said,
"Sanctify them through thy truth: thy word is truth."
John xvii. 17. This is a matter of vital importance, but
as the subject of Sanctification is considered elsewhere,[1]
it is not dwelt upon here. I only ask the reader to remember that Jesus intercedes for his disciples that
they may be sanctified.

(*c*) Their unity. "Neither pray I for these alone, but
for them also which shall believe on me through their
word; that they all may be one; as thou, Father, art in
me, and I in thee, that they also may be one in us: that
the world may believe that thou hast sent me." John xvii.
20, 21. In these precious words the first thing that strikes
us is the comprehensiveness of this prayer, which embraces all believers, all who shall believe in Christ
through the word of the apostles. It is delightful for

[1] See Chapter XXI

the saints in all generations and in all climes to know
that Jesus prayed for them on earth and intercedes for
them in heaven. In the verses just quoted Christ prays
for the oneness of his followers—"that they all may be
one." It seems most reasonable that there should be
unity among those who have the same faith in the same
Saviour. There was for a time in the church at Jerusalem an exemplification of this unity, for it is said that
"the multitude of them that believed were of one heart
and of one soul." Acts iv. 32. Christ recognizes, as the
model of the union for which he prays, the oneness between the Father and himself—"as thou, Father, art in
me and I in thee, that they also may be one in us." John
xvii. 21. He refers also to the effect which unity among
his disciples would have upon the world—"that the world
may believe that thou hast sent me." How important to
the best interests of the world is unity among those who
believe in Christ! For this unity, Christ intercedes in
heaven, and we look for the day when his people shall
be one—one in their loyalty to truth, one in faith, one
in love, one in hope, and one in consecration to the work
of the Lord.

(*d*) Their admittance into heaven. "Father, I will
that they also, whom thou hast given me, be with me
where I am ; that they may behold my glory." John
xvii. 24.

This, so far as we know, is the last petition offered on
earth by Christ for his disciples, and it is doubtless
repeated in his intercessions in heaven. When this
request is granted the work of intercession will cease,
or, at any rate, we can see no reason for its continuance.
Christ does not in so many words pray that those given
him by the Father shall be glorified in heaven, but he
says that which is in substance the same—"be with me

where I am." What heaven other than that created by the presence of Christ can the saints desire? Was not this Paul's leading conception of heaven? He wrote, " absent from the body, and present with the Lord " (2 Cor. v. 8) ; " having a desire to depart, and to be with Christ ; which is far better." Phil. i. 23. The same apostle, referring to glorified saints after the resurrection, and including himself among them, says, " And so shall we ever be with the Lord." 1 Thess. iv. 17. Christ so loves those who believe in him that he desires to have them with him. He will never see of the travail of his soul, so as to be satisfied, till they are in his immediate presence. His intercession based on his death will secure their admittance into glory. "For if, when we were enemies, we were reconciled to God by the death of his Son, much more, being reconciled, we shall be saved by his life." Rom. v. 10. Yes, " saved by his life," for he lives to intercede, lives to carry into full accomplishment the purposes of his death. Prominent among these purposes was the glorification of his saints in the presence of his Father. He said to his first disciples, and through them to all his disciples, " I go to prepare a place for you. And if I gc and prepare a place for you, I will come again, and receive you unto myself; that where I am, there ye may be also." John xiv. 2, 3. The preparation of this place is, doubtless, connected with the intercession of Christ. What a place it will be! Bright with glory, with what Christ calls, "my glory;" and it is his will that those ransomed by his blood shall behold this glory and exult in its splendors for evermore.

CHAPTER XVIII.

REGENERATION, WITH ITS ATTENDANTS, REPENT-
ANCE AND FAITH.

It is evident that the Scriptures refer to a great change in all who become Christians—a change denoted by such forms of expression as the following: "Born again" (John iii. 3); "Born of the Spirit" (John iii. 5); "Born of God" (John i. 13); "Created in Christ Jesus" (Eph. ii. 10); "Quickened together with Christ" (Eph. ii. 5); "A new creature" (2 Cor. v. 17); "Renewed after the image of him that created him" (Col. iii. 10); "Dead unto sin, . . . alive unto God." Rom. vi. 11. This change is, in theological writings, usually called Regeneration, and it is inseparable from "repentance toward God and faith toward our Lord Jesus Christ." Acts xx. 21. For this reason the heading of this chapter has been selected, and I purposely present in closest connection Regeneration, Repentance, and Faith. Nor is it my intention to dwell on what has been termed "the order of time." Indeed, if the view of Calvin and Jonathan Edwards is correct, regeneration and repentance are in substance the same so that the question as to the order of time is ruled out. Calvin says:

"In one word, I apprehend repentance to be regenera- tion, the end of which is the restoration of the divine image within us; which was defaced, and almost obliterated by the transgression of Adam."[1] The words of Edwards are these: "If we compare one scripture with another, it will be sufficiently manifest that by regeneration, or being *begotten* or *born again*, the same change in the state of the mind is signified with that which the Scripture speaks of as effected by true *repentance* and *conversion.* I put repentance and conversion together, because the Scripture puts them together (Acts iii. 19), and because they plainly signify much the same thing."[2]

Without fully endorsing the view of these great men, I may say that if regeneration and repentance are not identical, they are so closely connected that it is not worth while to inquire whether the one precedes or follows the other. As to regeneration and faith, a plausible argument may be made in favor of the priority of either. For example, if we turn to John i. 12, 13 it seems natural to suppose that those who believed in Christ were those who had been born of God. So also according to the correct rendering of 1 John v. 1, "Whosoever believeth that Jesus is the Christ is [has been] born of God." Some use this passage as it reads in the Common Version, "is born of God," to prove that faith is prior to regeneration, because the means of it; but the argument fails in view of the fact that not the present, but the perfect, tense is used in the original—"has been born of God." But if we turn to Galatians iii. 26, "For ye are all the children of God by faith in Christ Jesus," the obvious view is that we become God's children by faith, or, in other words, that faith is instrumental in effecting regeneration. We see, therefore, that there may be a plausible argument on either side of the question. It is, perhaps, in view of this

---

[1] *Institutes*, vol. i. p. 541, edition of Presbyterian Board of Publication.

[2] *Works*, edition of 1809, vol. vi. p. 410.

fact, wisest and safest to consider regeneration and faith simultaneous, or so nearly so that the question of precedence should not be considered at all. The adoption of this theory will save us from perplexities which will otherwise annoy. For instance, those insisting on the precedence of regeneration are not a little perplexed when asked if there can be a regenerate unbeliever, and those taking the opposite view are equally perplexed when asked if there can be an unregenerate believer. That regeneration and faith are not separable in point of time is, all things considered, the most satisfactory position. One thing is certain—wherever we see a regenerate person, we see a believer in Christ; and wherever we see a believer in Christ, we see a regenerate person.

After these explanatory matters I proceed to a discussion of the subject of regeneration in the following order :

1. *The nature of regeneration.* The change which the term implies does not pertain primarily to the physical nor to the intellectual faculties. The regenerated man has the same bodily conformation after this change as before, and his mental peculiarities remain. The intellect, like the body, is affected only so far as the moral powers exert an influence over it. This leads me to say that regeneration is a spiritual change. I call it a spiritual change, not only because it is produced by the Spirit of God, as will be shown, but because it takes place in the spirit of the subject. The heart is the theatre of the operation, and the change is in the *disposition* of the heart. This disposition, I suppose, lies below or back of the affections and the will, controlling the exercise of the affections and the choice of the will. That is to say, the affections love as they do, and the will chooses as it does, because of the *state* of the heart. I will not enlarge, lest I become meta-

physical. Regeneration involves the illumination of the un derstanding, the consecration of the affections, and the rectification of the will. To use Paul's language, " Ye were once darkness, but now are ye light in the Lord." Eph. v. 8. The affections of the unrenewed soul are placed on unworthy objects, and cleave to them with the greatest tenacity. There is no relish for things spiritual and divine, no appreciation of moral excellence, no love of holiness and of God. Regeneration recalls the affections from unworthy objects, and places them supremely on the ever-blessed Jehovah—enshrines them in his infinitely perfect character. It is therefore written, " Every one that loveth is born of God." 1 John iv. 7. The will of the unregenerate man is perverse, for it conflicts with the will of God. It chooses cursing and death rather than blessing and life. In regeneration its obliquity is overcome and rectified, its perverted action is arrested and changed. " Thy people shall be willing in the day of thy power." Ps. cx. 3. The will of the regenerate, being conformed to the divine will, gladly chooses the objects on which the consecrated affections are placed.

The definition to be given of regeneration must depend on the point of moral observation we occupy. If, for example, we contemplate the sinner as the enemy of God, regeneration is the removal of his enmity and the creation of love in its stead. If we consider the sinner the " child of the devil," regeneration is the change which makes him the " child of God." If we regard the unregenerate as totally destitute of the moral image of God, regeneration consists in stamping that image upon them. Or if we view them as " dead in trespasses and sins " (Eph. ii. 1), regeneration is the beginning of divine life in their souls. It is what Paul means by being " quickened together with Christ " (Eph. ii. 5)—that is, made spiritually alive in union with Christ. Thus various definitions, not conflicting but harmonious, may be given of regeneration, according to the points of moral observation of which we avail ourselves.

2. *The necessity of regeneration.* This part of the subject has been somewhat anticipated in what has been said of the depravity of our nature, for it is depravity that renders regeneration necessary. Depravity has sundered man from God, so that, in the expressive language of Scripture, he is "alienated from the life of God." Eph. iv. 18. How is a reunion to be brought about? There must be a reunion if man is to be saved; and as the two parties, God and man, are at variance, a change must take place in one or both of the parties before there can be reconciliation. But God is unchangeable, and the change, if it takes place at all, must take place in man. We therefore clearly see the necessity of regeneration. It is as necessary as the salvation of the soul is desirable, for there can be no salvation without reconciliation with God.

The necessity of regeneration appears also in the fact that without it we cannot become the children of God. Those who are new creatures in Christ Jesus have been "born, not of blood, nor of the will of the flesh, nor of the will of man, but of God." John i. 13. Being born of God is necessary to our partaking of his nature, and this participation of his nature is implied in our being his children. "That which is born of the Spirit is spirit" (John. iii. 6)—that is, partakes of the nature of its Author. If we cannot become the children of God without it, how important is regeneration! No language can adequately set forth its importance.

The necessity of regeneration is likewise apparent, because the unregenerate cannot enter heaven; and if they could, they would be miserable there. It is one of the fun-

damental laws of social existence that we enjoy the society of those only whose dispositions are similar to our own.
On the other hand, social enjoyment results from conge-
nial taste and feeling. We see this principle illustrated
every day. We see it in the gay assemblies of the lovers
of pleasure, in the vulgar carousals of the dissipated, in
the associations of the educated and the intellectual, and
in the companies of the saints who take "sweet counsel
together." In all these there is similarity of feeling, con-
geniality of disposition. Now, suppose unregenerate sinners were admitted into heaven and required to join in
the devotions of the sanctified. Would they be happy in
the presence of a God they do not love? Would they be
happy in rendering reluctant ascriptions of praise to his
name? Would they be happy in mingling in society for
which they feel no partiality? Surely not. Jesus labored
under no mistake when he said, " Ye must be born again."
John iii. 7. It has been well said, that "heaven is a prepared place for a prepared people." Regeneration furnishes the moral preparation to relish and enjoy the bliss
of heaven. This of itself is sufficient to show its great
necessity.

3. *The Author of regeneration.* Who accomplishes this
work? It is effected by divine agency. The phrase
"born of God" is of frequent occurrence in the New Testament. We have also the expression " born of the Spirit." No language could more clearly indicate the agency
employed in regeneration. The Spirit of God alone can
renew the soul. It is his prerogative to quicken, to give
life. All is death in the moral world without his influence. What air or breath is to animal life, that his operation is to spiritual life. "It is the Spirit that quicken-
eth." John vi. 63. Paul says of the Corinthians, " Ye are
manifestly declared to be the epistle of Christ, ministered

by us, written not with ink, but with the Spirit of the living God; not in tables of stone, but in fleshly tables of the heart." 2 Cor. iii. 3. The same apostle, after telling us that those who are "in Christ are new creatures," that "old things are passed away," and "all things are become new," immediately adds, "and all things are of God." 2 Cor. v. 17, 18. Regeneration, in several passages of Scripture, is referred to under the imagery of creation. Who but God possesses creative power, the power to bring something out of nothing? To create is his inalienable prerogative, and it is also his inalienable prerogative to regenerate. He says himself, "A new heart also will I give you, and a new spirit will I put within you: and I will take away the stony heart out of your flesh, and I will give you a heart of flesh." Ezek. xxxvi. 26. In the provisions of the new covenant he says, "I will put my laws into their mind, and write them in their hearts." Heb. viii. 10.

4. *The means of regeneration.* The instrumentality employed is the gospel, the word of God. This is a controverted point. Some argue that God renews the soul without the intervention of means. Others suppose that the term "regeneration" may be used both in a limited and in an enlarged sense. They concede that in the latter sense the word of God is the means of regeneration. Without dwelling on these different views, I quote the following passages in proof of the instrumentality of divine truth in regeneration: "In Christ Jesus I have begotten you through the gospel" (1 Cor. iv. 15); "Of his own will begat he us with the word of truth" (James i. 18); "Being born again, not of corruptible seed, but of incorruptible, by the word of God, which liveth and abideth for ever." 1 Pet. i. 23. There is, as we have seen, a sense in which we are born of the Spirit, and these passages teach

that there is a sense in which we are begotten or born of the word of God. I know of no way of harmonizing the two views but by attributing regeneration to the agency of the Spirit and the instrumentality of the truth.

God uses means in the natural world, and why should he act on a different principle in the moral world? He does not. The gift of the Bible and the institution of Christian churches with a gospel ministry prove that he does not. I suppose that the Spirit of God, in regenerating the heart, makes use of scriptural truth previously lodged in the understanding. But if I am asked how truth can influence and instrumentally change a heart that does not love it, I answer I do not know. If asked how the Spirit operates on the heart so as to change it, either with or without the word of truth, I must still say I do not know. I can give no other answer while I remember what Jesus said to Nicodemus: "The wind bloweth where it listeth, and thou hearest the sound thereof, but canst not tell whence it cometh and whither it goeth: so is every one that is born of the Spirit." John iii. 8. Spiritual birth is a blessed reality, but the processes of this birth are among "the secret things" that "belong unto the Lord our God." Deut. xxix. 29. We must remember, however, that its importance justifies the startling words, "To be born is an everlasting calamity unless we are born again."

REPENTANCE.

No one can attentively read the New Testament without receiving the impression that great importance is attached to repentance. When John the Baptist came "preaching in the wilderness of Judea," the burden of his message was, "Repent ye: for the kingdom of heaven is at hand" Matt. iii. 1, 2. When Jesus entered on his ministry he said,

" The time is fulfilled, and the kingdom of God is at hand repent ye, and believe the gospel." Mark i. 15. The twelve disciples, in obedience to the command of the Lord Jesus, " went out, and preached that men should repent." Mark vi. 12. After the resurrection of Christ, Peter preached repentance at Jerusalem, and Paul dwelt upon it in his one discourse at Athens and in his many discourses at Ephesus. (See Acts ii. 38; iii. 19; xvii. 30; xx. 21.)

It is, then, a question of great importance, What is repentance? The word of which it is a translation in the New Testament has as its primary meaning *after-thought*, and as its secondary meaning *a change of mind*. It is easy to see how the secondary followed the primary signification, for in all ages *after-thought* has discovered reasons for *a change of mind*. The discovery has had a close connection with the depravity of human nature and the fallibility of human opinions. Alas, how frequent have been the occasions for a change of mind! In this change of mind, so far as scriptural repentance is concerned, a great deal is involved, as we shall see; but I wish first to show that repentance is internal. I mean by this that it is a change of the mind, the heart, and not of the life, except so far as a change of life results from a change of mind or heart. Dr. George Campbell and others have not been happy in substituting " reform " and " reformation " for " repent " and " repentance." John the Baptist made a clear distinction between " repentance " and " fruits meet for repentance;" and by the " fruits meet " he meant reformation of life. Repentance is the tree, and reformation the fruit it bears. Paul too, as well as John, distinguished between " repentance " and " works meet for repentance." Acts xxvi. 20. Repentance belongs to the sphere of the mind, and reformation to the sphere of the life; or, in other words, the former is inward, and the latter is outward. Let no one, therefore, suppose that the command to "repent" is obeyed by a reformation of life; and let no one think his repentance genuine, unless it leads to reformation of life. I trust I have made this important distinction plain.

There are in Greek authors many instances of the use of the words translated in the New Testament *repent* and *repentance*. Dr. Conant gives several examples in his notes on Matt. iii. 2, in his revised version. It is evident from these examples that the Greeks knew what it was to exercise *after-thought*, so as to change their minds and in dulge sorrow of heart. There was, however, in their af ter-thought, change of mind, and sorrow of heart, no con sciousness of the evil of sin as committed against God. Nor is this strange, as they enjoyed not the light of di vine revelation.

Of the repentance enjoined in the gospel, the following things may be said—namely, that it involves—

1. *A consciousness of personal sin.* It is a state of mind that cannot exist without conviction of sin. Of what are persons to repent if they are not sinners? The angels in heaven cannot repent, for they have never sinned. Nor could Adam and Eve repent in their state of innocence. Sin precedes repentance, and not only sin, but a con sciousness of it. A sense of sin must take hold of the soul and pervade all its faculties. I have used the epi thet *personal*, and by it I mean that the individual sin ner must repent of his own sins. I mean that one man cannot repent for another, but that each man must repent for himself. I suppose, therefore, that those persons labor under a mistake who say that they have repented of Adam's sin. They may deeply regret the apostasy of Adam, and bitterly deplore the miseries in which his race is involved, but in strictness of speech they cannot

23

be said to repent of his sin. They cannot have a person al consciousness of his sin: they can only have such a consciousness of their own, and without personal con sciousness of sin there is no repentance.

2. *That sin is a great evil committed against God, for which there is no excuse.* All sin is committed against God, against his nature, his will, his authority, his law, his justice, his goodness; and the evil of sin arises chiefly from the fact that it is opposed to God, and out of harmony with his character. Truth does not require me to say, and I do not say, that the repenting sinner has no fear of the consequences of sin; but I do affirm that the evil of sin as committed against God is the thing which gives the true penitent special anxiety and trouble. He justifies God and condemns himself. He makes David's words his own: "Against thee, thee only, have I sinned, and done this evil in thy sight: that thou mightest be justified when thou speakest, and be clear when thou judgest.' Ps. li. 4. David had committed atrocious sins against his fellow-creatures, but the thing which absorbed his thoughts and broke his heart was the fact that he had sinned against God. The repenting sinner does not regard his sin as a misfortune merely, but as a crime, involving deep, personal blameworthiness. He knows that Satan has tempted him, but he does not lay his sins to the charge of Satan, so as to excuse himself. No, he feels that he has sinned without cause and deserves to die without mercy. There is a deep sense of shame, arising from a consciousness of guilt and ill-desert.

3. *Hatred of sin.* This is an essential element in repentance. The hatred is inseparable from the *change of mind* already referred to. The change of mind is in view of sin, and the mind undergoes the change, because sin is seen to be a great evil. Regarded in this light, it becomes

an object of abhorrence. At this point, repentance and regeneration coincide. Hatred of sin is among the primary impulses of regeneration, and it cannot be abstracted from repentance without changing its character. The repenting sinner hates the sin and the sins of which he repents. I use the singular and the plural with a purpose, meaning by *sin* depravity, corruption of nature, and by *sins* actual transgressions prompted by a sinful nature. There is hatred of sin as it inheres in the nature; there is self-loathing on account of it; and there is hatred of sins committed in heart and life. The salvation of the gospel consists chiefly in deliverance from sin; nor can we conceive how God can save his creatures from their sins without saving them from the love of sin—without inspiring in them such hatred of sin as will lead them to turn from it. Penitential hatred of sin may be said to be both general and specific: it is general in the sense that it embraces all sins, and it is specific in the sense that it embraces every sin. Sin is not really hated unless it is hated in all its forms—hated in its inward workings and in its outward manifestations. Sin is the abominable thing which God hates, and it is the object of the repenting sinner's hatred.

4. *Sorrow for sin.* This accompanies the hatred. He who repents hates the sins he is sorry for, and is sorry for the sins he hates. The hatred and the sorrow are reciprocal. Indeed, each may be regarded as either the cause or the effect of the other, so close is their relation.

Those who would substitute the term " reformation " for repentance virtually exclude the element of sorrow, or at least they give it no prominent place in the change denoted by their favorite word. There is one fact which proves beyond doubt that repentance involves sorrow for sin. That fact is found in the words of Jesus: "Then began he to upbraid the cities wherein most of his mighty works were done, because they repented not Woe unto thee, Chorazin! woe unto thee, Bethsaida! for if the mighty works, which were done in you, had been done in Tyre and Sidon, they would have repented long ago in sackcloth and ashes." Matt. xi. 20, 21.

"Sackcloth and ashes" are scriptural symbols of sorrow, and of no common sorrow. They certainly signified deep contrition and grief in the Ninevites. (See Jon. iii. 5, 6.) History, profane as well as sacred, refers to them as emblems of mourning. Now, that Jesus mentioned "sackcloth and ashes" in connection with repentance for ever settles the question that sorrow enters into it as its central element. This fact was so significant in the view of Dr. George Campbell, that he could not venture, in his *Translation of the Gospels*, to substitute in the above passage *reformed* for *repented*, but left the latter word as in the Common Version.

It is as unreasonable as it is unscriptural to suppose that there is not sorrow in the change of mind denoted by repentance. How and why does the mind change at all in regard to sin, unless there is in it something to excite sorrow? Whatever calls for a change of mind concerning sin calls for sorrow on account of sin. The heart of the true penitent is a broken and a crushed heart—broken with sorrow and crushed with grief. How can it be otherwise when sin is looked at in contrast with the purity of the divine character, and its turpitude is seen in the light which shines from the cross on Calvary?

5. *A purpose to forsake sin.* This purpose is, of course, internal, and repentance is internal. He in whom is exemplified the four preceding things is obliged to form

this purpose. It is a necessity of his moral constitution. The execution of the purpose is reformation, but the purpose itself is a part of repentance. It is not necessary to elaborate a point so plain as this, for no one can feel hatred and sorrow for sin without forming the resolution to abandon it.

In dismissing the subject of repentance, I may say that it is a reasonable, important, universal, and immediate duty. " God commands all men everywhere to repent," and all men should have that change of mind in regard to sin which repentance implies.

FAITH.

Faith, as well as repentance, accompanies regeneration. But what is faith ? The term is used in the Scriptures in more senses than one. For example, an apostle says, " What doth it profit, my brethren, though a man may say he hath faith, and have not works? can faith save him ?" James ii. 14. In the last clause the insertion of the definite article is required by the original Greek— " can *the* faith save him ?" That is, the faith which is not productive of works. There is a faith, then, which is fatally defective as to the matter of salvation ; for the question, " Can the faith save him ?" is a strong denial of the power of such faith to save. The apostle further says, " Thou believest that there is one God ; thou doest well: the demons also believe, and tremble." ver. 19. Here we see that faith in the unity of God is commended, but this faith does not save ; and the proof that it does not is seen in the fact that demons, while they believe this great truth and tremble under what it implies, remain unsaved. In the last verse of the same chapter the apostle gives an impressive illustration of what he means by a "faith without works:" "For as the body without the spirit is dead, so faith without works is dead also." This illustration all can understand, for all know that when the spirit leaves the body nothing remains but a mass of inanimate clay. There is no life; the vital principle is gone. So faith which is without works is worthless, for it has in it no saving quality. Such faith is a mere intellectual assent to the truth, or rather to some parts of the truth, leaving the heart unmoved, and therefore creating no motives to action. Alas, there are many who have this faith, and who have no other faith!

Jesus, in explaining the parable of The Sower, says: "They on the rock are they which, when they hear, receive the word with joy; and these have no root, which for a while believe, and in time of temptation fall away." Luke viii. 13. Here the reference is to a temporary faith, embracing not only the assent of the intellect, but exciting superficially the feelings of the heart. Who has not seen persons fitly represented by the seed that fell on the rock thinly covered with soil? The faith of such persons has fatal defects, and therefore it is transient. They "for a while believe," but they do not believe with the whole heart. "They draw back unto perdition," and do not "believe to the saving of the soul." Heb. x. 39.

In view of the considerations now presented, it is manifest that there may be a faith that has no connection with salvation. It therefore becomes a question of the greatest importance, What is the faith of the gospel, the faith which secures the salvation of the believer? There is but one answer: It is faith in Jesus Christ. This differs very widely from a belief in the existence of God and in the historical truth of the Bible. Many believe both of these facts who do not believe in Christ, do not accept him as the Saviour. Christ is emphatically the object of

faith. He so represented himself during his earthly ministry, as we may see from his words:

"And as Moses lifted up the serpent in the wilderness,
even so must the Son of man be lifted up: that whosoever believeth in him should not perish, but have eternal
life. For God so loved the world, that he gave his only-
begotten Son, that whosoever believeth in him should not
perish, but have everlasting life. . . . He that believeth
on him is not condemned" (John iii. 14–18); "He that
cometh to me shall never hunger; and he that believeth
on me shall never thirst" (vi. 35); "He that believeth in
me, though he were dead, yet shall he live: and whosoever liveth and believeth in me shall never die." xi. 25,
26.

It is needless to multiply quotations from our Lord's
sayings. The foregoing show him to be the object of
faith in such a sense that those who believe in him are
saved from perishing and put into possession of everlasting life. It is also supremely worthy of notice that unbelief, which is a rejection of Christ as the Saviour, is the
great sin of which the Holy Spirit convinces men. "He
will reprove the world of sin, and of righteousness, and
of judgment: of sin, because they believe not on me."
John xvi. 8, 9. This language of Christ teaches the
greatness of the sin of unbelief. This sin is the opposite
of faith, and as faith receives Christ, unbelief rejects him.
As we read of "an evil heart of unbelief" (Heb. iii. 12),
we know that faith has to do with the heart as well as
the intellect.

I have referred to Christ as the object of faith; and as
illustrative of this point there is one passage of Scripture
worthy of special consideration: "Testifying both to the
Jews, and also to the Greeks, repentance toward God, and
faith toward our Lord Jesus Christ." Acts xx. 21. The

terms "repentance" and "faith" are just where they should be. Repentance is toward God—that is, it has reference to God as a Lawgiver whose law has been broken; but faith is toward our Lord Jesus Christ—that is, it has reference to him as the Saviour. The reason is obvious: Christ by his obedience and death has satisfied the claims of the law, so that the Lawgiver can consistently pardon sinners who by faith receive Christ as the Saviour. Indeed, it is God the Lawgiver who offers his Son to guilty men as the only Saviour, and faith is the heart's response to that offer. In other words, the believer accepts the offer, accepts Christ, who is made to him "wisdom, and righteousness, and sanctification, and redemption." 1 Cor. i. 30.

In ascertaining the exact import of faith in Christ, it is well to remember that the word commonly translated "believe" in the New Testament is, in several passages, rendered "commit." (See Luke xvi. 11; John ii. 24; Rom. iii. 2; 1 Cor. ix. 17; Gal. ii. 7; 1 Tim. i. 11; Tit. i. 3.) Everybody knows the meaning of *commit*, and those who believe in Christ commit themselves to him to be saved by him—commit all the interests of their salvation into his hands. There is nothing kept back; the surrender to Christ is unconditional and entire. As in the gospel he is offered as the only Saviour, he is received as he is offered, and relied on as the only Saviour. When Paul in 1 Thess. ii. 4 says, "But as we were allowed of God to be put in trust with the gospel," he uses the same verb, in the passive voice, which is usually translated "believe." Paul was put in trust with the gospel—that is, the gospel was entrusted to him; so Christ is put in trust with the salvation of the believer—that is, the believer trusts in him. I know of no word in our language which expresses more fully than the term "trust" the central idea of the word "faith.' According to the gospel, faith is personal trust in a personal Saviour. No act can be more personal than the act of faith. It is as personal as dying. As every human being dies for himself, so every man must believe for himself—must trust in Christ for himself. I know of no better definition of gospel faith than this: *It is a trustful reception of the Lord Jesus as the only Saviour.*

When the trembling jailer said to Paul and Silas. "What must I do to be saved?" they said, "Believe on the Lord Jesus Christ, and thou shalt be saved." Acts xvi. 30, 31. They gave the only answer that could be given to the question. It is faith in Christ that puts the soul in possession of the benefits of redemption. "To him give all the prophets witness, that through his name whosoever believeth in him shall receive remission of sins" (Acts x. 43); "He that believeth on the Son hath everlasting life." John iii. 36.

As the subject of Faith will be referred to in connection with Justification, it is not deemed necessary to dwell on it at greater length in this chapter.

CHAPTER XIX.

JUSTIFICATION.

THERE is no doctrine of the gospel more important than Justification. It must ever be a question of intense interest, "How shall man be just with God?" Various answers have been given to this question. Some have insisted that justification is of grace; others have supposed it to be of works; while a third party have virtually attempted to commingle grace and works in a sinner's restoration to the favor of God. The adoption of correct views on this subject is highly necessary, not only on account of the importance of justification itself, but on account of the relation it bears to the other doctrines of Christianity. For it is obvious that our views of other doctrines will be influenced by the conclusions to which we come in regard to the way of acceptance with God.

But it is time to approach the question, *What is justification?* Let a Roman Catholic answer; and, availing himself of the decision of the Council of Trent, he will say that "justification is not only the remission of sin, but also sanctification and the renovation of the inward man." This definition is plainly incorrect, for if it does not identify justification with regeneration and sanctification, it is so explained as to include both. These three acts, though connected together, are distinguishable, and

should never be confounded. There is no passage of
Scripture which teaches that justification consists, either
in whole or in part, in renewing the heart and making
it holy. Justification never has this signification, in the
Bible or out of it. It never means to renovate, it never
means to make holy; it does not even signify *to make just,*
though the etymology of the word may suggest such a
definition. Let us illustrate this point as follows: There
was a custom among the ancients, as Ovid and others
inform us, of this kind: When a person was charged
with crime he was arraigned before judges, who, after
considering all the testimony in the case, proceeded to pro-
nounce judgment by depositing small stones in an urn.
If, in their opinion, the accused was guilty, they put black
stones into the urn; but if they regarded him innocent,
they deposited white stones. Thus the black stones were
symbols of condemnation, and the white ones symbols
of justification or innocence. Now, it is plain that the
ceremony of putting white pebbles into an urn did not
make the accused individual either just or innocent, but
it *formally declared* him just and innocent. It was a
judicial announcement of acquittal. If, then, justification
is, by universal consent, a forensic term, we are author-
ized to say that it is the act of *declaring* or *accounting* a
person just or righteous. In the evangelical use of the
word, it is the act of God wherein he declares or accounts
us just or righteous. This act involves a change of state,
not of heart. The justified stand in a new relation to
the divine law. They are treated as if they had not
broken it. Its thunders, so far as they are concerned,
are hushed into eternal silence.

In the Scriptures, both of the Old Testament and the
New, the terms "condemn" and "justify" are used as opposite to each other. Thus Solomon savs. "He that justifieth

the wicked, and he that condemneth the just, even they both are an abomination to the Lord." Prov. xvii. 15. Paul declares, " It is God that justifieth," and asks, " Who is he that condemneth?" Rom. viii. 33, 34. Here the momentous question presents itself: How is a sinner justified before God? Is it by works or by grace? If, as the Bible teaches, " all have sinned, and come short of the glory of God " (Rom. iii. 23), there can be no satisfac tory argument in favor of justification by works. The law of God demands perfect obedience. There must be compliance with all its requisitions. There must be no imperfection in the obedience rendered. There must be continuity of obedience till the period of probation closes. If any man can be found to whose obedience the epithet *perfect* can be applied, he may lay claim to justification by works. I may go further and say, that the divine law will allow the validity of the claim. The law interposes no obstacle to the justification of the perfectly obedient man. Its language is, " This do "—obey perfectly—" and thou shalt live." But where shall such a man be found? What nation can produce him? In what clime does he live? To these questions we need not wait for affirmative answers, for they cannot be given. When God looked down from heaven " to see if there were any that did understand and seek God," he reported the result of his world-wide observation in there words: ' There is none righteous, no, not one." Ps. xiv. 2, 3; Rom. iii. 10. The Gentiles were addicted to the most degrading superstitions. Their idolatries were multiplied and multiform. Every nation worshipped its own gods, and forgot the God of heaven Such was the condition of the Gentiles; and the Jews were trampling the authority of Jehovah under their feet. They were rebelling against him, in defiance of the thunders of Sinai. All had gone out of the way—all, Jews and Gentiles, had become unprofitable.

"Now we know," says Paul, "that what things soever the law saith, it saith to them who are under the law · that every mouth may be stopped, and all the world may become guilty before God." Rom. iii. 19. This is the condition of the children of men. Need it be said that they are exposed to the penalty of the law they have transgressed? If so, how can they be justified by the works of the law? The law condemns; can it also justify? Can it perform two incompatible operations? Surely not. Its province is to condemn the transgressor; it cannot, therefore, justify him. Again and again the Scripture says, "By the deeds of the law there shall no flesh be justified in his sight." ver. 20. The truth of this declaration may be shown in the clearest manner. Let us see: The possibility of a sinner's justification by works of law—if such possibility exists—must arise from ability to atone for past sins by present or future obedience. In this statement, is included every conceivable theory of justification by works, for every such theory recognizes the ability referred to. But does the ability exist? It does not. Two considerations will make this plain: *First*, no man can do more than his duty. *Secondly*, no act of man can have a retrospective bearing, and thereby change the past.

What says the first and great commandment of the law?—"Thou shalt love the Lord thy God with all thy heart, and with all thy soul, and with all thy mind, and with all thy strength." Mark xii. 30. So far as the present argument is concerned, it is a matter of no consequence what may be the measure of man's strength. Angels no doubt excel him in strength. The fact in which we are now interested is that man is under obliga-

24

tion to exercise *all* his strength, to employ *all* his ability in the love and service of God. How, then, can he do more than his duty? Let the love and the service continue till death, still they would come strictly within the limits of duty. How manifest, then, that there can be no present or future superfluous obedience to make up for past failures! Past sins cannot be atoned for by present or future performances. This results inevitably from man's inability to do at any moment more than his duty.

That no act of man can have a retrospective bearing, and thereby change the past, results from man's inability to do more than his duty. It is, therefore, needless to dwell on this point. It is as clear as the light of day that "by the deeds of the law there shall no flesh be justified." Rom. iii. 20.

But it is proper to consider another aspect of the case. Some theologians have, either intentionally or otherwise, so expressed themselves as to justify the inference that, in their judgment, repentance is the basis of a sinner's acceptance with God. They disconnect repentance from the works of the law, and hence admit that legal justification is impossible. Let us notice this theory of repentance: To say that repentance can atone for sin is absurd, because there would be no repentance independent of the atonement of Christ. I assume, without argument, that the agency of the Holy Spirit and the instrumentality of the truths of the gospel are involved in the production of repentance. But this agency and this instrumentality are both secured by the mediatorial work of the Lord Jesus. Irrespective of his atonement, therefore, there would be no repentance, for there would be an entire absence of the agency and the means necessary to its exercise. It follows that the reasoning which assumes that repentance is a kind of atoning expedient is false, for repentance in every instance results from influences which proceed from the atoning work of Christ. This fact shows, too, that the supposed necessity of ascribing to repentance anything like atoning merit is entirely superseded.

But, again, if repentance could be exercised without respect to Christ's work of mediation, it would possess no saving efficacy. Repentance is not atonement. Reparation of injury is not its province. Common sense and common law teach this. Let a man throw himself from a house and break an arm or a leg, and though he may repent bitterly of his reckless folly, it does not repair the injury. Let the murderer plunge the bloodthirsty dagger into his neighbor's heart, and then indulge the most excruciating sorrow for what he has done. Does it restore to life the murdered man? It does not, and the execution of the penalty of the law is declarative of the fact that it does not. Now, if human governments do not recognize the principle that repentance atones for crime, why should it be supposed that the divine government does? If the principle belongs to the divine government, it ought to be incorporated into the constitution of every human government, for all human governments approach perfection as they become more and more conformed to the government of God. But the principle is false, and receives no sanction in heaven or on earth. We see, then, that there is no repentance disconnected from the atonement of Christ; and if there were, it would not possess the first element of expiation. Here, then, we may dismiss the consideration of the topic.

The question returns, How is a sinner justified before God? I answer, in the language of Paul: "Being justified freely by his grace through the redemption that is in Christ Jesus;" "Much more, then, being now justified by his blood, we shall be saved from wrath through him;"

"Christ is the end of the law for righteousness to every one that believeth " (Rom. iii. 24 ; v. 9; x. 4); "For he hath made him to be sin for us, who knew no sin ; that we might be made the righteousness of God in him " (2 Cor. v. 21) ; "And be found in him, not having mine own righteousness, which is of the law, but that which is through the faith of Christ, the righteousness which is of God by faith." Phil. iii. 9.

These are but a few of the passages of Scripture which teach the method of a sinner's justification before God. They direct our attention to the interposition of Jesus Christ in man's behalf. He was "made under the law, to redeem them that were under the law." Gal. iv. 4, 5. He "was delivered for our offences, and was raised again for our justification." Rom. iv. 25. The obedience and death of Christ constitute the meritorious basis of a sin ner's justification before God. They constitute such a basis, because they answer the demands of the divine law. Nor was there a relaxation of the demands of the law when Jesus engaged in the work of mediation. An abatement of its claims would not have comported with the perfection of the Lawgiver. The law, retaining its un- alterable strictness and its immaculate purity, must be magnified and made honorable. Its rectitude must be maintained, its majesty vindicated ; and there must be established a medium through which justifying mercy can be consistently extended to the guilty and the con- demned. All this was done by the obedience and death of Christ. It was so done that "Christ is the end of the law for righteousness to every one that believeth." Rom. x. 4. It was so done that God can be "just, and the jus- tifier of him which believeth in Jesus." Rom. iii. 26.

The obedience of Christ, his obedience unto death, is usually termed his righteousness. This righteousness must be imputed to sinners, in order to their justification. "Imputed righteousness" is a phrase to which many object. It must be admitted that many absurd things have been said and written on the subject of imputation, but Christ has consecrated the principle, and the doctrine, properly understood, is replete with comfort. While our sins were imputed to Christ, and he died for them because they were imputed to him, they were not so imputed as to make him a sinner; and though his righteousness is imputed to believers, it is not imputed in such a sense as to render them personally worthy of the favor of God. Christ, having assumed our legal responsibilities, was treated *as if he had been a sinner;* and we, having received his righteousness, are treated *as if we were righteous.* He was so treated *for our sakes,* because our sins were charged to his account, and he "bare our sins in his own body on the tree" (1 Pet. ii. 24); we are so treated *for his sake,* because the robe of his righteousness adorns us. None who have examined the subject will say that either sin or righteousness is transferable, except in its effects. A transference of character, of moral qualities, is plainly impossible Christ died, the *just* for the *unjust.* Surely, the moral character of those for whom he died was not transferred to him; for, in that case, he could not have remained *just,* nor could they have remained *unjust.* The awful consequence of their guilt—namely, exposure to the curse of the law—was transferred to him; the glorious effect of his righteousness—namely, a full satisfaction of the law's demands—is transferred to them. As moral qualities are not susceptible of transfer, as justification changes our state, but not our hearts I venture to say that there is no way in which Christ's righteousness can become ours, except by imputation. It may be and is *accounted* ours, and God deals with us accordingly This, I imagine, is the

24 *

correct view of imputation, and it may be illustrated by reference to the Epistle to Philemon. Paul, in writing of Onesimus, says, " If he hath wronged thee, or oweth thee anything, put that on my account "—literally, " charge that to me." ver. 18. The apostle uses the same word when he says, " Sin is not imputed when there is no law." Rom. v. 13. Christ's righteousness is put to the account of those who believe in him. It is accounted or imputed to them. They are reckoned as righteous for Christ's sake. He is made to them righteousness. They are justified by his obedience unto death, accepted in the Beloved, and experience the blessedness referred to in Rom. iv. 6-8: " Even as David also describeth the blessedness of the man to whom God imputeth righteousness without works, saying, Blessed are they whose iniquities are forgiven, and whose sins are covered. Blessed is the man to whom the Lord will not impute sin."

The period at which justification takes place, and the means by which it is effected, may now be considered. Some have advocated the doctrine of eternal justification. They say that "God from eternity purposed to justify sinners through the obedience and death of his Son." I gladly concede the fact, but what then? Surely, a purpose is one thing, and its execution another. Men are not accustomed to confound a design with its accomplishment. I see not why eternal regeneration, or eternal adoption, or eternal sanctification may not be as consistently advocated as eternal justification. The purpose of God will furnish as plausible arguments in the one case as in the other; that is to say, it will furnish no arguments at all. Justification, according to the teaching of the Scriptures, always implies previous condemnation. If, then, justification dates back from eternity, shall we say that condemnation was antecedent to eternity? This would be absurd, and the doctrine of eternal justification is replete with absurdity. I therefore dismiss it as unworthy of further consideration.

The position which we may unhesitatingly assume is that sinners are justified by faith in Christ, and are therefore justified when they believe on him. That this position can be maintained is manifest from the following portions of the word of God: "He that believeth on him is not condemned: but he that believeth not is condemned already, because he hath not believed in the name of the only-begotten Son of God" (John iii. 18); "And by him all that believe are justified from all things, from which ye could not be justified by the law of Moses" (Acts xiii. 39); "Therefore being justified by faith, we have peace with God through our Lord Jesus Christ" (Rom. v. 1); "With the heart man believeth unto righteousness" (Rom. x. 10); "For by grace are ye saved through faith; and that not of yourselves: it is the gift of God." Eph. ii. 8.

These passages are very explicit, and they conclusively prove that faith in Christ is the hinge on which turns a sinner's justification. Nor is the method of justification by faith liable to the charge of novelty. It is as old as the patriarchal age. Paul argues that Abraham was justified by faith. The Jews supposed that circumcision had much to do in the matter, but the apostle shows that he was justified before he was circumcised, and that his circumcision was "a seal of the righteousness of the faith which he had, yet being uncircumcised." Rom. iv. 11. Paul refers to Abraham's justification before God, which was by faith. The apostle James refers to this faith as developed in works, and very naturally mentions the offering of Isaac on the altar. Abraham's justification by faith was a private transaction between God and his own soul, and was therefore unknown to the world; but when he offered his son, his faith, by which he had been previously justified before God, exhibited its vitality and power. The world saw it, and all succeeding generations have conceded its genuineness and admired its strength. The faith to which Paul referred contained in it the germ of universal obedience; James referred to the same faith as manifested in a remarkable act of obedience. Thus, taking into account the different objects which the two apostles had in view in calling attention to different parts of Abraham's history, we shall see that there is no conflict between their statements.

We are not to suppose that there is anything meritorious in faith, because the justification of the believer is ascribed to its instrumentality. It is our duty to believe in Christ, for we are commanded to do so. But there is no merit in the performance of duty. When we have done all that is required of us, we are taught by the Saviour to say of ourselves, "We are unprofitable servants; we have done that which was our duty to do." Luke xvii. 10. Faith, then, being a duty, the principle which Christ has established divests it of the merit which some would vainly attempt to attach to it. We are justified *by* faith, not *for* faith. There is in faith nothing for the sake of which we can be justified. Whatever justifies must meet the demands of the law. This, faith cannot do. Love, hope, zeal, humility, and other graces of the Spirit are as competent to do this as faith. They are all incompetent. Why, then, it may be asked, is justification spoken of by the sacred writers in connection with faith, rather than with other Christian graces? I answer, Because it is emphatically the province of faith to *receive Christ.* God in the gospel offers his Son as the Saviour of sinners. Faith is the believer's act of acceptance, for it is

a state of heart responsive to God's proposal. It takes
him at his word and welcomes a gratuitous salvation.
There is no more merit in it than in a beggar's reception
of alms. The essential elements of justifying faith are to
be found in a cordial reception of the Lord Jesus and an
unreserved reliance on his righteousness. When faith is
said to be "counted for righteousness" it is so counted
objectively; that is, it is so regarded in reference to its
object, the atoning Mediator. Hence Abraham's faith,
which was "counted to him for righteousness," embraced
the promised Messiah. The blessings of salvation flow,
not from faith, but from the *object* of faith. Irrespective
of its reference to Christ faith could avail nothing. This
may be illustrated by a New Testament incident. Not to
detail all the particulars of this incident, it is sufficient
to say, that Jesus on a certain occasion said to a blind
man, "What wilt thou that I should do unto thee? The
blind man said unto him, Lord, that I might receive my
sight. And Jesus said unto him, Go thy way; thy faith
hath made thee whole." Mark x. 51, 52.

It is evident that the blind man's faith possessed no
power to restore his sight. The restoring virtue proceeded from Christ *through* faith. Thus it is in the justification of a sinner before God. The justification is by
faith instrumentally; it is by the righteousness of Christ
meritoriously. Faith is the instrument of justification,
because it receives Christ, and for no other reason. We
are "accepted in the Beloved" (Eph. i. 6), and we must
be "in the Beloved" before we can be accepted in him
or for his sake. Faith is the means of bringing us into
union with Christ. It is the spiritual ligament that binds
the soul to Christ. When united to the Saviour by faith,
God accepts us. We are reinstated in his favor. We are
justified; not pardoned merely, but justified. There is

a gracious remission of sins, while, at the same time, a title to everlasting life is conferred   Faith has been termed—and very properly too—"the appropriating grace," for by it we appropriate to the purposes of our personal salvation the benefits of the atonement of Christ.   Prominent among these benefits is justification "Being justified freely by his grace through the redemp.ion that is in Christ Jesus." Rom. iii. 24.

This method of justification furnishes a bright display of the grace of God; and faith, as the means of justifica tion, is in perfect harmony with the wondrous plan. Paul therefore says, "It is of faith that it may be by grace." Rom. iv. 16. So far is faith from being a work for the sake of which we are justified, it is, in the evangelical scheme, perfectly adjusted to the doctrine of salvation by grace. It is even spoken of in contrast with works: "If Abraham were justified by works, he hath whereof to glory, but not before God. For what saith the scripture? Abraham believed God, and it was counted to him for righteousness. Now to him that worketh is the reward reckoned, not of grace, but of debt. But to him that worketh not, but believeth on him that justifieth the ungodly, his faith is counted for righteousness." Rom. iv. 2–5.

Here working and believing are referred to as opposite, while working not and believing are represented as in perfect harmony. He who "works" with a view to justify himself by his own deeds cannot believe, cannot receive Christ. He who does not "work" with a view to a legal justification is prepared to believe in Christ, and thereby obtain evangelical justification. Grace and faith go together. Grace gives, and faith receives; and as there is no merit in receiving, justification by faith excludes boasting. Grace and faith are perfectly harmonious in their operations; for justification by faith pre-eminently illustrates the fact, that "grace reigns through righteousness unto eternal life by Jesus Christ our Lord." Rom. v. 21.

"It is God that justifieth." Rom. viii. 33. This is Jehovah's prerogative, for guilt and condemnation are incurred by a violation of his law. Whether that guilt and condemnation shall be removed, he must decide. He has graciously determined to justify those who believe on Jesus Christ. As man believes with the heart unto righteousness, as faith has to do with the heart, it is morally certain that no "priest" or "minister," whether Romish or Protestant, can come between God and the soul in the great matter of justification. The doctrine of "sacramental efficacy" cannot be tolerated here. No bodily act can be called into requisition. The transaction is between God and the soul of man. There is no room for human mediators. Faith embraces the one Mediator Christ Jesus; and God justifies for his sake. In the act of believing, the sinner is justified. He passes from condemnation to a state of acceptance with God.

The plan of justification by faith is wisely and graciously adapted to meet most effectually the necessities of our fallen race. If salvation depended on "priestly absolution," and the priest should refuse to say, "I absolve thee," his refusal would be the precursor of damnation If justification was inseparable from baptism, and it was physically impossible to be baptized, then the soul must be lost. If church membership was indispensable to salvation, then the members composing a church would have it in their power to say whether the applicant for membership should be saved or lost. If partaking of the Lord's Supper was essential to justification, then without eating bread and drinking wine at his table there could be no restoration to the favor of God. In view of these considerations, the method of justification by faith is surely a wise and gracious one. According to this method, justification has no connection with "priestly absolution;" it precedes baptism, church membership, an observance of the Lord's Supper, and is not, therefore, dependent on any one of these things, nor on all of them combined. The unjustified have nothing to do with church ordinances or church membership.

It is proper to notice, in the close of this chapter, an objection which has been often urged against the views now presented. The substance of the objection is, that the doctrine of justification by grace through faith is njurious to the interests of holiness. That the objection is not valid will appear if we consider the following points:

The death of Christ, which with his obedience is the meritorious basis of a sinner's justification, furnishes the universe with a most impressive exhibition of the evil of sin. Indeed, an exhibition equally affecting and appalling is vainly looked for away from the cross. It cannot be seen in any of the consequences of sin, so far as either fallen men or fallen angels are concerned. It cannot be seen on earth or in hell. Now, if God's method of justification shows the odiousness of sin, and by consequence the beauty of holiness, then it is as unreasonable as it is unscriptural to insist that his plan of restoring lost sinners to his favor is in any respect injurious to the interests of holiness. It is a blessed truth, that justification presupposes the pardon of sin, but, strange as it may appear to the carnal mind, God shows his hatred of sin in forgiving it. The reason is, sin is invariably pardoned through the death of Christ. How, then, can the doctrine of justification by grace through faith operate in juriously on the interests of holiness? It is morally impossible.

Again, those who are justified by faith in Jesus Christ are said by the apostle Paul to be "dead to sin," and he inquires with indignant eloquence, "How shall we that are dead to sin, live any longer therein?" Rom. vi. 2. In his view, the doctrine of justification by grace, so far from giving countenance to sin, emphatically condemns it, and eminently promotes the interests of holiness. There is evidently a moral absurdity in supposing that those who are dead to sin will live any longer therein. The objection under review is not valid.

Once more: The faith to which justification is ascribed is a living faith. It purifies the heart and prompts to holiness of life. Its vitality indicates itself in the good works to which it prompts. "As the body without the spirit is dead, so faith without works is dead also." James ii. 26. We are here plainly taught, that a faith which is not productive of works is as incompetent for purposes of justification as is a corpse to perform the functions of a living body. It was often said by the "old theologians," that "good works are the fruits of faith and the evidences of justification." This is undoubtedly true. Justification by faith precedes good works, but the works inevitably follow. Now, if justifying faith prompts its possessor to walk in the pathway of obedience, it cannot be that the doctrine of justification by grace through faith is inimical to the interests of holiness. Other arguments might be employed to demolish the objection I have been refuting, but it is deemed unnecessary. I close this chapter in the words of some writer whose name I cannot now remember: "We are justified by faith alone, but not by a faith which is alone."

25

CHAPTER XX.

ADOPTION.

WHILE regeneration denotes a change of heart, and justification a change of state, Adoption seems to be a complex term, which represents the believer as regenerated and justified. So far as this term is expressive of the *feelings* of God's children toward him, it coincides with regeneration; and so far as it expresses a *relation* of acceptance with God through Christ, it is identical with justification. Taking this view of the matter as regeneration and justification have been discussed at some length, I shall not elaborate the topic of adoption.

It may shed some light on the subject to say, that ancient nations—Egyptians, Greeks, Romans, and others —were familiar with the process of civil adoption. By this process, children were taken from families of which they were natural members, introduced into other famil ies, and made to sustain a legal relation thereto—a relation similar in its results to those of the natural relation. Such children were recognized as the children of those who had adopted them, and became their heirs. In view of this definition of civil adoption we can easily see that spirit-ual adoption is the act by which God takes those who were by nature children of wrath into a new relation to himself—a filial relation—involving their recognition and treatment as children. They are distinguished by the appellation " sons and daughters " of the " Lord Almighty." (See 2 Cor. vi. 18.)

Civil adoption and spiritual are in some respects similar, in others dissimilar. The points of similarity are such as these :

1. In each kind of adoption, the child is *taken from another family.* The fact that the child belongs to another fami'y renders the adopting process necessary. Sinners, we know, are estranged from God, children of the devil, members of another family.

2. In each, the adopted child sustains a *new relation to the adopter.* This relation is a filial one, which cannot possibly exist until the adopting act is performed.

3. In each, the adopted becomes the *heir of the adopter.* By the law of nature, and by the civil law too, the child is regarded as the heir of the father. The adopted one is in the place of a child. Christians, having been adopted by God, are his heirs. They inherit from him, and their inheritance is incorruptible, undefiled, and unfading.

But there are points of dissimilarity :

1. Civil adoption, it is supposed, was first permitted for *the benefit and comfort of the childless.* There is nothing like this in spiritual adoption. Jehovah is not childless. The angels are " the sons of God," and they constitute " an innumerable company." These " sons of God shouted for joy " when the omnipotent Creator laid the foundations of the earth. Job xxxviii. 7.

2. In civil adoption, something *amiable and attractive in the adopted excites the regard of the adopter.* Hence, Pharaoh's daughter was charmed with the infant loveliness of Moses, had compassion on him, and adopted him as her son. We are told also, that Mordecai, because Esther was " fair and beautiful " and her parents were dead, " took her for his own daughter." Esth. ii. 7. To instances like

these, there is nothing similar in spiritual adoption. In the moral character of those whom God adopts, there is nothing attractive, but everything repulsive. They are his enemies, guilty of high treason against the King of glory. They bear the image of Satan, for they are of their father, the devil. The wickedness of their lives is only an expression of the greater wickedness of their hearts. Surely, God, in adopting such creatures into his family, is prompted by nothing good or amiable in them, but by his amazing and infinite love.

3. In civil adoption, *though a filial relation is established, there is not necessarily a filial disposition.* Adopted children sometimes become moral monsters in human form. So base is their requital of the kindness of their benefactors, as to sicken every benevolent heart. Spiritual adoption is always connected with a filial temperament. It is inseparable from regeneration, by which we are born of God and become his children through faith in Jesus Christ. Where the filial relation is established the filial affections are exercised. All whom God adopts love him as their gracious Father.

The privileges of adoption claim attention. They are many, and I name the following:

1. *Unobstructed access to God.* The child can approach the father when a stranger would be repulsed. The son can gain admittance when the servant would ask a hearing in vain. The people of God may draw near to him at all times. He ever bids them welcome. They may approach him with confidence. He invites them to "come boldly unto the throne of grace." Heb. iv. 16. Paul says, "For ye have not received the spirit of bondage again to fear; but ye have received the Spirit of adoption, whereby we cry, Abba, Father." Rom. viii. 15. How delightful to feel the sublime joy resulting from

fellowship with God! How cheering is his fatherly smile! Who that has experienced the blessedness of free access to God as a Father would exchange it for all that "earth calls good or great"?

2. *The adopted are brethren of Christ.* "Having predestinated us unto the adoption of children by Jesus Christ to himself, according to the good pleasure of his will." Eph. i. 5. The whole of the process of spiritual adoption is through Christ, and the fatherhood of God is inseparable from brotherhood in Christ. All the adopted can claim the Lord Jesus as their Brother. He is said to be "the first-born among many brethren." Rom. viii. 29 There is a numerous family, but he is the Elder Brother. All others are adopted for his sake. Nor is he ashamed of the relation he sustains to them. "For both he that sanctifieth and they who are sanctified are all of one; for which cause he is not ashamed to call them brethren." Heb. ii. 11. What an honor is this! To claim Christ, not only as a Friend, but as a Brother, and to know that this fraternal relation is cemented and sanctified by the blood of the cross!

3. *They enjoy the Spirit of adoption.* We are told, that "God sent forth his Son, made of a woman, made under the law, to redeem them that were under the law, that we might receive the adoption of sons. And because ye are sons, God hath sent forth the Spirit of his Son into your hearts, crying, Abba, Father." Gal. iv. 4–6. The Spirit is a Comforter. He comforts the adopted by bearing testimony to their adoption. We therefore read in Rom. viii. 16 as follows: "The Spirit itself beareth witness with our spirit, that we are the children of God." He enables us to appropriate the promises made to the adopted. When we are conscious that we possess the evidences of adoption our spirits also bear witness

25 *

There is concurrent testimony, for the Spirit of God bears witness with our spirit. To enjoy the Spirit of adoption is an inestimable privilege. This Spirit cries— that is, prompts the adopted to cry—"Abba, Father." They claim relationship with God. The beloved disciple therefore says, " Behold, what manner of love the Father hath bestowed upon us, that we should be called the sons of God: therefore the world knoweth us not, because it knew him not. Beloved, now are we the sons of God, and it doth not yet appear what we shall be: but we know that, when he shall appear, we shall be like him; for we shall see him as he is." 1 John iii. 1, 2. How great the honor for Christians, while in this world of sin and sorrow, to enjoy the blessed consciousness that they are the children of God, with all the high possibilities of glory before them !

4. *They are the objects of divine care and protection.* A kind earthly father provides, according to his ability, what is needful for his children, and "like as a father pitieth his children, so the Lord pitieth them that fear him." Ps. ciii. 13. David, remembering his shepherd-life and his care of the flocks committed to his charge, said, "The Lord is my Shepherd; I shall not want. He maketh me to lie down in green pastures: he leadeth me beside the still waters." Ps. xxiii. 1, 2. The Psalmist, it is true, speaks here for himself, but elsewhere he uses language so general as to include all who love and serve God· "For the Lord God is a sun and shield: the Lord will give grace and glory: no good thing will he withhold from them that walk uprightly." Ps. lxxxiv. 11. Paul said to the Philippian church, " But my God shall supply all your need according to his riches in glory by Christ Jesus." Phil. iv. 19. He also said to the Romans, " And we know that all things work together for good to them that love

God, to them who are the called according to his purpose." Rom. viii. 28. If God, who has "all things" under his control, makes all things work together for good
to his people, what more can they ask or desire? Surely.
they may rejoice in his care and protection.

5. *They are chastened in love, for their spiritual good.* Some
may think it strange that I include paternal chastening
among the privileges of adoption, but it cannot be im-
proper to do so when we are told that our heavenly
Father chastens us "for our profit, that we might be
partakers of his holiness." Heb. xii. 10. Earthly fathers,
owing to their imperfection, often make mistakes in the
infliction of chastisement. They are prompted, it may
be, by passion or controlled by caprice, and they may
have unworthy ends in view. God is infinitely perfect
and infinitely wise. The motives which prompt his action are worthy of his nature. He doeth all things well.
We may safely say, that because of his great love for his
people he would never chasten them at all if their spiritual
good did not require it. "Whom the Lord loveth he chas-
teneth, and scourgeth every son whom he receiveth." Heb.
xii. 6. Chastening, then, is a proof of his love, for he
has in view the "profit" of those he chastens. The expression, "that we may be partakers of his holiness,"
contains a most precious truth. It indicates that the
chastenings which God inflicts on his people are promotive of their conformity to his moral image. To partake
of his holiness is to become holy. This is his will concerning his people. He says, "But as he which hath
called you is holy, so be ye holy in all manner of conversation; because it is written, Be ye holy; for I am
holy." 1 Pet. i. 15, 16. The highest good of creatures
is to be found in their holiness, in their likeness to God.
If, then, God chastens those whom he adopts into his

family that he may make them like himself surely chastening is to be classed among the privileges of adoption. The sanctification of suffering is provided for in God's covenant with his adopted children, and they should, therefore, regard all their afflictions as blessings in disguise.

6. *A glorious inheritance is in reserve for the adopted.* This inspiring truth is taught in the following passages: "And if children, then heirs; heirs of God, and joint heirs with Christ; if so be that we suffer with him, that we may be also glorified together" (Rom. viii. 17); "Blessed be the God and Father of our Lord Jesus Christ, which according to his abundant mercy hath begotten us again to a lively hope by the resurrection of Jesus Christ from the dead, to an inheritance incorruptible, undefiled, and that fadeth not away" (1 Pet. i. 3, 4); "He that overcometh shall inherit all things; and I will be his God, and he shall be my son." Rev. xxi. 7.

These precious Scriptures give assurance to the adopted of an inheritance so glorious that nothing more glorious can be desired or imagined. Who can adequately conceive how much is meant by the heavenly heirship—heirship with God and joint heirship with Christ? His adopted children are to inherit from God, their gracious Father, and they are to inherit in connection with their Elder Brother, Christ Jesus. They are to inherit all things, and their inheritance will be an immortal one. It is "incorruptible, undefiled, and fadeth not away." This is what Jesus means by "a treasure in the heavens that faileth not, where no thief approacheth, neither moth corrupteth." Luke xii. 33. How secure and how permanent! In the enjoyment of this heavenly treasure, the largest and highest aspirations of the saints will receive full gratification. The expanded faculties of every redeemed soul will be filled to a blessed repletion with joy inexpressible and eternal. God will recognize his adopted ones, smile upon them, and permit them through endless ages to draw on his infinite resources for happiness. They will appear before his throne in all the beauty of unblemished purity, reflecting the image of their Redeemer, even as the polished mirror reflects the image of the noonday sun. But why enlarge? It will require eternity to comprehend and eternity to enjoy this last great privilege of adoption—the possession of the incorruptible inheritance.

CHAPTER XXI.

SANCTIFICATION.

THE term *sanctify* is frequently used in the Bible. Without attempting an exhaustive examination of all the senses in which it is employed, I may say that it has two prominent meanings. As first used, it signifies to set apart for a special purpose. In proof of this, the following passages may be quoted: "And God blessed the seventh day, and sanctified it" (Gen. ii. 3); "Seven days thou shalt make an atonement for the altar, and sanctify t; and it shall be an altar most holy: whatsoever toucheth the altar shall be holy" (Ex. xxix. 37); "And it came to pass on the day that Moses had fully set up the tabernacle, and had anointed it, and sanctified it, and all the instruments thereof, and had anointed them, and sanctified them," etc. Num. vii. 1. Here we are plainly taught that the seventh day was distinguished from other days, set apart and in this sense sanctified. During a period of seven days an atonement was to be made for the altar that it might be sanctified, rendered ceremonially holy, and thus set apart for a special purpose in connection with the Mosaic economy. The atonement was ceremonial, and the sanctification of the altar was ceremonial, and whatever touched the altar was to be holy. or sanctified in the sense of special designation. Not only the tabernacle, but all its "instruments" and "vessels" were to be sanctified. They were

298

sanctified by being set apart from common to special purposes.

The other prominent meaning of *sanctify* is to make holy morally—that is, really. The ceremonial holiness of the Mosaic dispensation was a type of the moral holiness of the Christian economy. The Jews were a holy people in a national sense; that is, they were ceremonially separated from other nations, and set apart as the peculiar people of God. Many of them, we doubt not, were saints in reality as well as in form, but the great mass of the nation from age to age exemplified only a ritual, formal saintship.

Sanctification, according to the gospel and as the term is used in theology, is a precious reality, involving holiness of heart, which leads to holiness of life. It has its origin in regeneration, for regeneration is the beginning of holiness in the soul. I concede that unregenerate persons may possess amiable instincts and commendable social qualities, may illustrate what are called natural virtues; but I say with strongest emphasis that there is no spark of holiness in any unregenerate heart. Where holiness exists in its most incipient form it is a supernatural production, the effect of regeneration. Now, while regeneration implants the germ of holiness in the heart, sanctification is the unfolding of that germ. This being the case, it follows that regeneration and sanctification are essentially the same in nature, and may be regarded as two parts of the moral process by which depraved man is restored to the image of God. A reference to the figurative language of the apostle Paul will shed some light on this point. He refers to "babes in Christ" (1 Cor. iii. 1) and also to the "perfect man." Eph. iv. 13. What are we to understand by these forms of expression? We know very well that *babe* in its literal sense means an infant.

and that a perfect man has reached the maturity of developed manhood. "Babes in Christ" are spiritual infants; and as birth by generation brings forth the natural babe in possession of all the members of the body, though these members are feeble, so birth by regeneration brings forth the spiritual babe, possessed of all the parts of the "new man," but needing spiritual diet, exercise, strength development. In regeneration, then, the "new creature" is formed, comes into being, and exhibits all the conditions of a babe, while sanctification nourishes the babe and promotes its growth to spiritual maturity. Sanctification is therefore a progressive work, going on by degrees till finally accomplished. Regeneration breaks the power of sin and destroys the love of sin, so that "whosoever is born of God doth not commit sin" (1 John iii. 9), in the sense of being the slave thereof, but it does not free the soul from the presence and the pollution of sin. Alas. the regenerate know full well that sin is in their hearts and that it stamps with imperfection whatever they do This accounts for the Christian warfare, which begins in regeneration and is carried on in sanctification. "The flesh lusteth against the spirit, and the spirit against the flesh: and these are contrary the one to the other: so that ye cannot do the things that ye would." Gal. v. 17. This conflict implies the remains of sin in the believer, while the fact itself must be taken into account in any consistent interpretation of the much-controverted passage in Rom. vii. 14–25. These verses are true of a regenerate man sanctified in part, and they are true of no other man. This, of course, is not the place for critical exposition, but I may say the things which follow:

No regenerate man, perfectly sanctified, can say in truth, "For that which I do, I allow not: for what I would, that do I not; but what I hate, that do I;" "For the good that

I would, I do not: but the evil which I would not, that de
I ;" " But I see another law in my members, warring against
the law of my mind, and bringing me into captivity to
the law of sin which is in my members;" " O wretched
man that I am! who shall deliver me from the body of
this death ?"

No unregenerate man can truly say, " I consent unto
the law that it is good;" "To will is present with me;"
' For I delight in the law of God after the inward
man ;" "So then, with the mind I myself serve the law
of God."

But a regenerate man, imperfectly sanctified, can in
truth repeat all these declarations. Because he is regenerate, and for no other reason, he " delights in the law of
God after the inward man ;" and because he is sanctified
only in part there is " another law warring against the
law of his mind." Paul, I doubt not, referred to himself,
in the verses quoted, as an imperfect Christian, struggling
with the remains of depravity, and seeing hope of triumph only in the grace of God through the Lord Jesus
Christ.

Sanctification implies *the crucifixion of sin.* "For if ye
live after the flesh, ye shall die: but if ye through the
Spirit do mortify the deeds of the body, ye shall live."
Rom. viii. 13. To mortify is to put to death, and there
must be an earnest and a constant effort to put sin to
death, to crucify it. The warfare against sin must be impartial. There must be no favorite sins. A war of exter-
mination must be waged against every sin. Temptations
to the commission of outward sins must be resisted, and
our inward enemies, the sins of the heart, must be dragged
forth from their lurking-places and slain before the Lord
Sin is so great an evil that if the right hand " offends " or
leads to sin, it is better to cut off that right hand than to

retain it. If the right eye involves its possessor in sin, it is the part of wisdom to pluck it out, however severe the excision may be. These are the teachings of Christ concerning sin. What a fearful evil it must be! The death of crucifixion was usually a lingering death, and the crucifixion of sin is often a lingering process. How many Christian soldiers have fought the battle against sin from the freshness of youth, through the vigor of manhood, down to the decrepitude of age! They have done so under the impulses created by regeneration and projected through the whole process of sanctification. The spirit of Christianity calls for the crucifixion of sin in all its forms.

Again, sanctification implies *the growth and improvement of the Christian graces.* These graces enter into the formation of the Christian character, but they are susceptible of increase in strength. The most prominent of them are faith, hope, and love ; for it is written, "And now abideth faith, hope, charity [or love], these three ; but the greatest of these is charity." 1 Cor. xiii. 13. That faith is capable of growth is clearly taught in the following passage : "We are bound to thank God always for you, brethren, as it is meet, because that your faith groweth exceedingly." 2 Thess. i. 3. There was not only a growth, but a remarkable growth, in the faith of the Thessalonian church. What was true in apostolic times is true at this day. Faith may still grow, and in proportion to its growth does the work of sanctification advance. The connection between faith and sanctification is taught in such scriptures as these : "And put no difference between us and them, purifying their hearts by faith " (Acts xv. 9); "That they may receive forgiveness of sins, and inheritance among them which are sanctified by faith that is in me " (Acts xxvi. 18); "Who is he that overcometh the world

but he that believeth that Jesus is the Son of God?"
1 John v. 5. The first of these passages teaches that
the heart is purified by means of faith; the second, that
sanctification, as well as forgiveness of sins, is dependent
on faith in Christ; and the third, that victory over the
world is achieved through faith in Jesus as the Son of
God. As faith increases, the heart becomes purer, and
therefore less accessible to the influences of the world.
This shows how it is that faith overcomes the world, and
it shows also that the degree of faith is the measure of
sanctification.

Hope, as well as faith, may be increased. In proof of
this I need only quote Rom. xv. 13: "Now the God of
hope fill you with all joy and peace in believing, that ye
may abound in hope, through the power of the Holy
Ghost." Here the fact is recognized that Christians not
only entertain hope, but that they may abound in hope.
This will be readily admitted, in view of the fact that
hope springs from faith. A weak faith, therefore, inspires a feeble hope, and a strong faith a vigorous hope.
When faith, with a firm grasp, embraces the facts of the
gospel, hope confidently looks for the accomplishment
of the promises of the gospel. The great promise, the
culmination of all the promises, is eternal life. "This
is the promise that he hath promised us, even eternal
life." 1 John ii. 25. The hope of a blissful immortality
is of necessity influential. Its sanctifying tendency is
positively asserted as follows: "And every man that
hath this hope in him purifieth himself, even as he is
pure." 1 John iii. 3. I doubt not that *upon* should take
the place of *in* if we would have the meaning of the
original; that is to say, the hope of the believer rests *upon*
Christ. True, the hope is in the believer, but Christ is
the foundation on which it rests. The point, however,

which claims special attention is the purifying influence of Christian hope. While the followers of Christ are animated with the hope of seeing him as he is, and of being like him, it is morally certain that they will "follow holiness" and use all the means in their power to promote their purification. Thus does it appear that there is a union between hope and sanctification, and that the advance in sanctification is to be measured by the vigor of hope.

Love "abides," as well as faith and hope; that is, while the gift of tongues and other miraculous gifts answered a temporary purpose in the establishment of Christianity, faith, hope, and love are permanent, so that wherever a Christian is found to the end of the world there will be found in him these three graces. The greatest of these is love, but its pre-eminence is not the thing now to be noticed. Its capability of increase is the matter which claims attention. "And the Lord make you to increase and abound in love one toward another, and toward all men, even as we do toward you: to the end he may stablish your hearts unblamable in holiness before God, even our Father, at the coming of our Lord Jesus Christ with all his saints." 1 Thess. iii. 12, 13. If Christian love and love toward all men can increase and abound, then surely love to God can increase and abound. Indeed, this must be so, for Christian love and love toward all men grow out of love to God. Jesus teaches us that love may "wax cold;" and if so, it may wax warm, even to fervent heat. The spark may kindle into a flame which will burn with increasing brightness on the altar of the heart. "God is love;" and the more of love there is in his people the greater their moral nearness and likeness to him. It is therefore written, "He that dwelleth in love dwelleth in God, and God in him."

1 John iv. 16. If God is love, and if those who dwell in love dwell in him, then love seems to be the blessed element in which sanctification takes place. This being the case, an increase of love is an increase of sanctification; and while God causes his people to abound in love he "establishes their hearts unblamable in holiness."

Once more: In the work of sanctification *the will of the Christian is more and more conformed to the divine will.* If sin had not disturbed the harmony of the universe, there would have been but one will—the will of God. All creatures, being in a state of holiness, would have been in a state of conformity to the will of the Creator. That this is not the case we have mournful proof in the apostasy of some of the angels and in the universal apostasy of men. Of Adam's race it is true, that "all have sinned and come short of the glory of God." Rom. iii. 23.

The divine will, according to our best conception of it, grows out of the divine nature, and is inseparable from it. That is, God wills as he does because he is what he is. The crowning glory of his nature is his holiness, and his will is a recognition and an expression of his holiness. God's will, however manifested, is the rule of action for his rational creatures. The method of its manifestation in heaven we know not, but that it is made known in some way is evident, because Jesus has taught us to pray "Thy will be done in earth, as it is in heaven." Matt. vi. 10. The essence of sin consists in the conflict of the creature's will with the will of the Creator. I refer to the will of the creature in an enlarged sense of the term, not only as including volition, but the state of heart in which volition has its origin. The will of man in his natural state is in rebellious collision with the will of God. Regeneration, therefore, includes among other

26 *

things a rectification of the will, so as to conform it to the will of God; but the conformity is incipient, and not perfect. Sanctification, as we have seen, carries on what regeneration begins; and hence the will of the Christian, as the work of sanctification goes on, is assimilated more and more to the will of God. Partial conformity to the divine will is partial sanctification, and perfect conformity is perfect sanctification. Some suppose that the latter is attainable in this life, but the whole tenor of Scripture seems to indicate that more or less imperfection will cleave to the saints as long as they are "in the body." Still, they should earnestly strive to be " holy as God is holy," and such striving would no doubt lead to higher degrees of sanctification. They should regard the character of Christ as the standard of moral excellence, and devoutly aspire to perfect conformity to that standard. In other words, Christians should, "forgetting those things which are behind, and reaching forth unto those things which are before, . . . press toward the mark for the prize of the high calling of God in Christ Jesus." Phil. iii. 13.

While in the threefold definition now given of sanctification several points have been referred to which are in truth evidences of the progress of the gracious work, it may be well to refer more definitely to some other evidences. I name the following:

1. *A deep sense of unworthiness.* In all dispensations true piety has exalted God and humbled man. The humiliation has ever resulted from conscious unworthiness induced by reverential views of the divine character. Of this, we have two striking specimens in the Old Testament. Job, in meeting the charges made against him by his professed friends and "comforters," went too far in his own vindication. He thought too well of himself, and exhibited in some measure a spirit of self-righteousness. But

when " the Lord answered Job out of the whirlwind, and said, Who is this that darkeneth counsel by words without knowledge?" then it was that Job said, " Behold I am vile; what shall I answer thee? I will lay my hand on my mouth." . . . "I have heard of thee by the hearing of the ear; but now mine eye seeth thee: wherefore I abhor myself, and repent in dust and ashes." (See Job xxxviii. 1, 2; xl. 4; xlii. 5, 6.) Job had never had so deep a sense of his unworthiness as at that time, and never did the process of sanctification go on so rapidly as then.

Isaiah, as we learn from the sixth chapter of his prophecy, had a vision, and saw " the Lord sitting upon a throne, high and lifted up." He heard the six-winged seraphim cry one to another, " Holy, holy, holy is the Lord of hosts: the whole earth is full of his glory." The trembling prophet said, " Woe is me! for I am undone; because I am a man of unclean lips, and I dwell in the midst of a people of unclean lips: for mine eyes have seen the King, the Lord of hosts." The contrast between divine purity and human imperfection was so great that the prophet thought himself " undone," utterly ruined. His sense of ruin arose from a sense of unworthiness, and he referred, no doubt, to the uncleanness of his lips as symbolic of the uncleanness of his heart. Never before did Isaiah feel so unworthy, never before did he make such spiritual attainments.

In the New Testament we have in Paul a remarkable example of growth in grace, but who ever had a deeper sense of unworthiness? His words are, " Unto me, who am less than the least of all saints, is this grace given." Eph. iii. 8. These words were written when he was an old man, two years before his death; and one year before his martyrdom he referred to himself as " the chief of sinners." The work of sanctification most probably never went on with such blessed rapidity as during those two eventful years. I think I may safely say that as Christians make progress in sanctification the more unworthy do they appear to themselves. They are not more unworthy than those who have not these humbling views, but greater light shines into their souls and they make new discoveries.

2. *An increasing hatred of sin.* Sin is the opposite of holiness, and, so far as we know, God cannot make us holy without making us hate sin. He deals with us as rational creatures, susceptible of hatred and love. To hate sin, we must see what an evil it is, how odious and how bitter. This is the important object secured by conviction. It is in God's purpose that "sin by the commandment might become exceeding sinful." Rom. vii. 13. When the Holy Spirit convinces of sin, he so performs his work that sin becomes hateful. Hatred of sin enters into the essence of repentance, and the hatred becomes more intense as the sanctifying process advances. The epithet most frequently used to designate the Spirit of God is "*holy ;*" and this, doubtless, is the case because it is his province to make men holy. Hatred of sin implies love of holiness. The hatred and the love necessarily coexist, and they are exactly equal in strength. The Christian hates sin as much as he loves holiness, and no more. As the work of sanctification goes on, the Christian hates sin more intensely, and the attainments he makes in holiness are in proportion to his hatred of sin. Hence it is that one evidence of progressive sanctification is an increasing hatred of sin.

3. *A growing interest in the means of grace.* The word of God is more highly appreciated as the instrument of sanctification; for Jesus prayed, "Sanctify them through thy truth: thy word is truth." John xvii. 17. Nor is the

truth of this word brought into miraculous contact with the heart. The Scriptures must be read and studied. A superficial perusal will not do, for it would be like taking food into the stomach and permitting it to remain there undigested. The Christian must "desire the sincere milk of the word, that he may grow thereby." 1 Pet. .i. 2 The word of God is one of the prominent means of promoting holiness; and if it be asked, Who are advancing in sanctification? the answer must be, Those described by the Psalmist, whose "delight is in the law of the Lord," and who in his law "meditate day and night" (Ps. i. 2) —those in whose judgment and according to whose spiritual taste "the statutes of the Lord" are "more to be desired . . . than gold," "sweeter also than honey and the honeycomb." Ps. xix. 8, 10.

Prayer, also, is a precious means of grace. The Christian's closet is a sacred place, for there he holds communion with his God. The divine eye alone sees him, the divine ear alone hears him, while he pours forth his sou. in fervent supplication. It is in answer to prayer that the Holy Spirit is given, who carries on the work of sanctification. If the Christian neglects prayer, or engages in it in a heartless manner, the sanctifying process stops, for it cannot go on in a prayerless soul. Those Christians in whom has been most attractively illustrated the doctrine of progressive sanctification have been most given to prayer. Religious biography will support this declaration.

Did time and space permit, I might refer to the social and the church prayer-meeting, the Lord's Day, the public services of the sanctuary, and the observance of the Lord's Supper. These are means of grace of which those who desire spiritual progress must avail themselves. They cannot be safely dispensed with, unless Providence so orders. A growing interest in the means of grace is one of the evidences that sanctification is advancing in the soul.

4. *An increasing love of things heavenly.* "If ye, then, be risen with Christ, seek those things which are above, where Christ sitteth on the right hand of God. Set your affection on things above, not on things on the earth. For ye are dead, and your life is hid with Christ in God. When Christ, who is our life, shall appear, then shall ye also appear with him in glory." Col. iii. 1–4.

Christians profess to have died to sin and to have risen with Christ to a new life. If so, the impulses of their renewed souls should prompt them to seek the things that are above, where Jesus is. Heavenly objects should attract their love, for their citizenship is in heaven. Their names are written in heaven, and Christ himself teaches us, that this should be a source of the sublimest joy. He has also told his followers, that he has gone to prepare a place for them, and we know that he has entered into heaven itself. It is characteristic of Christians to love Christ and to think of the place he has gone to prepare Their treasure is in heaven and their hearts are there. They are pilgrims on earth, looking for the "city which hath foundations, whose Builder and Maker is God." Heb. xi. 10. Their permanent home is heaven.

Now, one of the effects of increasing sanctification is the weakening of the ties that bind Christians to this world, and the strengthening of their attachments to heavenly things. As they grow in grace they become less and less like men of the world, who, because they have "their portion in this life," are said to "mind earthly things." There is no better evidence of progressive sanctification than an increasing love of heavenly things.

It is a delightful thought that, as perfect sanctification

must precede admittance into heaven, those who appear before the throne of glory will be clothed with robes of spotless white, emblems of their immaculate moral purity. The last stain will have been washed from their souls by the blood of the Lamb, and they will stand before the throne in all the beauty of unblemished perfection. Every one of them can then say, as they now sing in anticipation,

> " Sin, my worst enemy before,
>   Shall vex my eyes and ears no more
>   My inward foes shall all be slain
>   Nor Satan break my peace again. "

CHAPTER XXII.

GOOD WORKS.

It is important to understand what is meant by ' good works." They have their proper place in the Christian scheme. They do not precede justification, so as to procure it, nor are they performed before regeneration, so as to effect it; but they follow both and are evidences of both. While the phrase "good works" implies a proper state of heart, from which they spring, it is evident from the New Testament that such works are chiefly outward acts of consecration to God. In proof of this, I quote the words of Christ, as follows: "Let your light so shine before men, that they may see your good works, and glorify your Father which is in heaven." Matt. v. 16. This is the first use of the words "good works" in the Scriptures, and it is plain that Christ refers to external performances, which could be seen. So also when he said to the Jews (John x. 32), "Many good works have I shewed you from my Father," he referred to his beneficent miracles which they had witnessed. In Acts ix. 36, it is said of Dorcas, "This woman was full of good works and almsdeeds which she did." These good works were visible, and therefore known. From Rom. xiii. 3 we learn that "rulers are not a terror to good works, but to the evil." Here, too, there must be a reference to external works. Paul taught likewise that an aged widow, before receiving assistance from a church fund, must be 'well reported of for good works; if she have brought up children, if she have lodged strangers, if she have washed the saints' feet, if she have relieved the afflicted, if she have diligently followed every good work." 1 Tim. v. 10. In the same Epistle, the rich are exhorted to be "rich in good works" (vi. 18), while in the letter to Titus he is urged to show himself "a pattern of good works.' Chap. ii. 7. When it is said in Heb. x. 24, "And let us consider one another to provoke unto love and good works," it is manifest that good works refer to outward acts, even as love refers to the heart. The good works of the life were to proceed from the love of the heart. Peter wrote to his brethren, "Having your conversation [behavior] honest among the Gentiles: that, whereas they speak against you as evil-doers, they may by your good works, which they shall behold, glorify God in the day of visitation." 1 Pet. ii. 12. Here, again, as in the first passage quoted, the visibility of good works is taken for granted.

I have now referred to a large majority of the places in the Scriptures where the phrase "good works" is used, and it cannot be denied that it denotes external acts.

Now, while there are good works and evil works, it is very important to know what are the qualities of good works. In other words, their nature must be defined. What, then, is the nature of good works? I give a threefold answer:

1. *They are prompted by supreme love to God.* The first and the great commandment of the law is, "Thou shalt love the Lord thy God with all thy heart." Matt. xxii. 37. This is the universal duty of creatures. Indeed, we are so constituted that we cannot conceive how God can create a rational being under no obligation to love him.

27

The obligation is as undeniable as the light of day or the darkness of night. It is true, also, that unless love to God is in the heart of man, no act of obedience rendered to any command can be acceptable. It is impossible for God to be pleased with such obedience. I will illustrate this point. Wives are required to obey their husbands and, according to the teaching of Scripture, "the husband is the head of the wife." Eph. v. 23. The husband, it is to be supposed, requires nothing unreasonable of the wife in the way of compliance with his wishes. She may perform any number of acts of external obedience, but if the husband is not assured of her love he is utterly dissatisfied. The want of love he considers a defect so great as to vitiate every act of obedience. In view of this conjugal illustration, I may surely say that want of love to God pollutes every act of obedience which man may perform. There can be no acceptable element in any obedience severed from love to God. This was the capital defect in "the righteousness of the Scribes and Pharisees." They were punctilious in paying tithes of herbs, but the Saviour told them, that they "passed over judgment and the love of God." Luke xi. 42. The love of God in their hearts did not prompt their obedience, and therefore the obedience did not secure the divine approval; so far from it, the frown of God was upon it.

No works are evangelically good unless they proceed from love to God, and there is no love to God in any unrenewed heart. Hence good works are performed by the regenerate alone, and are the evidences of regeneration. "Every one that loveth is born of God," and has been "created in Christ Jesus unto good works." 1 John iv. 7; Eph. ii. 10. The performance of good works follows the great change referred to under the imagery of a birth and a creation.

2. *They are conformed to the divine law.* This is an important point. It must not be imagined that if we love God, we can do anything we please and still be within the sphere of good works. This view is entirely wrong. A good work must not only proceed from love to God, but it must be conformed to his law; and if so, it will be performed in compliance with the moral obligation of the actor. For the law of God is the expression of his will, and of course recognizes the obligation of man to do that will. I would not indulge in conjecture, but I may say, that while moral distinctions are traceable to the divine nature as their supreme and original source, the divine will, as expressed in the divine word, is the standard and the measure of human obligation. It follows, therefore, that no work can be a good work the performance of which conflicts with the will of God and is a violation of moral obligation. No matter what motive may prompt such a work, it cannot be a good work. It is characteristic of a regenerate soul that it "consents to the law that it is good," and good works are performed in obedience and conformity to the law.

3. *They are performed for the divine glory.* This follows the two preceding points, for those who love God and are conformed to his law must desire his glory. They therefore act with reference to it. This is the highest object that mortal man can propose, and no loftier purpose controls the motives of an archangel. More than this, God himself acts with a view to his glory. The essential glory of God is alike incapable of increase or diminution, but there may be an increase of his declarative glory. His declarative glory is his manifested glory—the glory resulting from an exhibition of his character and perfections. All the good works of the saints have this tendency—to present the character of God in a favorable

light—for they are performed under his inspiring influence, and are feeble imitations of the good works which he is constantly doing. Let it never be forgotten that good works are performed by his people, in order that God may be glorified.

Having attempted to define the nature of good works, it is well to allude to two classes into which they may be divided; they refer to the bodies and to the souls of men. The acts of kindness mentioned in Matt. xxv. 35–40 pertain to the body: " For I was a-hungered, and ye gave me meat: I was thirsty, and ye gave me drink: I was a stranger, and ye took me in: naked, and ye clothed me: I was sick, and ye visited me: I was in prison, and ye came unto me. Then shall the righteous answer him, saying, Lord, when saw we thee a-hungered, and fed thee? or thirsty, and gave thee drink? When saw we thee a stranger, and took thee in? or naked, and clothed thee? Or when saw we thee sick, or in prison, and came unto thee? And the King shall answer and say unto them, Verily I say unto you, Inasmuch as ye have done it unto one of the least of these my brethren, ye have done it unto me."

It is the body that hungers, thirsts, is naked, sick, imprisoned. The good works specified in the verses quoted pertain to the body, and they will be approvingly recognized at the judgment of the great day. They will be referred to, not as meritorious of salvation, but as evidences of the Christian character of those who will be welcomed into the heavenly kingdom. The question was once asked in a company of Christians, " What is a good work?" and a pious woman, without learning, but with much common sense, said, " An act of kindness that we do to the needy for Christ's sake, and then forget it." Admirable answer!

It is written in James i. 27, " Pure religion and undefiled before God and the Father is this, To visit the
fatheress and widows in their affliction, and to keep
himself unspotted from the world " To visit, in the
sense of this passage, is, no doubt, to do acts of kindness
for widows and fatherless ones. Alas! in all ages, the
condition of widows and fatherless children has been a
sadly eloquent appeal for help. It is an appeal that is
practically regarded by those who carry into effect the
New Testament idea of good works. Jesus said, and his
words are full of meaning, " For ye have the poor always
with you." Matt. xxvi. 11.

Souls have supreme claims. The body has value as the
tenement of the soul. What must be the worth of the
immortal spirit? The question which Jesus asked has
remained unanswered through all the centuries: "For
what is a man profited, if he shall gain the whole world,
and lose his own soul? or what shall a man give in
exchange for his soul?" Matt. xvi. 26. This language
implies that if a man should gain the whole world and
lose his soul, the gain would be unspeakably paltry and
the loss infinitely great. Souls need salvation, and must
perish without it; and salvation, if obtained at all, must
be secured during this short life. When Jesus died on
the cross his estimate of the value of souls was written
in characters of blood. Surely, those who have the mind
of Christ must feel compassion for unsaved souls, and be
ready to labor to rescue them from ruin. It is often the
case that kindness shown to the needy and suffering body
opens an avenue through which the soul is reached.
" He that winneth souls is wise " (Prov. xi. 30); and the
soul-winner shows his wisdom in the sanctified tact to
which he resorts in gaining his purpose.

The phrase " good works," as descriptive of the efforts
27 *

of Christians for the salvation of sinners, has an enlarged meaning. It includes all the methods of Christian labor These methods are many; among which I may mention religious conversation, consistent example, circulation of the Holy Scriptures and the truths of the gospel in other forms, the support of the Gospel, home and foreign missions, and other Christian works.

The consecration of their tongues is a thing which Christians greatly need. They should talk of the things of God, and recommend the religion of Jesus to their dying fellow-men. How can the tongue be so usefully employed as in telling of salvation through the Crucified One?

What the tongue says, however, must be enforced by the power of Christian example. Words have but little influence when they are merely used to commend that which is not practised by the speaker. Christian usefulness depends greatly on the deportment which the Christian calling requires.

The word of God is the prominent means of conversion and salvation. The Holy Spirit makes use of it in enlightening the mind and renewing the heart. To disseminate this word as far as possible is one of the good works which Christians should be ever performing. "The seed is the word," and this seed should be sown far and near. The extent of the spiritual crop to be gathered from it will not be known till the great harvest-day. It will be seen then what good has resulted from the circulation of divine truth, whether in the large volume, the tiny leaflet, or the various intermediate grades of Christian publications.

The gospel must be supported. By this I mean "that they which preach the gospel should live of the gospel." 1 Cor. ix. 14. The most of those whom God calls to this work are taken from the poor of this world. Ministers of the word are sometimes placed in circumstances which require them, like Paul, to labor with their hands for the necessaries of life, and it is honorable for them to do so. Ordinarily, however, the people who enjoy a minister's labors can give him, at least, a moderate support.

We are accustomed to speak of home and foreign missions, but in truth the cause of missions is one, the spirit of missions is one. The language of Christ "that repentance and remission of sins should be preached in his name among all nations, beginning at Jerusalem" (Luke xxiv. 47), is the fullest authority for missions in the most enlarged sense of the term. "Beginning at Jerusalem" embraces the work of home missions in all the forms of that work; while the words "among all nations" direct attention to foreign missions in their world-wide operations. How sublime is the missionary enterprise! It contemplates the evangelization of the world, the salvation of immortal souls, the triumph of the Redeemer's kingdom, and the manifestation of God's glory in all the earth. This enterprise calls for the large pecuniary contributions of the rich and the smaller offerings of the poor. Every Christian who is not "an object of charity" should give conscientiously and systematically to this cause. How can money be so wisely used? How can gold be employed for a better purpose than in extending the gospel of salvation, which is more precious "than gold, yea, than much fine gold"? Among the good works of Christians pecuniary donations to the cause of God must never be forgotten. "The silver is mine, and the gold is mine, saith the Lord of hosts." Hag. ii. 8.

But while the good works embraced in the various fields of Christian labor are diligently performed, unceasing prayer must be offered to God for his blessing

Success depends on his benediction. Means, however earnestly used, accomplish nothing, unless he renders them effectual. "Not by might, nor by power, but by my Spirit, saith the Lord of hosts." Zech. iv. 6. Let "the sacramental host of God's elect" occupy a suppliant attitude. Prayer on God's footstool brings down blessings from his throne.

In view of the considerations presented in this chapter the words of the Holy Spirit through Paul are very impressive: "This is a faithful saying, and these things I will that thou affirm constantly, that they which have believed in God might be careful to maintain good works." Tit. iii. 8.

Such works are the appropriate fruits of faith, proving it to be a vital principle, which, while it justifies before God, prompts active consecration to his service. These works also are evidences of regeneration, for they show in the holiness of the life that the germ of holiness has been deposited in the heart.

In performing good works Christians have the satisfaction of knowing that they are copying the example of Jesus their Lord. We are told, that when personally on earth he "went about doing good." Acts x. 38. This was his business, his calling. He not only did good, but "went about" to find opportunities of doing good—to find objects on whom to confer his benefactions. There was no bodily suffering that did not excite his pity There was no sorrow in any heart that did not touch a responsive chord in his bosom. He has left his followers an example which it is their highest honor to copy. Let them, like him, go about doing good, making the world better by their beneficent labors; and when their work on earth is done they will be transferred to a sphere of more exalted service in heaven.

CHAPTER XXIII

PERSEVERANCE OF SAINTS.

It has been shown in former chapters, that those who
are saved by Christ are regenerated, justified, adopted, and
sanctified. That is to say, the changes denoted by regeneration, justification, and adoption have already taken
place, while the process of sanctification is going on. It
is a question of deep interest, whether all who are in a
state of acceptance with God will continue therein
through life, and finally reach heaven. To this question, two answers are given, the one affirmative, the
other negative. The affirmative answer is full of consolation, but the negative excites fear and disquiet.
The point, however, to be decided is, What do the Scriptures teach? Their utterance is decisive, whether the
decision be productive of comfort or of apprehension.
The word of God, as it seems to me, teaches the perseverance of saints in a state of grace to a state of glory.
It has been admitted in the chapter on Sanctification, that
Christians are imperfect, and will be while they are in the
body. Sometimes their imperfection shows itself in very
distressing forms, as, for example, in the case of Peter.
But as Peter's " faith failed not "—as he repented of his
great sin and obtained pardon—so there is scriptural
reason for believing that every child of God, however
grievously he may backslide, will be reclaimed from his

wanderings. As to those represented by the "stony-ground hearers," having "no root in themselves," they of course in time of temptation "fall away." Luke viii. 13. So those denoted by the unfruitful branches do who have no vital connection with the vine. Their union with Christ is professional—not real, not spiritual. They therefore fail of salvation. I refer only to those who "know the grace of God in truth." Nor do I put the question as it is sometimes put—namely, "*Can* a Christian fall from a state of grace?" I say he can, if God gives him up. There is no impossibility, but a positive certainty of his falling, unless he is "kept by the power of God through faith unto salvation." 1 Pet. i. 5. I put the question, "Will a Christian fall from a state of grace?" and in view of the guarantees of God's covenant with his people I humbly, gratefully, and boldly answer, No.

That saints will persevere through grace to glory may be argued from the following considerations:

1. *The purpose of God the Father.* This is a very comprehensive purpose. Taken in its full extent, it not only includes the predestination of the saved to eternal life, but also the predestination of everything necessary to salvation. We therefore read, "Forasmuch as ye know that ye were not redeemed with corruptible things, as silver and gold, . . . but with the precious blood of Christ, as of a lamb without blemish and without spot; who verily was foreordained before the foundation of the world, but was manifest in these last times for you." 1 Pet. i. 18–20. Here we are clearly taught that Christ, who was manifested by his incarnation, was foreordained to accomplish the work of redemption through his blood. The atoning sacrifice of Calvary, which lays the basis of human salvation, was offered in pursuance of the purpose of God—offered according to his determinate counsel and

foreknow.edge. The office-work of the Holy Spirit was also embraced in the divine purpose. This almighty Agent makes sinners " meet to be partakers of the inheritance of the saints in light." Col. i. 12.

That which now claims special notice in connection with the purpose of God is the fact, or rather the series of facts, recorded in Rom. viii. 30: " Moreover, whom he did predestinate, them he also called : and whom he called, them he also justified: and whom he justified, them he also glorified."

This has already been termed the golden chain of four links. The links are predestination, calling, justification, and glorification. The predestination is the divine purpose, and the purpose is executed in the calling—another name for regeneration, containing the germ of sanctification—and in justification. That is, the regenerated and the justified have been regenerated and justified in accordance with the purpose of God the Father, and in execution of it. In the absence of this purpose, there would have been no regeneration, no justification. The purpose by a blessed necessity secures the performance of these parts of salvation. Now the question arises, Will not the same purpose secure glorification ? In other words, Will not the same considerations which prompt God to regenerate and to justify, prompt him to glorify ? We must adopt this view, unless we believe in a suspension of the divine purpose before glorification is accomplished. Would not such a belief as this be arbitrary ? Would it not be more reasonable to believe in a suspension of the purpose before regeneration and justification ? Would it not be more consistent to believe in the formation of no purpose at all ? But those who deny the final perseverance of the saints admit that the purpose of God is effected in their regeneration and justification. Shall the purpose, then, be abandoned before it reaches its final point in the glorification of the redeemed? This, it may be said with reverence, would be unworthy of God. I insist, therefore, that the purpose of God the Father supplies a valid argument in favor of the perseverance of saints.

2. *Union with Christ.* That believers are united to Christ is a truth unspeakably important and infinitely precious. It is a truth which the New Testament affirms in a variety of ways. When, for instance, Christ is termed "the true Vine," his disciples are said to be "branches" of that Vine. John xv. 1, 5. When he is styled a "Foundation" and "Cornerstone, elect, precious," Christians are described as "living stones" out of which a spiritual house is built upon the foundation. (See 1 Cor. iii. 11; 1 Pet. ii. 7, 5.) When he is represented as the Head, his followers are declared to be members of his body. The union between husband and wife is referred to as illustrative of the relation between Christ and the subjects of his grace. It may be said that these forms of expression are highly figurative. This is true, but they surely mean something. Their pertinency and force arise from the fact that there is a union between a vine and its branches, between a foundation and its superstructure, between the head and the members of a body, between the husband and the wife. The strongest figures can only typify in a feeble manner the union between Christ and believers.

There is one phrase which expresses more fully than any other the intimacy of the union to which I refer. That phrase is composed of the two words—IN CHRIST. No merely human relation is thus expressed. There is a relation between pastor and church, physician and patient, lawyer and client; but no one says that the church is *in* the pastor, or the patient *in* the physician, or the client *in* the lawyer. Christians, however, are said to be *in Christ*, and he is said to be in them. They are in him, and he dwells in their hearts by faith as the hope of glory. It follows that the union between Christ and believers is a most intimate one. Should it be said, that faith is the bond of union, and that if faith fails, the union will be broken, I grant it. But what did Jesus say to Peter?—" I have prayed for thee, that thy faith fail not." Luke xxii. 32. His faith did not fail. The conflict between faith and unbelief in Peter's heart may have been, and no doubt was, severe, but there was no total and final failure of his faith. It would have failed if Jesus had not prayed that it might not fail. As Jesus prayed on earth for Peter, so he intercedes in heaven for all who believe in him. In his intercession, is involved the prayer that their " faith fail not." After Peter's experience it is not strange that he wrote, " Kept by the power of God through faith unto salvation." 1 Pet. i. 5. The preserving power is divine; it is exerted, not independently of faith, but through faith, and it is exerted " unto salvation." If, then, there is this connection between faith and salvation, the union between Christ and his disciples is indissoluble. This union, therefore, furnishes an argument for the perseverance of saints which cannot be invalidated. Who can question the power of this argument when Jesus himself says, " My sheep hear my voice, and I know them, and they follow me: and I give unto them eternal life ; and they shall never perish, neither shall any man pluck them out of my hand. My Father, who gave them me, is greater than all ; and no man is able to pluck them out of my Father's hand " ? John x. 27–29. Again he says, " Because I live, ye shall live also." John xiv. 19. Surely, if the life of the members depends on the life of the Head, while there is life in the Head there will be life in the members. The perse-

28

verance of saints through grace to glory is therefore secured by their vital union to Christ.

3. *The work of the Holy Spirit.* That the Spirit of God performs a great work in the hearts of all who become Christians is manifest from the words "born of the Spirit." It is a radical, revolutionary work, referred to under the imagery of birth, creation, resurrection. There is one scripture which may be specially considered in this connection. It is found in Eph. iv. 30: "And grieve not the Holy Spirit of God, whereby ye are sealed unto the day of redemption." There are two views of this passage. Some think that the words translated *whereby* should be rendered *in whom,* as denoting "the sphere and element of the sealing." Dr. Conant, taking this view, translates the verse accordingly. Dr. Noyes retains the "whereby" of the Common Version. The former view requires a belief that God the Father performs the sealing operation *in* the Holy Spirit; the latter view ascribes the sealing agency to the Spirit. Whichever view is adopted, the work of sealing is divine, and has reference to the day of redemption. The sealing is connected with "the earnest of the Spirit:" "Who hath also sealed us, and given the earnest of the Spirit in our hearts." 2 Cor. i. 22. If the sealing is setting apart, designating, as in John vi. 27, then believers are set apart, designated, as belonging to God, and the day of redemption will be the day of their public recognition as his. The sealing contemplates the period when Christ shall come "the second time without sin unto salvation." Heb. ix. 28. If, then, the purpose of the sealing is accomplished, saints must persevere unto the end. If the earnest of the Spirit is inseparable from the sealing, the argument in favor of perseverance is strengthened. The earnest of the Spirit is a pledge and a foretaste of the glory to be revealed. But of what value would be the pledge and the foretaste

without a certainty of the glory? There is certainty of the glory if the saints persevere to the end, but no certainty if they do not. "He that endureth to the end shall be saved." Matt. x. 22. Thus does it appear, from the conjoint work of the Father, the Son, and the Holy Spirit in the salvation of believers, that the perseverance of saints is provided for and secured. Much more might be said on this interesting topic, but I must forbear.

There are two prominent objections often urged against the final perseverance of saints. The one is, that the doctrine is inconsistent with the promises, the admonitions, the warnings, and the threatenings addressed to the people of God in his word. The answer to this objection is that Christians are dealt with as rational beings, and therefore susceptible of influence from motive. Hence their hopes and fears are appealed to, and the appeal is designed to stimulate their activity in working out their salvation. In other words, they are to be saved in the use of means, and not in neglect of means. No one sees inconsistency in the connection between means and physical results. Where, then, is the inconsistency between means and spiritual results? If God has made the cultivation of the soil and the sowing of seed necessary to a literal crop, it cannot be unworthy of him to make the "reaping of life everlasting" dependent on "sowing to the Spirit" Gal. vi. 8. The scriptural view of the matter is strongly expressed in these words: "For we are his workmanship, created in Christ Jesus unto good works, which God hath before ordained that we should walk in them." Eph. ii. 10.

The other leading objection to the doctrine of the perseverance of saints is, that it is unfriendly to the interests of holiness. That is, it is supposed that if Christians were certain of getting to heaven at last, they would not strive to live lives of holiness on earth. But is it not true that the love of holiness which regeneration creates, must prompt to holy obedience in the life? Is there not a sacred necessity in the case? If so, where is there anything unfriendly to the interests of holiness? Is not a love of holiness the best security for obedience?

As to those professing Christians who fail to show their faith by their works of obedience, I may say that they deprive themselves of all scriptural proof that they are Christians. The doctrine advocated in this chapter is the perseverance of *saints.* Those, therefore, who do not persevere should not consider themselves saints. This view of the matter shows that the doctrine is not unfriendly to the interests of holiness, but, on the other hand, contains a stimulus to obedience, that the scriptural evidence of saintship may be possessed and enjoyed.

It is a delightful thought that " the righteous, obtaining help from God, shall hold on his way " (Job xvii. 9) and ultimately reach the bright mansions of glory in heaven. He who, when standing on the verge of eternity, can say with Paul, " I have fought the good fight," can also say with him, " Henceforth there is laid up for me a crown of righteousness which the Lord, the righteous Judge, shall give me at that day." 2 Tim. iv. 7, 8.

CHAPTER XXIV.

THE CHURCH. [1]

THE term *church* frequently occurs in the New Testament. It may be found there more than a hundred
times. The word thus translated means congregation or
assembly, but it does not indicate the purpose for which
the congregation or assembly meets. Hence it is used
Acts xix. 32, 39, 41, and rendered *assembly*. In every
other place in the New Testament it is translated *church*.
In its application to the followers of Christ it is usually,
if not always, employed to designate a particular congregation of saints or the redeemed in the aggregate. It is
used in the latter sense in several passages, as, for example, when Paul says, "Christ also loved the church, and
gave himself for it; . . . that he might present it to himself a glorious church, not having spot or wrinkle, or any
such thing." Eph. v. 25–27. In these places and in several others it would be absurd to define the term "church"
as meaning a particular congregation of Christians meeting in one place for the worship of God.

The other signification of the word claims special at-

[1] If any are disposed to say that this chapter should immediately
follow the one on Regeneration, I shall not deny it. Still, all things
considered, I have thought it best to present in unbroken connection
the topics of Regeneration, Justification, Adoption, Sanctification,
etc.

tention. In a large majority of instances it is used in the Scriptures to denote a local assembly convened for religious purposes. Thus we read of "the church at Jerusalem," "the church of the Thessalonians," "the church of Ephesus," "the church in Smyrna." Nor are we to suppose that it required a large number of persons to constitute a church. Paul refers to Aquila and Priscilla, and "the church that is in their house;" to "Nymphas, and the church which is in his house." 1 Cor. xvi. 19; Col. iv. 15. A congregation of saints, organized according to the New Testament, whether that congregation is large or small, is a church. The inspired writers, as if to preclude the idea of a church commensurate with a province, a kingdom, or an empire, make use of the following forms of expression: "the *churches* of Galatia," "the *churches* of Macedonia," "the *churches* of Asia," "the *churches* of Judea." But they never say "the *church* of Galatia," "the *church* of Macedonia." Wherever Christianity prevailed in apostolic times there was a plurality of churches.

In answer to the question, What is a church? it may be said, A church is a congregation of Christ's baptized disciples, acknowledging him as their Head, relying on his atoning sacrifice for justification before God, depending on the Holy Spirit for sanctification, united in the belief of the gospel, agreeing to maintain its ordinances and obey its precepts, meeting together for worship, and co-operating for the extension of Christ's kingdom in the world. If any prefer an abridgment of this definition, it may be given thus: A church is a congregation of Christ's baptized disciples, united in the belief of what he has said, and covenanting to do what he has commanded.

If this definition of the term "church" is correct, it is

manifest that membership is preceded by important qualifications. These qualifications may be considered as *moral* and *ceremonial*. All moral qualifications are embraced in Regeneration, with its attendants, Repentance and Faith, already discussed.[1]

It is obvious that the purposes of church organization can be carried into effect by regenerate persons alone. Those who become members of a church must first have exercised "repentance toward God and faith toward our Lord Jesus Christ." They are "called to be saints," and must "walk worthy of the vocation wherewith [they] are called."

Baptism is the *ceremonial* qualification for church membership. There can, according to the Scriptures, be no visible church without baptism. An observance of this ordinance is the believer's first public act of obedience to Christ. Regeneration, repentance, and faith are private matters between God and the soul. They involve internal piety, but of this piety there must be an external manifestation. This manifestation is made in baptism. The penitent, regenerate believer is baptized into the name of the Father, and of the Son, and of the Holy Spirit. There is a visible, symbolic expression of a new relationship to the three persons of the Godhead—a relationship entered into in repentance, faith, and regeneration. As Baptism will be the topic of a distinct chapter, it is briefly referred to here.

OFFICERS OF A CHURCH.

It cannot be said that officers are essential to the existence of a church, for a church must exist before it can appoint its officers. After this appointment, if, in the providence of God, they should be removed by death

[1] Chapter XVIII.

it might affect the interests, but not the *being*, of a church. It has been well said that "although officers are not necessary to the *being* of a church, they are necessary to its *well-being*." Paul, refering to Christ's ascension gifts, says: "And he gave some, apostles ; and some, prophets, and some, evangelists; and some, pastors and teachers, for the perfecting of the saints, for the work of the minis- try, for the edifying of the body of Christ." Eph. iv. 11, 12. Apostles, prophets, and evangelists filled extraordi- nary and temporary offices. There are no such offices now. Pastors and teachers, the same men, are the ordi- nary and permanent spiritual officers of the churches, while the office of deacon has special reference to the sec- ular interests of the churches. Of these two offices, the following things may be said :

1. PASTORS.— This term was first applied to ministers having oversight of churches. The reason, no doubt, was in the resemblance between the work of a pastor and that of a literal shepherd. A shepherd has under his charge a flock, for which he must care and for whose wants he must provide. The sheep and the lambs must be looked after. The Lord Jesus, "that great Shepherd of the sheep" (Heb. xiii. 20), virtually says to all his under- shepherds, as he did to Peter, "Feed my lambs," "Feed my sheep." John xxi. 15, 16. It is worthy of remark that this language was not addressed to Peter until the Saviour had obtained from him an affirmative answer to the question, "Lovest thou me?" As if he had said, "I love my spiritual flock so well that I cannot entrust the sheep and lambs composing it to any man who does not love me." Love to Christ must be regarded in all ages and in all places as the pastor's supreme qualification. All other qualifications are worthless if this is absent. Talent and learning are not to be undervalued, but they

must be kept under the control of piety and receive its sanctifying impress.

The work of pastors is referred to by Paul when he says, "If a man desire the office of a bishop, he desireth a good work." 1 Tim. iii. 1. It is indeed a good work—the best work on earth—but a *work*. The term *bishop* must not be suffered to suggest any such idea as its modern acceptation implies. In apostolic times there were no bishops having charge of the churches in a district of country, in a province, or a kingdom. A bishop was the pastor of a church, and the New Testament, so far from encouraging a plurality of churches under one pastor, refers in two instances at least to a plurality of pastors in one church. (See Acts xx. 28; Phil. i. 1.) In the former passage the elders of the church of Ephesus are called *overseers*, and the word thus translated is the same rendered *bishop* in Phil. i. 1; 1 Tim. iii. 2; Tit. i 7; 1 Pet. ii. 25. Thus does it appear that pastor, bishop. and elder are three terms designating the same office This view is further confirmed by a reference to 1 Pet. v 1, 2, where elders are exhorted to "feed the flock of God'—that is, to perform the office of pastor—"taking the oversight thereof;" that is, acting the part of bishops, or overseers. For the word translated "taking the oversight" belongs to the same family of words as the term rendered "bishop" in the passages cited. It is plain, therefore, that a pastor's work is the spiritual oversight of the flock, the church he serves. Like a good literal shepherd, he must care for the feeble and the sick as well as for the healthy and the vigorous. Some he can feed with "strong meat," while others can digest nothing but "milk." He must exercise a sanctified discretion, and "study to show" himself "approved unto God, a workman that needeth not to be ashamed, rightly dividing the word of truth." 2 Tim. ii. 15. Much depends on dividing the word of truth *rightly;* hence the necessity of study, prayerful study, imbued with the Spirit of the Master.

The administration of the ordinances—which are two, baptism and the Lord's Supper—as well as the preaching of the word, is the proper business of the pastor. As it does not accord with the plan of this volume to elaborate any topic, the work of the pastor cannot be enlarged on, nor is there room to present the many motives to pastoral fidelity. The mention of two must suffice: The church over whose interests the pastor watches has been bought with "the precious blood of Christ," and the faithful pastor will, when "the chief Shepherd" comes, "receive a crown of glory that fadeth not away." 1 Pet. v. 4. What motives to diligence and faithfulness could possess more exhaustless power?

2. DEACONS.—The office of deacon originated in a state of things referred to in the sixth chapter of the Acts of the Apostles. It is said, that "when the number of the disciples was multiplied, there arose a murmuring of the Grecians against the Hebrews, because their widows were neglected in the daily ministration." The "Grecians" were Jews as well as the Hebrews, but they spoke the Greek language, and were probably not natives of Palestine. The members of the church at Jerusalem "had all things in common," and a distribution was made out of the common stock "as every man had need." Acts iv. 35. This seems to have been done at first under the immediate direction of the apostles; and the intimation is that the large increase of the church interfered with an impartial distribution of supplies. The apostles saw that if they made it their business to "serve tables," it would greatly hinder their work in its spiritual aspects

They said, "It is not reason that we should leave the word of God, and serve tables. Wherefore, brethren, look ye out among you seven men of honest report, full of the Holy Ghost and wisdom, whom we may appoint over this business. But we will give ourselves continually to prayer, and to the ministry of the word." Acts vi. 3, 4.

Thus the creation of the office of deacon recognizes the fact that the duties of pastors are pre-eminently spiritual, and that they should not be burdened with the secular interests of the churches.

The words "men of honest report, full of the Holy Ghost and wisdom," applied to the first deacons, indicate that they were men of unblemished reputation, ardent piety, and good common sense. The phrase "full of the Holy Ghost" is an admirable definition of fervent, elevated piety; and in the selection of deacons their spirituality must be regarded, for their duties are not exclusively secular. Their secular duties, however, should be performed in a spiritual frame of mind, and in this way they "purchase to themselves a good degree, and great boldness in the faith which is in Christ Jesus." 1 Tim. iii. 13. In visiting the poor to distribute the charities of the church, deacons must not perform the duty in a *formal* manner, but must inquire into the spiritual as well as the worldly circumstances of the recipients of the church's bounty. They will often witness such an exhibition of faith, patience, gratitude, and resignation as will richly repay them for their labor of love. As occasion may require, they should report to the pastor such cases as need his special attention, and thus they will become a connecting link between the pastor and the needy ones of the church.

As deacons were first appointed "to serve tables," it

may be well to say that there are three tables for them
to serve:

1. *The table of the poor;* 2. *The table of the Lord;* 3. *The*
table of the pastor. The pecuniary supplies to enable them
to serve these tables must be furnished by the church.
The custom of taking a " collection " for the poor after
the celebration of the Lord's Supper is a good one. It is
suitable at the close of the solemn service to think of the
pious poor whom sickness or some other misfortune may
have kept from the sacred feast.

As some pecuniary expenditure is necessary in furnish-
ing the table of the Lord, this should be made through
the deacons; and it is eminently proper, though not indispensable, for them to wait on the communicants in the
distribution of the elements.

Deacons should serve the pastor's table. It is not for
them to decide how liberally or scantily it shall be supplied. The church must make the decision, and enlarged
views should be taken when it is made, for the energies of
hundreds of pastors are greatly impaired by an incompetent support. The pastor's compensation having been
agreed on by the church, the deacons must see that it
is raised and paid over. They may appoint one of
their number acting treasurer, who shall receive and
pay out funds; but it should never be forgotten that
deacons were originally, by virtue of their office, **the**
treasurers of the church.

As all pecuniary expenditures are to be made through
deacons, they should at the end of every year make a report to the church of what moneys they have received during the year, and how they have been expended. This
will keep everything straight and plain, while it will
do very much for the promotion of a church's influence
and efficiency.

Deacons as well as pastors should be ordained to office by prayer and the laying on of hands.

Church Government.

In the language of theology, and in popular language too, there are three forms of church government, known by the terms Episcopacy, Presbyterianism, and Independency.

Episcopacy recognizes the right of bishops to preside over districts of country, and one of its fundamental doctrines is that a bishop is officially superior to other ministers. Of course, a modern bishop has under his charge the "inferior clergy," for it is insisted that the "ordaining power" and "the right to rule" belong to the episcopal office. The modern application of the term "bishop" to a man who has under his charge a district of country is very objectionable. It has almost banished from Christendom the idea originally attached to the word. In apostolic times, as we have seen, "bishop," "pastor," and "elder" were terms of equivalent import.

Presbyterianism recognizes two classes of elders—*preaching* and *ruling* elders. The pastor and ruling elders of a congregation constitute what is called "the session of the church." The "session" transacts the business of the church, receives, dismisses, and excludes members. From the decisions of a session there is an appeal to the Presbytery, from the action of the Presbytery an appeal to the Synod, and from the action of the Synod an appeal to the General Assembly, whose adjudications are final and irresistible.

Independency is in irreconcilable conflict with Episcopacy and Presbyterianism, and distinctly affirms these three truths:

1. *That the governmental power is in the hands of the members of a church.* It resides with the members in contra distinction from bishops or elders; that is to say, bishops, or elders, can do nothing strictly and properly ecclesiastical without the concurrence of the members.

2. *The right of a majority of the members of a church to rule in accordance with the law of Christ.* The will of the majority having been expressed, it becomes the minority to submit.

3. *That the power of a church cannot be transferred or alienated, and that church action is final.* The power of a church cannot be delegated. There may be messengers of a church, but there cannot be, in the proper use of the term, delegates.

These are highly important principles; and while the existence of the independent form of church government depends on their recognition and application, it is an inquiry of vital moment, Does the New Testament inculcate these principles? For if it does not, whatever may be said in commendation of them, they possess no obligatory force. Does the New Testament, then, inculcate the foundation-principle of Independency—namely, that the governmental power of a church is, under Christ, with the members? Let us see.

It was the province of the apostolic churches to admit members into their communion. In Rom. xiv. 1, it is written: "Him that is weak in the faith receive ye." The import of this language is, "Receive into your fellowship and treat as a Christian him who is weak in faith." There is a command: "receive ye." To whom is this command addressed? Not to bishops, not to the pastor and "ruling elders," but to the church, for the Epistle was written "to all that be in Rome, beloved of God, called to be saints."

New Testament churches had the right to exclude un-worthy members, and they exercised the right. Paul, in referring to " the incestuous man " at Corinth, says to the church: " In the name of our Lord Jesus Christ, when ye are gathered together, and my spirit, with the power of our Lord Jesus Christ, to deliver such an one to Satan, for the destruction of the flesh, that the spirit may be saved in the day of the Lord Jesus." 1 Cor. v. 4, 5. It is worthy of remark that while Paul "judged" that the guilty man should be excluded from the church, *he* did not exclude him. He did not claim the right to do so and when he said to the " churches of Galatia," " I would they were even cut off who trouble you," he did not cut them off, though he desired that it should be done. With regard to "the incestuous man," Paul said, " Put away from among yourselves that wicked person." 1 Cor. v. 13. Here is a command, given by an inspired man, requiring the exclusion of an unworthy member from the church at Corinth. To whom was the command addressed? " Unto the church of God, which is at Corinth, to them that are sanctified in Christ Jesus, called to be saints." 1 Cor. v 1. The right of a church to exclude unworthy members is taught in Matt. xvii. 17; 2 Thess. iii. 6, and in other places.

The apostolic churches had the power and the right to restore to fellowship excluded members who gave satis-factory evidence of penitence. In 2 Cor. ii. 6–8 "the in-cestuous man " is again mentioned as follows: "Sufficient to such a man is this punishment, which was inflicted of many. . . . Wherefore I beseech you that ye would con-firm your love toward him." Paul could no more restore him than he could expel him in the first instance, but he says, " I beseech you." The great apostle bowed to the majesty of the doctrine of church independence. He virtually admitted that nothing could be done unless the church chose to act. Now, if the New Testament churches had the right to receive, exclude, and restore members they must have had the right to transact any other business coming before them. There surely can be nothing more vital to the interests of a church than the reception, exclusion, and restoration of members. Here I rest the argument for the foundation-principle of church independency, though many other passages might be adduced in favor of it.

A second principle of Independency, already announced, is the right of a majority of the members of a church to rule in accordance with the law of Christ. I refer again to 2 Cor. ii. 6: "Sufficient to such a man is this punishment, which was inflicted of many." A literal translation of the words rendered "of many" would be "by the more"—that is, by the majority. Dr. MacKnight's translation is, "by the greater number." If, as has been shown, the governmental power of a church is with the members, .t follows that a majority must rule. This is so plain a principle of Independency and of common sense, that it is needless to dwell upon it.

A third truth involved in the independent form of church government is, that the power of a church cannot be transferred or alienated, and that church action is final. The church at Corinth could not transfer her power to the church at Philippi, nor could the church at Antioch convey her authority to the church of Ephesus. Neither could all the apostolic churches combined delegate their power to an association or synod or convention. That church power is inalienable results from the foundation-principle of Independency—namely, that this power is in the hands of the people, the membership. If the power of a church cannot be transferred, church action is final. That there is no tribunal higher than a church is evident from Matt. xviii. 15–17. The Saviour lays down a rule for the adjustment of private differences among brethren : "If thy brother shall trespass against thee, go and tell him his fault." If the offender, when told of his fault, does not give satisfaction, the offended brother is to take with him " one or two more, that in the mouth of two or three witnesses every word may be established." But if the offender "shall neglect to hear them," what is to be done? Tell it to the church. What church? Evidently the particular congregation to which the parties belong. If the offender does not hear the church, what then? "Let him be unto thee as a heathen man and a publican." But can there be no appeal to an association or presbytery or conference or convention? No; there is no appeal. Shall any kind of organization put the offender back in church fellowship when the church by its action classed him with heathen men and publicans? This is too absurd. What sort of fellowship would it be?[1]

---

[1] It was my design to present the subject of church discipline in this connection, but, finding that I cannot do so without making this chapter too long, I abandon my purpose. The topic is very important, and I take the liberty of referring the reader to chapter vi. of my *Church Manual*, where this subject is discussed at some length. (See pp. 118–147.)

29 *

CHAPTER XXV.

BAPTISM.

IF, as has been stated in the preceding chapter, a church is a congregation of Christ's baptized disciples, then we must consider two important questions, What is baptism? and Who are to be baptized? In other words, What is the act of baptism? and who are subjects of the ordinance? These two points now claim consideration.

I. THE ACT OF BAPTISM.

Baptism is the immersion in water, by a proper administrator, of a believer in Christ, into the name of the Father, and of the Son, and of the Holy Spirit. Immersion is so exclusively the baptismal act that without it there is no baptism; and a believer in Christ is so exclusively the subject of baptism that without such a subject there is no baptism.[1] That immersion alone is the baptismal act may be shown by the following considerations:

1. *Greek lexicons give immerse, dip, or plunge, as the primary and ordinary meaning of baptizo.* Here it is proper to say that *baptizo* and *baptisma*, being Greek words, are,

---

[1] In these two statements all Baptists agree. As to a proper administrator, there is some difference of opinion. By a proper administrator, in the above definition, is meant a person who has received authority from a scriptural church to administer baptism. It does not comport with my design to enlarge on this point.

in the Common Version of the Scriptures, *anglicized*, but not translated. By this it is meant that their termination is made to correspond with the termination of English words. In *baptizo*, the final letter is changed into *e;* and in *baptisma*, the last letter is dropped altogether. To make this matter of *anglicism* plain, it is only necessary to say that if the Greek verb *rantizo* had been anglicized, we should have *rantize* in the New Testament where we now have *sprinkle.* King James I. of England, by whose order the Common Version was made in the year 1611, virtually forbade the translation of *baptize* and *baptism.* This has been sometimes denied, but it is susceptible of conclusive proof. The king's third instruction to his translators reads thus: "The old *ecclesiastical words* to be kept, as the word *church* not to be translated 'congregation.'" It is absurd to say that this rule had exclusive reference to the word "church," for this term is plainly given as a specimen of "old ecclesiastical words." Why should plurality of idea be conveyed by the phrase "ecclesiastical *words*," if the rule had respect to but one word? The question, then, is, Are *baptism* and *baptize* "old ecclesiastical words"? They were *words* when the Bible was translated or they would not be found in it. They had been used by church historians and by writers on ecclesiastical law, and were therefore *ecclesiastical.* They had been in use a long time, and were consequently *old.* They were "old ecclesiastical words." Such words the king commanded "to be kept," "not translated." It is worthy of remark, too, that the Bishop of London at the king's instance, wrote to the translators, reminding them that His Majesty "wished his *third* and *fourth* rule to be specially observed." This circumstance must have called special attention to the rule under consideration. In view of these facts, it may, surely, be said that the translators knew what were "old ecclesiastical words." Let their testimony, then, be adduced : In their " Preface to the Reader " they say that they had, " on the one side, avoided the scrupulosity of the Puritans, who left the *old ecclesiastical words* and betook them to other, as when they put *washing* for *baptism*, and *congregation* for *church ;* and, on the other hand, had shunned the obscurity of the Papists." Is not this enough? Here there is not only an admission that baptism was an old ecclesiastical word, but this admission is made by the translators themselves—made most cheerfully—for it was made in condemnation of the Puritans and in commendation of themselves.

The king's fourth rule was this : " When any word hath divers significations, *that* to be kept which hath been most commonly used by the most eminent Fathers being agreeable to the propriety of the place and the analogy of faith."

Baptizo is not a word of divers significations ; but if it were, the king's translators, if they had translated it at all, would have been compelled by the fourth rule to render it *immerse ;* for every man of ordinary intelligence knows that it was " most commonly used " in this sense " by the most eminent Fathers." But it will be seen that the king's *third* rule makes inoperative the *fourth*, so far as old ecclesiastical words are concerned. Whether such words have one meaning or a thousand meanings, they are " to be kept," " not translated." The translators were not at liberty to refer to the signification always attached by the Greeks to *baptizo*—a signification which received the cordial endorsement of " the most eminent Fathers." They might have examined the endorsement if the royal decree had not said, " Hitherto, but no far-ther "—" the old ecclesiastical words to be kept."

Some Baptist authors have expressed themselves as if King James had a special antipathy to immersion and forbade the translation of *baptize* and *baptism* with a view to encourage *sprinkling*, which had been introduced from Geneva into Scotland in the reign of Elizabeth, and was in the early part of the seventeenth century making its way into England. There is, so far as I know, no historical evidence that the king was opposed to immersion; but he was bitterly opposed to the "Genevan Version" of the Bible, in which *baptism* was rendered *washing*. Most probably his dislike of this version led him to give his *third* rule. The Genevan Version was made by exiles from Scotland, who during the reign of "Bloody Mary" fled to Geneva and became acquainted with John Calvin.

The fact that *baptize* is an anglicized, and not a translated, word makes an appeal to Greek lexicons necessary in ascertaining its meaning. Lexicons do not constitute the *ultimate* authority, but their testimony is very valuable. There is a remarkable unanimity among them in representing *immerse*, or its equivalent, as the primary and ordinary meaning of the word. On this point Professor Moses Stuart, for many years the chief glory of the Andover Theological Seminary, shall speak. In his treatise on the *Mode of Baptism*, page 14, he says: "*Bapto* and *baptizo* mean to *dip*, *plunge*, or *immerge* into anything liquid. All lexicographers and critics of any note are agreed in this." This quotation is made to supersede the necessity of giving the meaning of *baptizo* as furnished by Greek lexicons, of which there is a large number. Professor Stuart's testimony will be received.

2. *Distinguished Pedobaptist theologians concede that baptize*

---

[1] The extracts I have made concerning the king's rules, etc. may be verified by reference to Lewis' *History of Translations*, pp. 317, 319, 326.

means to immerse. John Calvin, in his *Institutes*, says : " But whether the person who is baptized be wholly immersed, and whether thrice or once, or whether water be only poured or sprinkled upon him, is of no importance ; churches ought to be left at liberty, in this respect, to act according to the difference of countries. The very word *baptize*, however, signifies to immerse ; and it is certain that immersion was the practice of the ancient church." [1]

We have here some of Calvin's opinions, but what concerns us is his positive testimony as to the meaning of *baptize.*

Dr. George Campbell, a distinguished Presbyterian of Scotland, in his notes on Matt. iii. 11, says: "The word *baptizein* [infinitive mode of *baptizo*], both in sacred authors and in classical, signifies *to dip, to plunge, to immerse,* and was rendered by Tertullian, the oldest of the Latin Fathers, *tingere*, the term used for dyeing cloth, which was by immersion. It is always construed suitably to this meaning."

Dr. Chalmers, in his *Lectures on Romans*, says : " The original meaning of the word *baptism* is immersion ; and though we regard it as a point of indifferency whether the ordinance so named be performed in this way or by sprinkling, yet we doubt not that the prevalent style of the administration in the apostles' days was by an actual submerging of the whole body under water. We advert to this for the purpose of throwing light on the analogy that is instituted in these verses. Jesus Christ, by death, underwent this sort of baptism—even immersion under the surface of the ground, whence he soon emerged again by his resurrection. We by being baptized into his death are conceived to have made a similar translation." [2]

[1] Vol. ii. ●. 491, edition of Presbyterian Board of Publication.
[2] *Lectur* xxx., on chap. vi. 3-7.

This is but a specimen of the concessions of learned Pedodaptists in regard to the meaning of *baptizo.* These concessions are of great value, for it may be said, in the language of another, " This testimony of theirs to me is worth a thousand others, seeing it comes from such as in my opinion *are evidently interested to speak quite otherwise."* Who will testify to that which condemns his own practice, unless compelled by the force of truth to do so?

3. *The classical usage of baptizo establishes the position that immersion is the baptismal act.* It has been already stated that lexicons are not the ultimate authority in settling the meaning of words. Lexicographers are dependent on the sense in which words are used to ascertain their meaning. But it is not impossible for them to mistake that sense If they do, there is an appeal from their definitions to *usage,* which is the ultimate authority. It is well to go back to the ultimate authority. Want of room forbids the insertion of extracts from classical Greek authors, but it will be sufficient to refer to the treatise of Professor Stuart on the *Mode of Baptism.* The reader will see that the learned professor, in proving that *baptizo* means immerse, gives the word as used by various Greek authors—namely, Pindar, Heraclides Ponticus, Plutarch, Lucian, Hippocrates, Strabo, Josephus, etc. Dr. Conant has investigated the meaning of *baptizo* much more exhaustively than Professor Stuart. No use is made of his learned work, because Pedobaptist testimony is preferred. Seven hundred years intervened between the birth of Pindar and the death of Lucian. During those seven centuries usage shows that *baptizo* meant to immerse. Most of the classic Greek writers lived before baptism was instituted, and consequently knew nothing of immersion as a religious ordinance. Those who lived after its institution cared nothing for it. There was no con-

troversy as to the meaning of *baptizo* during the classic period of Grecian history. There was no motive, therefore, that could so operate on Greek writers as to induce them to use the word in any but its authorized meaning. That meaning was most obviously to immerse.

It is said by some that, though *baptizo* in classic Greek means *immerse*, it has a different meaning in the New Testament. Let them prove it. On them is the burden of proof, and they will find it a burden indeed. Let every man who takes this view answer this question : Could the New Testament writers, *as honest men*, use *baptizo* in a new sense without notifying their readers of the fact? It is certain that they could not, and equally certain that no such notification was ever given.

4. *The symbolic import of baptism furnishes a conclusive argument in favor of immersion.* There is in baptism a representation of the burial and resurrection of Jesus Christ. Paul says, " Know ye not that so many of us as were baptized into Jesus Christ were baptized into his death? Therefore we were buried with him by baptism into death ; that like as Christ was raised up from the dead by the glory of the Father, even so we also should walk in newness of life. For if we have been planted together in the likeness of his death, we shall be also in the likeness of his resurrection " (Rom. vi. 3-5); " Buried with him in baptism, wherein also ye are risen with him, through the faith of the operation of God who raised him from the dead." Col ii. 12. Peter says, "The like figure whereunto even baptism doth also now save us (not the putting away of the filth of the flesh, but the answer of a good conscience toward God), by the resurrection of Jesus Christ.' 1 Pet. iii. 21.

It is clear from these passages that baptism has a commemorative reference to the burial and resurrection of Christ. The two ordinances of the gospel symbolically procl..im the three great facts of the gospel. These facts, as Paul teaches (1 Cor. **xv. 3, 4**), are that Christ died, was buried, and rose again. The Lord's Supper commemorates the first fact. At his table the disciples of Jesus are solemnly reminded that he, for their sakes, submitted to the agonies of death. They weep over him as crucified, *dead.* In baptism they see him *buried* and *raised again,* just as they see him dead in the sacred Supper. Baptism is therefore a symbolic proclamation of two of the three prominent facts of the gospel—the burial and resurrection of Christ.

Baptism also expresses, in emblem, the believer's death to sin and resurrection to newness of life. In " repentance toward God and faith toward our Lord Jesus Christ " there is a spiritual death to sin and a spiritual resurrection to a new life. These two facts are emblematically set forth in baptism. Hence the absurdity of baptizing any who are not dead to sin. We are baptized into the death of Christ. We profess our reliance on him, in his atoning death, for salvation, and we profess also that as he died *for* sin, we have died *to* sin. As burial is a palpable separation of the dead from the living, so baptism is a symbolic separation of those dead to sin from those living in sin; and as a resurrection from the dead indicates an entrance into a new sphere of existence, so baptism, in its similitude to a resurrection, denotes an entrance upon a new life. Dr. Chalmers, therefore, in the lecture already referred to, says that we " are conceived in the act of descending under the water of baptism to have resigned an old life, and in the act of ascending to emerge into a second or new life."

Baptism is likewise a symbol of remission of sins and
30

of moral purification. We read of being baptized " for
the remission of sins." Acts ii. 38. The remission surely
is not actual, but symbolic and formal. That baptism
symbolizes purification is evident from Acts xxii. 16
" And now why tarriest thou? arise, and be baptized,
and wash away thy sins, calling on the name of the
Lord." Sin is referred to as that which defiles. " Wash
away thy sins." How? literally? No, but symbolically.
The blood of Jesus really washes away sins. Hence the
language " washed us from our sins in his own blood."
Rev. i. 5. But the sins which the blood of Jesus has
really washed away are symbolically and formally
washed away in baptism.

Once more: Baptism anticipates the believer's resurrection from the dead. This we learn from 1 Cor. xv. 29:
" Else what shall they do who are baptized for the dead,
if the dead rise not at all? Why are they then baptized
for the dead?" These questions are proposed in the
midst of an argument on the resurrection of the dead
Some of the Corinthians, it seems, denied the doctrine
of the resurrection, yet it does not appear that they questioned the propriety of an observance of the ordinance
of baptism. Paul virtually tells them that baptism
has an anticipatory reference to the resurrection of the
saints. It has this reference because it has a commemorative reference to the resurrection of Christ. It anticipates because it commemorates. The reason is obvious
The resurrection of the Lord Jesus procures the resurrection of his followers, and is an infallible pledge of
it. The two resurrections are inseparable. Baptism
therefore, while it commemorates the resurrection of
Christ, anticipates, of necessity, the resurrection of his
followers.

Now, if these views of the symbolic import of baptism

are correct, it follows inevitably that the immersion in water of a believer in Christ is essential to baptism—so essential that there can be no baptism without it. If baptism represents the burial and resurrection of Christ, it must be immersion. If it sets forth in emblem the believer's death to sin and resurrection to a new life, it must be immersion. If it in symbol remits and washes away the sins which Christ has really washed away in his blood, still it must be immersion. If it anticipates the resurrection, nothing but immersion justifies the anticipation. We are "buried by baptism"—that is, by means of baptism. When the baptismal process takes place there is certainly a burial. The two are inseparable, and therefore where there is no burial there is no baptism.[1]

II. The Subjects of Baptism.

While the import of the word "baptize" indicates what is the baptismal act, it does not determine *who* are to be baptized. We must therefore look elsewhere than to the meaning of the word to ascertain who are scriptural subjects of baptism. Where shall we look? Evidently to the commission given by Christ to his apostles, for this commission is the supreme authority for the administration of baptism. Apart from it there is no authority to baptize. The circumstances connected with the giving of this commission were replete with interest. The Saviour had finished the work which he came down from heaven to accomplish. He had offered himself a sacri-

[1] Other considerations in favor of immersion might be presented, suggested by the places selected for the administration of baptism and the circumstances attending its administration, but the limits of this volume forbid. The reader is referred to the many books that treat of baptism.

fice for sin. He had exhausted the cup of atoning sor
row. He had lain in the dark mansions of the grave
He had risen in triumph from the dead, and was about to
ascend to the right hand of the Majesty on high. In
vested with perfect mediatorial authority, he said to his
apostles :

"All power is given unto me in heaven and in earth.
Go ye, therefore, and teach all nations, baptizing them in
the name of the Father, and of the Son, and of the Holy
Ghost ; teach'ng them to observe all things whatsoever I
have commanded you" (Matt. xxviii. 18-20); "Go ye
into all the world, and preach the gospel to every creature. He that believeth and is baptized shall be saved;
but he that believeth not shall be damned" (Mark xvi.
15, 16); "Thus it is written, and thus it behoved Christ
to suffer, and to rise from the dead the third day; and
that repentance and remission of sins should be preached
in his name among all nations, beginning at Jerusalem."
Luke xxiv. 46, 47.

Surely the language of this commission is plain. Matthew informs us that making disciples (for the word
translated "teach" means to make disciples) is to precede baptism; Mark establishes the priority of faith to
baptism ; and Luke connects repentance and remission
of sins with the execution of the commission. No man
can, in obedience to this commission, baptize an unbeliever or an unconscious infant. The unbeliever is not a
penitent disciple, and it is clearly impossible for the infant to repent and believe the gospel.

It may be laid down as a principle of common sense
which commends itself to every candid mind, that a commission to do a thing authorizes only the doing of the
thing specified. There is a maxim of law to the effect
that "the expression of one thing is the exclusion of

another." It must be so, for otherwise there could be no definiteness in contracts and no precision in legislative enactments or judicial decrees. This maxim may be illustrated in a thousand ways. Numerous scriptural illustrations are at hand. For example: God commanded Noah to make an ark of *gopher-wood.* Gen. vi. 14. The command forbade the use of any other kind of wood. Abraham was commanded to offer his son Isaac for a burnt-offering. Gen. xxii. 2. He was virtually forbidden to offer any other member of his family. Ay, more—he could not offer an animal till the order was revoked by him who gave it, and a second order was given requiring the sacrifice of a ram in the place of Isaac. The institution of the Passover furnishes an illustration, or rather a series of illustrations. Ex. xii. A lamb was to be killed —not a heifer; it was to be of the first year—not of the second or third; a male—not a female; without a blemish—not with a blemish; on the fourteenth day of the month—not on some other day; the blood was to be applied to the door-posts and lintels—not elsewhere.

The Constitution of the United States supplies many Illustrations, one only of which will be mentioned. It provides that "the President shall have power, by and with the advice and consent of the Senate, to make treaties, provided two-thirds of the Senators present concur." In view of this language, can any man believe that the Supreme Court and the House of Representatives can make treaties? Or that the President without the Senate, or the Senate without the President, can make treaties?

In application of the principle laid down, and of the law-maxim now illustrated, I may say that the commission of Christ, in enjoining the baptism of disciples, believers, forbids in effect the baptism of all others. It will not do to

30 *

say that we are not forbidden, in so many words, to bap
tize infants. The same may be said of unbelievers;
ay, of horses, cattle, and bells.

It will be said by those who oppose the views of Baptists
—for it has been said a thousand times—that if infants
are not to be baptized because they cannot believe, they
will not be saved because they cannot believe. If the
salvation of infants depends on their faith, they cannot
be saved. They are incapable of faith. They are, doubtless, saved through the mediation of Christ, but it is not
by faith. Our opponents fail to accomplish their object
in urging this objection to our views. They must intend
to make us admit the propriety of infant baptism or force
us to deny infant salvation. But we make neither the admission nor the denial. When we say that infants are
saved, not by faith, but without faith, their objection is
demolished.

In considering the commission of Christ it is well to
observe how it was understood and carried into effect in
apostolic times. The first practical interpretation of it
was given on the day of Pentecost. Acts ii. The gospel
was preached, the people were pierced to the heart, and
cried out, " Men and brethren, what shall we do?" Peter
replied, " Repent and be baptized, every one of you." No
man will say that the command "repent" is applicable to
infants, and it is certain that the same persons were called
on to repent and be baptized. The result of Peter's sermon is given in the following words : " Then they that
gladly received his word were baptized : and the same
day there were added unto them about three thousand
souls." ver. 41. The baptism was limited to those who
gladly received Peter's words ; and as infants were not of
that number, to infer that they were baptized is utterly
gratuitous. The Pentecostal administration of baptism

shows that penitent believers were considered the only subjects of the ordinance.

Philip's labors in Samaria indicate his understanding of the great commission. He preached Christ to the people. What then? The people "believed Philip preaching the things concerning the kingdom of God and the name of Jesus Christ." What next? "They were baptized both men and women." Acts viii. 12. Here, again, baptism was restricted to believers.

Was there a deviation from this rule among the Gentiles? Certainly not. When Peter preached to Cornelius and his family there was a restriction of baptism to those who received the Holy Spirit; and when Paul preached in Corinth "many of the Corinthians hearing, believed, and were baptized." Acts x. 47; xviii. 8.

Thus it appears that among Gentiles, as well as Samaritans and Jews, baptism was preceded by faith in Christ. The commission was practically expounded in the same way both in Europe and Asia.

Nor do the household baptisms mentioned in the New Testament furnish any argument against the baptism of believers alone, for something is said of every household which could not be said of unconscious infants. For example, it is said of Cornelius (Acts x. 2) that he "feared God with all his house;" of the jailer (Acts xvi. 32, 34), that Paul and Silas "spoke to him the word of the Lord and to all that were in his house," and that he "rejoiced believing in God with all his house." It is said of Lydia (Acts xvi. 40) that Paul and Silas, having been released from prison, entered into her house, "and when they had seen the brethren they comforted them." Doubtless, "the brethren" were persons in Lydia's employ who constituted her "household," and were baptized as well as herself. Infants would not have been referred to as "brethren " nor as " comforted." The intimation, in Acts xviii 8, is that the family of Crispus was baptized, but it is said, that " he believed on the Lord with all his house." Paul, as we learn from 1 Cor. i. 16, baptized the household of Stephanas, but he says in the same Epistle (xvi. 15), ' Ye know the house of Stephanas, that it is the first-fruits of Achaia, and that they have addicted themselves to the ministry of the saints." These are all the household baptisms mentioned in the New Testament, and we see in them no deviation from the commission of Christ, which requires *discipleship* as a prerequisite to baptism. On the other hand, they confirm the position that believers alone are scriptural subjects of baptism.

In closing this chapter, which might be lengthened almost indefinitely, I may say that the allusions to baptism in the apostolic Epistles forbid the supposition that infants were baptized. The baptized are referred to as " dead to sin," rising from the baptismal waters to " walk in newness of life," " having put on Christ," " baptized for the dead," or in the belief of the resurrection. Rom. vi. 11, 4; Gal. iii. 27; 1 Cor. xv. 29. Not one of these forms of expression can be applied to speechless infants. Moreover, baptism is defined to be " the answer of a good conscience toward God." 1 Pet. iii. 21. This is a definition which precludes the idea that baptism was, in apostolic times, administered to any except accountable agents. What conscience has an infant? There can be no operation of conscience prior to accountability. Baptism, then, in its administration to unconscious babes, cannot be what an inspired apostle declares it to be.

Without enlarging on these topics, what is the conclusion of the whole matter? Clearly this: The commission of Christ, as understood and exemplified in the apostolic age, requires the baptism of believers, disciples; and the baptism of all others, whether unbelievers or unconscious infants, is utterly unwarranted. There is, as Paul has written in the Epistle to the Ephesians, "one Lord, one faith, one baptism." ch. iv. 5. The one Lord is the object of the one faith, the one faith embraces the one Lord, and the one baptism is a profession of the one faith in the one Lord.

The baptism is *one* in the action involved, and *one* in the subjects of the action. I can see it in no other light.

CHAPTER XXVI.

THE LORD'S SUPPER.

WHAT Paul says of the institution and design of the Lord's Supper is the substance of what the evangelists had recorded. These are his words: "For I have received of the Lord that which also I delivered to you, That the Lord Jesus the same night in which he was betrayed took bread: and when he had given thanks, he brake it, and said, Take, eat: this is my body which is broken for you: this do in remembrance of me. After the same manner also he took the cup, when he had supped, saying, This is the new testament in my blood: this do ye, as often as ye drink it, in remembrance of me. For as often as ye eat this bread and drink this cup, ye do show the Lord's death till he come." 1 Cor. xi. 23–26.

From this inspired account of the origin of the Lord's Supper it is plainly a commemorative ordinance. It is a memorial service. It commemorates the death of Christ and nothing else. "Ye do show the Lord's death." We do not show the birth or baptism or burial or resurrection or ascension of our Redeemer, *but his death.* If ever the tragedy of Calvary should engross the thoughts of the Christian to the exclusion of every other topic, it is when he sits at the table of the Lord. Then the death of his Saviour should occupy all his thoughts, monopolize all the power of his memory.

Some will perhaps say that in the Lord's Supper we express our Christian fellowship for our fellow-communicants. This is done only in an indirect and incidental manner. Our communion, according to the teaching of Paul, is the communion of the body and the blood of Christ. It is a solemn celebration of his atoning death. The broken bread is the emblem of the Saviour's broken body; for he said, "Take, eat; this is my body." He manifestly used language as he had done in his ministry. He had said, in explaining the parable of the Sower, "The seed is the word of God" (Luke viii. 11); and in interpreting the parable of the Wheat and Tares, "The field is the world." Matt. xiii. 38. He meant, "The seed *represents* the word of God"—"The field *represents* the world." So when he said of the bread which he held in his hands, "This is my body," he meant, "This *represents* my body." The Romish view, that the bread and wine are changed into the real body and blood of Christ, is utterly indefensible; as is also the Lutheran view, that "the body and blood of Christ are materially present in the sacrament of the Lord's Supper, though in an incomprehensible manner."

The Romish theory is called "transubstantiation," and the Lutheran dogma is styled "consubstantiation," neither of which has a rational claim to credence. The bread used in the supper of the Lord is bread before it is put on his table, it is bread while on the table, and it is bread when eaten. There is no sense in which it is the body of Christ, except the figurative sense in which it represents his body. So also of the wine which represents his blood. The bread and the wine are impressive, striking emblems, but they are only emblems. They are solemn mementos of the Saviour's crucified body and of his shed blood. They are memorials of his death, designed to perpetuate a remembrance of the greatest event which has ever taken place in the universe. It is to be deeply regretted that many persons entertain views of the Lord's Supper which, to say the least, do in a great degree ignore the purpose of its original appointment. It seems to be regarded as a suitable way for Christians to express their opinion of each other's piety. Some appear even to think that the Lord's Table is the proper place for those to come together who are allied by ties of blood or ties of marriage. Alas, that opinions so dishonorable to Christ should be held by any who profess to be his disciples! The important truth should echo and re-echo throughout Christendom, that the Lord's Supper is a memorial service—that the central idea in its observance is the commemoration of Christ's death. This must never be forgotten.

By whom is the Lord's Supper to be observed? We answer, By the members of a visible church of Christ. That is to say, it is a church ordinance. It cannot be properly administered to persons in their individual capacity—for example, to the sick at their homes. The meeting of a *church* is indispensable to a scriptural observance of the solemn rite. As none can be members of a visible church without baptism, it follows that baptism is a prerequisite to the Lord's Table. It will be seen from this statement of the case that baptism is a prerequisite to the Lord's Supper, because it is a prerequisite to church membership. It is a condition precedent, in the sense that it precedes, and is essential to, church membership It would be well for Baptists to make this view more prominent. Let them not say less of baptism, but more of church membership. In Acts ii. 41 it is said, "Then they that gladly received his word were baptized: and the same day there were added to them about three thousand souls." The three thousand were, no doubt, added to the church, "the hundred and twenty disciples," mentioned in the preceding chapter; for in the last verse of the second chapter it is written, "And the Lord added to the church daily the saved." The adding in the two verses was the same in kind; that is, it was an adding to the church. It will be perceived that the *baptized* were added to the church, and that this was done before the "breaking of bread"—a phrase descriptive of the Lord's Supper. A refusal on the part of Baptists to unite in the Lord's Supper with Pedobaptists grows out of the fact that the latter have ever been considered by the former as unbaptized, and consequently without a scriptural church membership. — *no baptism, no church*

Even the celebrated Robert Hall, who advocated the joint participation of Baptists and Pedobaptists with an eloquence and an energy of argumentation rarely to be found in the annals of controversy, does not hesitate to express the opinion that Pedobaptists are unbaptized. He says:

"We certainly make no scruple of informing a Pedobaptist candidate that we consider him as unbaptized, and disdain all concealment on the subject." Again, "If we join with those whom we are obliged to consider as unbaptized, they unite with persons who, in their judgment, repeat an ordinance which ought not to be performed but once, nullify a Christian institute, and deprive their children of the benefit of a salutary rite."[1]

But while Mr. Hall considered Pedobaptists unbaptized, he insisted on their right as *unbaptized* persons to come to the Lord's Table. He did not admit baptism to be a prerequisite to the Lord's Table. Had he conceded this,—a

[1] *Works*, vol. i. pp. 455, 456.

point almost universally conceded by Baptists and Pedo-baptists,—he would not have written his *Terms of Communion* at all.

To give a summary answer to all that Robert Hall ever wrote in favor of "mixed communion," it is only necessary to show the scriptural priority of baptism to the Lord's Supper. It surely is not difficult to do this. That baptism was first instituted is a significant fact. No one will deny that John, the harbinger of Christ, baptized multitudes, and that Jesus through his disciples (John iv. 1, 2) baptized before the institution of the Lord's Supper. It is morally certain that those present at its institution, the night of the betrayal, had been baptized. Jesus himself had been baptized, and it is too much for credulity itself to believe that he selected unbaptized persons as his apostles. Does the subsequence of the Lord's Supper, in its original appointment, to baptism mean nothing? But it was said by Mr. Hall, that "John's baptism was not Christian." It was gospel baptism. It was not an ordinance of the Mosaic economy. John certainly introduced the gospel dispensation. His preaching was "the beginning of the gospel" (Mark i. 1), and "the law and the prophets were until John." Luke xvi. 16. If any one chooses to deny that his baptism was *Christian* because it is not so termed, the denial may be so enlarged as to embrace all the baptisms of the New Testament; for the epithet "Christian" is not applied to any of them. But while firmly believing that John's was a gospel ministry and a gospel baptism, all this might be waived by Baptists for argument's sake, and then they can show the unavoidable priority of baptism to the Lord's Supper. Let them go at once to Christ's last commission: "Go, teach all nations, baptizing them." Matt. xxviii. 19. Every scholar knows that the Greek word translated "teach" means *disciple* or *make disciples.* Disciples to Christ were to be made through the preaching and teaching of the apostles. This is plain. The discipling process was first, and then the baptismal act was to be performed. "Go, disciple all nations, baptizing them." Now, according to this commission, it is evident that the process of discipleship is to be followed so immediately by the administration of baptism as to leave no room for an observance of the Lord's Supper to intervene. Baptism is the first thing after a person is discipled to Christ. It is the believer's first public duty. It is an open avowal of faith in Christ and of allegiance to him. It is, therefore, inevitably prior to the Lord's Supper, an observance of which is no doubt included in the expression, "Teaching them to observe all things whatsoever I have commanded you." Matt. xxviii. 20. The baptized disciples of Christ are to be taught to observe all things which he has commanded, and under his commission his ministers are not required to say anything to the unbaptized about the Lord's Supper. The baptized disciples are to be instructed. How, then, can the Lord's Supper precede baptism when the commission enjoins the mention of it only to the baptized?

But how did the apostles understand and carry into effect this commission? This is a question of capital importance in this discussion. On the day of Pentecost, Peter said to the convicted Jews, "Repent, and be baptized." Acts ii. 38. The baptism was to succeed the repentance. There is no intimation that the Lord's Supper was to come between; and it is added, that the baptized "continued steadfastly in the apostles' doctrine and fellowship, and in breaking of bread, and in prayers." Acts ii. 42. The breaking of bread—the Lord's Supper

—was preceded by baptism. When Philip went down to Samaria and preached, the people believed and were baptized both men and women." Acts viii. 12. The narrative plainly indicates that baptism, and not the Lord's Supper, immediately followed a belief of Philip's preaching. When the Ethiopian eunuch avowed his faith in Christ, Philip at once baptized him. There was no celebration of the Lord's Supper before they left the chariot and "went down both into the water." Acts viii. 38. When Cornelius and his family received the Holy Spirit, Peter did not ask, " Who can forbid their coming to the Lord's Table?" but "Can any man forbid water, that these should not be baptized?" Acts x. 47. When Paul and Silas, at the hour of midnight, preached to the jailer and his house, and they believed, what was then done? Did they come to the Lord's Table? No, but "he was baptized, he and all his, straightway." Acts xvi. 33.

Thus does it appear that the men who first acted under the commission of Christ understood it as enjoining baptism before the Lord's Supper. They have left an instructive example, which we are not at liberty to disregard. In view of this example it may be boldly affirmed that the whole tenor of the New Testament indicates the priority of baptism to the commemoration of the Redeemer's death at his table. Nothing is plainer.

Pedobaptists concede the precedence of baptism to the Lord's Supper. Indeed, their practice of infant baptism extorts the concession from them.

Dr. Wall, of the Church of England, expresses himself in strong terms as follows:

" No church ever gave the communion to any persons before they were baptized. Among all the absurdities that ever were held, none ever maintained that any per-sors should partake of the communion before they were baptized."[1]

Dr. Doddridge, Independent, remarks:

"It is certain that Christians in general have always been spoken of by the most ancient Fathers as baptized persons. And it is also certain that, as far as our knowledge of primitive antiquity extends, no unbaptized person received the Lord's Supper."[2]

Dr Dwight, Congregationalist, says:

"It is an indispensable qualification for this ordinance that the candidate for communion be a member of the visible church of Christ in full standing. By this I intend that he shall be such a member of the church as I have formerly described—to wit, that he should be a person of piety, that he should have made a public profession of religion, and that he should have been baptized."[3]

Dr. John Dick, Presbyterian, uses this language:

"An uncircumcised man was not permitted to eat the Passover, and an unbaptized man should not be permitted to partake of the Eucharist."[4]

Dr. Hibbard, Methodist, expresses himself thus:

"It is but just to remark that in one principle the Baptist and the Pedobaptist churches agree. They both agree in rejecting from communion at the table of the Lord, and in denying the rights of church-fellowship to, all who have not been baptized. Valid baptism they consider as essential to constitute visible church membership. This, also, we hold. The only question, then, that here divides us is, What is essential to valid baptism? The Baptists, in passing a sweeping sentence of disfranchisement upon all

---

[1] *History of Infant Baptism*, Part ii. chap. ix.

[2] *Miscellaneous Works*, p. 510.

[3] *Theology*, Sermon 160.   [4] *Lectures on Theology*, Lecture 93.

other Christian churches, have only acted upon a principle held in common with all other churches—viz., that baptism is essential to church membership. . . . Of course, they must be their own judges as to what baptism is. It is evident that, according to our views, we can admit them to our communion, but with their views of baptism it is equally evident they can never reciprocate the courtesy; and the charge of *close communion* is no more applicable to the Baptists than to us, inasmuch as the question of church membership is determined by as liberal principles as it is with any other Protestant churches—so far, I mean, as the present subject is concerned; that is, it is determined by valid baptism."[1]

This extract from Dr. Hibbard exhibits a spirit of controversial candor and fairness not often witnessed in the discussion of the qualifications for participating in the Lord's Supper. It explodes the charge of "Baptist bigotry and exclusiveness," and establishes the fact that the point in dispute between Baptists and others is not about so-called "*close communion*," but about "*close baptism.*" The controversy is supremely and intensely baptismal.

Every visible church of Christ may be considered a sacred enclosure that can be entered only in one way. In that enclosure is set the table of the Lord. The Lord of the table has prescribed the terms of admittance into that enclosure. Those who have complied with the terms, and have entered in, are the guardians of the table. They must see that it is approached only in the way which the Lord of the enclosure has specified. If they are appealed to to change the way of entrance, or to make a new way, or to allow those without to make ways of entrance to suit themselves, they must say with strongest emphasis

[1] *Christian Baptism*, pp. 171, 175.

" THERE IS ONE LAWGIVER "—" WE HAVE NO SUCH CUSTOM, NEITHER THE CHURCHES OF GOD."

It will be said—for it has been said no one knows how often—the table is the Lord's. This all will concede. But how different are the reasonings based on this concession ! Pedobaptists say, that, as it is the Lord's Table, they have a right to approach it; that, as it is not the table of Baptists, the Baptists ought to place no obstructions in the way of their approach. Baptists say, that, as it is the Lord's Table, it must be approached in the way HE directs; that his proprietorship of the table furnishes the reason of their course; that if it was their table, they would have discretionary authority, whereas they now have none; that they do not place obstructions in the way of Pedobaptists, but that the Lord of the table has done it. This is a specimen of the reasoning employed by the two parties in the controversy. Which species of reasoning indicates greater loyalty to Christ, the reader may determine.

Did space permit, I should be glad to argue the precedence of baptism to the Lord's Supper from the symbolic import of the two ordinances. What the argument would be I indicate as follows : Baptism symbolizes spiritual birth—the beginning of spiritual life in the soul; the Lord's Supper symbolizes the nourishment and support of that life by union with Christ in his death. Life in its manifested form is preceded by birth. As we are born once, we are baptized once; but as we need food continuously to sustain life, we observe the Lord's Supper continuously so long as we are in the body. Thus does it appear that the symbolism of the two ordinances inexorably demands that baptism shall precede the Lord's Supper

CHAPTER XXVII.

DEATH OF CHRISTIANS, AND THE INTERMEDIATE STATE.

PRECIOUS and numerous as are the blessings of the covenant of salvation, exemption from natural death is not included among them. The saints of all generations—with the two notable exceptions of Enoch and Elijah—have passed through the gate of death into the eternal world. Christians still die, and the stroke of mortality will, doubtless, fall on believers as well as on unbelievers till Christ comes "the second time."

We need not curiously inquire why the saints are subject to death. It is more becoming to us to accept the fact, and be silent as to the philosophy of it. When, however, we remember that Jesus died and was buried, we almost involuntarily exclaim,

> "Where should the dying members rest
> But with their dying Head?"

As God is with his people during the pilgrimage of life, so he is with them in the hour of death; and, as it is their great business to glorify him in life, they should also glorify him in death. When Jesus, after his resurrection, told Peter of certain things connected with the martyr-death before him, it is added, "This spake he, signifying by what death he should glorify God." John xxi. 19 Glorifying God in death is a topic wh'ch may well en gage the attention of Christians. How may they thus glorify him? I answer:

1. *By their preparation for the dying hour.* All men must die, yet none by Nature are prepared to die. How is preparation to be secured? How may an exit from earth be rendered safe and happy? These questions, Nature cannot answer. We may interrogate her ever so rigidly, catechise her ever so earnestly, entreat her ever so imploringly, and she maintains an unbroken silence. All inquiries, instituted in whatever department of Nature, concerning preparation for death, are instituted in vain and prosecuted in vain.

Nor can reason and philosophy tell how a sinner can be pardoned, sanctified, prepared for death and heaven. Among their many utterances, there is not one on the subject of salvation. Their realm is a wide one, but it does not embrace the science of redemption. The grave is not more silent than they as to the way of a sinner's restoration to the divine favor.

The gospel does what Nature cannot do, what reason and philosophy cannot do. It answers every perplexing question as to a sinner's justification, sanctification, preparation for death, and fitness for heaven. One passage of Scripture makes this plain: "The sting of death is sin; and the strength of sin is the law. But thanks be to God. which giveth us the victory through our Lord Jesus Christ!" 1 Cor. xv. 56, 57. Here we learn that everything fearful in death is ascribed to sin. Sin furnishes death with its dreadful sting. But the strength of sin is the law; and why? Because, as sin is the transgression of the law, it follows that the law gives sin its power to condemn. But God has sent his Son into the world on an errand of saving mercy. Jesus has "magnified the law"—has sustained its dignity and honored its claims—

by obeying its precepts and bearing its penalty. Sin, therefore, can be pardoned consistently with law. Now when the guilt of sin is cancelled by the blood of atonement, and the soul is purified from its moral pollution by "the sanctification of the Spirit," there is in death nothing to excite alarm, for there is nothing which can do real injury. The removal of sin is the extraction of the sting of death. Believers in Christ can, therefore, die safely, peacefully, and even triumphantly. God gives them the victory through the Lord Jesus Christ. No process of philosophical discipline gives it. Reliance on self-righteousness does not give it. Dependence on morality does not give it. God gives it. His grace alone prepares for the dying hour. The dying Christian's preparation for death is so manifestly the work of God that HE is glorified thereby. All the glory redounding from the preparation is the Lord's; and he so presides over the death of his people as to glorify his own name.

2. *By bearing testimony to the power of Christianity to sustain them in the dying hour.* This testimony has been often borne. It has been no uncommon thing for the dying saint to say, "God is with me, and I fear not." The doctrine of the Scriptures is, that divine grace is sufficient for the saints in all circumstances. Whether it is sufficient in death must be tested when death comes. Let the dying pilgrim testify that he who has been with him along the journey of life is with him at its close— that his promises support, that his grace sustains, that his presence cheers; and then God is glorified. In the dying chamber of the saint it sometimes occurs that men as wicked as Balaam adopt Balaam's words: "Let me die the death of the righteous, and let my last end be like his." Num. xxiii. 10. Infidelity trembles, turns pale, wonders, and renders a reluctant tribute of admiration

to the majesty of the religion of Jesus. The votaries of Christianity may well felicitate themselves that they "have not followed cunningly-devised fables," but have embraced a system of religion all divine. According to the teachings of this system, "to die is gain," and "blessed are the dead which die in the Lord." Phil. i. 21; Rev xiv. 13. In the sublime inventory of the Christian's possessions, as made out by Paul, "death" has a place: "All things are yours: whether Paul, or Apollos, or Cephas, or the world, or life, or death, or things present, or things to come: all are yours, and ye are Christ's, and Christ is God's." 1 Cor. iii. 21–23. That Christianity can sustain when "flesh and heart fail" has been proved in numberless instances. It has been proved at home and abroad, in civilized and savage lands, in the palaces of the rich and the cottages of the poor, on the land and on the sea, in the dungeon and at the stake. Whether the religion of the Bible can support in death is no longer a debatable question. It has been long settled, and settled to the consolation of living Christians, who know full well that they must soon fall into the arms of death.

As to the physical act of dying, there is in it nothing desirable. Nature recoils from the dissolution of soul and body. Even the grace of God does not make death welcome for its own sake, but for the sake of the blessed results that follow it. "To die is gain." Something is gained when the expiring struggle is over, and the struggle is willingly encountered because of the advantages that succeed it. This directs our attention to what has been called

THE INTERMEDIATE STATE.

By this state is meant the period that intervenes between the death and the resurrection of the body. All, therefore, who believe in the resurrection believe in such a state, but there are differences of opinion in regard to it. The differences do not pertain to the body, but to the disembodied spirit. All agree that the body will remain in the grave till Christ appears "the second time without sin unto salvation." Heb. ix. 28. The three leading views concerning the separate spirits of the pious dead are the following:

1. *That the soul is unconscious from the death to the resurrection of the body.* Those who hold this view have been led to embrace it by supposing that, as the soul now acts through the body, it is restricted to this method of action. It is inferred that upon its exit from the body it falls into a state of inactivity and unconsciousness, from which it cannot awake till the body is raised from the dead. Even Archbishop Whately, in his volume on the *Future State*, evidently inclines to this theory. His reasoning, however, is by no means conclusive. He does not positively deny the activity of the soul during the interval between the death and the resurrection of the body, but he insists that if the soul is active, it cannot act as it does while connected with the body. This may be granted—indeed, no one will deny it—but what then? Will any one say, that the soul's activity and consciousness are so dependent on its connection with the body as to be destroyed when that connection is broken? This would be assuming the very point in question. It surely does not follow that the action of the soul is to be stamped with unvarying uniformity in all the states of its being. Why may not the disembodied souls of the redeemed be as conscious and as active as are angelic spirits? The latter have no bodies, yet how intense their consciousness, how unwearied their activity! They hold intercourse with kindred intelligences, and enjoy the most exquisite

social bliss. Why may it not be so with the spirits of departed saints? Stephen, when dying a martyr's death, prayed, "Lord Jesus, receive my spirit." Did he ask his Lord to receive an unconscious spirit? Or did he labor under a mistake? Strange time to make a mistake, when he saw heaven opened and the glory of God shining brighter than ten thousand suns, while Jesus stood waiting to receive his spirit! Did it enter into the thoughts of the stoned martyr that the Lord Jesus in receiving his spirit would receive an unconscious thing? This is utterly incredible. The account given in Luke xvi. 19–31 of "the rich man and Lazarus" defies interpretation if the spirits of both good and bad men are not intensely conscious after they leave the bodies in which they dwelt on earth. The body of the rich man was buried, but after the burial there was something belonging to him that was susceptible of torment. So Lazarus is said to have been conveyed to Abraham's bosom, and to have been "comforted" there. This was after the death of his afflicted body, which no one supposes was "carried to Abraham's bosom." If any one shall say, that this narrative is a parable and full of terms used figuratively, I answer, What if it be so? Did not Jesus teach something by all his parables? What does he teach here if not the consciousness of the soul after the death of the body? As to words used figuratively, why is there force in them? Plainly, because there is meaning in them when used literally.

With regard to those passages of the divine word which refer to death under the imagery of *sleep*, I need say but little. The sleep is clearly the repose of the body, and cannot be identified with the unconsciousness of the soul. I think that, in view of the teachings of Scripture, it may be safely said, that there is no evidence to justify the belief that the soul is unconscious from the death to the resurrection of the body. We should thank God that the gloomy theory has no scriptural support.

2. *That the soul goes to paradise, there to abide till the resur·rection of the body.* Many theologians entertain this opinion. They think that the redeemed will not enter into heaven till after the judgment. This is by no means a satisfactory theory, and the arguments relied on for its support are not conclusive. It is said, that the soul will be happy, that all its powers will be actively employed, but that it will not be in heaven. Paradise, it is argued, will be the abode of happy spirits till the consummation of all things, but that paradise and heaven are not identical. All that can be said in favor of this view proceeds on the supposition that paradise is not heaven. What does Paul say? —" I knew a man in Christ above fourteen years ago (whether in the body, I cannot tell, or whether out of the body, I cannot tell: God knoweth); such an one caught up to the third heaven. And I knew such a man (whether in the body, or out of the body, I cannot tell: God knoweth); how that he was caught up into paradise, and heard unspeakable words, which it is not lawful for a man to utter." 2 Cor. xii. 2–4. It is manifest from this language that the third heaven and paradise are the same place. This is so undeniable that even Dean Alford, who might have been expected to take the opposite view, says in his commentary, " The paradise here spoken of cannot be the Jewish paradise, . . . where the spirits of the just awaited the resurrection, . . . but the paradise of which our Lord spoke on the cross—the place of happiness into which he at his death introduced the spirits of the just." In reply to this it may be said that the word *paradise* is used but three times in the New Testament (Luke xxiii. 43; 2 Cor. xii. 4; Rev. ii. 7), and

that it is gratuitous to assume that it has different meanings. If it has, let it be shown, for it has not yet been done. Paul was a Jew, and he expressed himself in accordance with the prevalent opinion of his nation. The Jews believed in three heavens, the atmosphere constituting the first. Hence we read of the birds of heaven. The apparent abode of the sun and stars they considered the second heaven. Far above the sun and stars they supposed the throne of God to be established. This they regarded as the third heaven. The Jewish opinion sheds light on such scriptural phrases as "heaven of heavens," "above all heavens." It was to the third heaven, the highest heaven, even into paradise, that Paul was caught up. There is in the term paradise, as used in the New Testament, nothing that requires us to believe it a place distinct from heaven. With this view there is no objection to the belief that the souls of the pious dead go to paradise; but if by paradise is meant a place different from heaven, a place like the elysium of the ancient heathen, there are insuperable objections to the doctrine. I now refer to another prominent view of the intermediate state, which I regard as satisfactory, because it is the scriptural one :

3. *That the departing spirit is at once taken into the presence of Christ in heaven.* It will not be denied that Christ is in heaven. Stephen saw him there. Luke tells us, that Christ, while blessing his disciples, "was parted from them and carried up into heaven." Luke xxiv. 51. Peter, in Acts iii. 21, says of Christ, "Whom the heaven must receive until the times of restitution of all things;" and in his First Epistle (iii. 22), "Who is gone into heaven, and is on the right hand of God." Surely, if Christ is on the right hand of God, he is in heaven. Now, Paul taught that Christians have a home in heaven. He says, "For

we know that if our earthly house of this tabernacle were dissolved, we have a building of God, a house not made with hands, eternal in the heavens." 2 Cor. v. .. The " earthly house of this tabernacle " refers, of course, to the body, and it is the earthly abode of the soul. This house is contrasted with the heavenly house. The former is a temporary, the latter an everlasting, habitation. The natural inference from the apostle's words is, that as soon as the spirit leaves its earthly house it enters its heavenly dwelling-place. This point is made even clearer in verses 6, 7, 8 of the same chapter: " Therefore we are always confident, knowing that whilst we are at home in the body, we are absent from the Lord (for we walk by faith, not by sight): we are confident, I say, and willing rather to be absent from the body, and to be present with the Lord."

The apostle assumes that there is in Christians some thing different from the body, something which he calls " we "—" while we are in the body." The reference is to the spirit, for " the body without the spirit is dead." James ii. 26. We are plainly taught that the spirit's abode in the body is the period of its absence from the Lord. " At home in the body," " absent from the Lord," are expressions equivalent in duration, however much they differ in other respects. When Paul says, " We are willing rather to be absent from the body, and to be present with the Lord," the irresistible inference is, that just as soon as the spirit makes its exit from the body, so as to be absent from it, just so soon is it in the presence of the Lord. The glorious presence of the Lord is doubtless referred to, and this is enjoyed only in heaven. The language of Paul in Phil. i. 23 deserves special notice: " Having a desire to depart, and to be with Christ; which is far better." Here we see that the departure, including death, was to precede introduction into the presence of Christ. If Paul had believed in the soul's unconsciousness from the death to the resurrection of the body, could he have said anything of being "with Christ"? Or if so, could he have thought it "far better" for his spirit to be with him in an unconscious state, than to enjoy the sacred pleasures of piety in its earthly tenement? We cannot for a moment suppose it. Nor could Paul, knowing Christ to be in heaven, desire to go to paradise without believing it to be identical with heaven. The glorified body of Jesus is in heaven, and therefore heaven is a *place*. To this glorious place, Paul desired to go, and restrained his desire only by considerations of usefulness on earth.

It is perfectly consistent with the foregoing views to believe that the saints will receive, at the resurrection, large accessions of bliss. The thing insisted on is, that the separate spirits of believers in Christ will enjoy unspeakable happiness while the bodies they have left are sleeping in the grave. I close this chapter with the precious words, "ABSENT FROM THE BODY—PRESENT WITH THE LORD."

32 *

CHAPTER XXVIII.

THE RESURRECTION.

THOUGH, in the preceding chapter, the death of Christians has been specially referred to, it is not to be forgotten that all men die: "It is appointed unto men once
to die." Heb. ix. 27. This appointment is of God. It is
universal and inevitable. The stroke of death falls on all
the human race. As the body is a part of the complex
nature of man, it is a matter of no little interest to inquire
what becomes of it after death, and what is to be its final
destiny. What becomes of it we learn from Eccles. xii.
7: "Then shall the dust return to the earth as it was."
This takes place in fulfilment of the sentence, "Dust thou
art, and unto dust shalt thou return." Gen. iii. 19. The
body, having been made "of the dust of the ground," is
resolved into its original elements. The work of disorganization is complete in the grave. But will the body
remain evermore in the grave? The ancient heathen
philosophers and people, would have answered in the
affirmative. They had some confused notions of the immortality of the soul, but of the resurrection of the body
they had no conception. They did not believe that any
or all of their gods had power sufficient to raise the dust
of mortality from the cold embraces of the tomb. Hence
when Paul at Athens preached "the resurrection of the
dead, some mocked." Acts xvii. 32. Indeed, apart from

the teachings of the Bible, the resurrection of the body is incredible. Rev. Dr. Richard Fuller has well said:

"I am not unmindful of certain analogies as to which poets and philosophers have discoursed with great beauty. I remember the butterfly rising from the chrysalis and spreading its gaudy wings to the sun; but was there any death there? This is nothing but a new form of existence. And so, too, as to the coming forth of bud and leaf and flower in spring-time; vegetation never was dead, it only slept. The vernal rays pour no life into the trunk which is hewn or decayed. They cannot give it vital growth again.

"The resurrection of the body is no such renewal of suspended vitality; it is the re-infusion of life into a corpse, and these fancies only mock the earnest soul seeking anxiously for truth."[1]

The body in the grave is *dead*, and how is it to live again? There is nothing in the wide realm of nature and reason which intimates the possibility of its living again. Paul's question, in his defence before King Agrippa, is full of meaning: "Why should it be thought a thing incredible with you, that God should raise the dead?" Acts xxvi. 8. The apostle does not suggest, as on another subject (1 Cor. xi. 14), that "nature itself" teaches something. No, the point he makes is, that God can raise the dead, and therefore the doctrine of the resurrection is perfectly credible. The power of God is specially concerned in the resurrection, and this is the reason why Jesus said to the Sadducees, "Ye do err, not knowing the Scriptures, nor the power of God." Matt. xxii. 29. It was not only their ignorance of the Scriptures, but their inadequate idea of the power of God, that led them to deny the resurrection. The Spirit of inspiration seems to have anticipated

[1] *Sermon on The Incredulity of Thomas.*

and obviated all objections to the doctrine of the resurrection in these words: "Who shall change cur vile body, that it may be fashioned like unto his glorious body, according to the working [energy] whereby he is able even to subdue all things unto himself." Phil. iii. 21. The energy, the power which can "subdue all things," can raise the dead. "The things which are impossible with men are possible with God." Luke xviii. 27. The term "resurrection" literally means *rising again.* This implies that the body which rises again had fallen. It is needless to discuss the question of the identity of the body, for the fact of the resurrection irresistibly implies it. The same body which dies and is buried is raised up in possession of all the properties essential to its identity. The same spirit which had left it at its death re-enters it, and thus the complete personality will be preserved for ever. So true will it be that "whatsoever a man soweth, that shall he also reap." Gal. vi. 7. The same man who sows in time shall reap in eternity.

As to the period of the resurrection, the whole tenor of Scripture indicates that it will take place at the end of the world, at the second coming of Christ, and as preparatory to the general judgment. It is supposed by many that there will be two resurrections—the one of the righteous, preceding and introducing the millennium; the other of the wicked, following the millennium and in immediate connection with the last judgment. The two passages of Scripture chiefly relied on in support of this view are 1 Thess. iv. 16; Rev. xx. 6. In the first of these passages—that is to say, in the words, "The dead in Christ shall rise first"—there is obviously no reference to the wicked. The apostle teaches that when the Lord descends from heaven the dead saints will rise first; that is, before the living saints are transformed and "caught up with them to meet the Lord in the air." As to the second passage, it may be said, that while there are great and good men who understand it to teach a literal resurrection, there are weighty objections to this view. If it is correct, it seems quite plain that all the righteous will not rise at the same time. John in his wonderful vision saw "the souls of them that were beheaded for the witness of Jesus and for the word of God." The reference is to the noble army of martyrs, and if the resurrection is literal, it must be restricted to martyrs, for of them it is said, that they "reigned with Christ a thousand years." What is to become of the millions of the righteous who were not "beheaded for the witness of Jesus"? Will there be a distinct resurrection for them? or will their resurrection be postponed until the wicked are raised? Again, if in the passage under consideration a literal resurrection is referred to, it is passing strange that John did not see the *bodies*, but "the souls of them that were beheaded for the witness of Jesus." Rev. xx. 4. It is to be remembered that the book of Revelation abounds in figurative language. Many of its figures are very bold and strong. It cannot be said that the import of the "first resurrection" is clear beyond a doubt, for men differ in opinion concerning it. This being the case, it is not consistent with the rules of sound interpretation to make Rev. xx. 6 the basis of a theory in conflict with other plain passages of the divine word. That the obscure must yield to the clear, and the indistinct to the luminous, should be regarded an axiom in exposition. How, then, are we to interpret what is said of the "first resurrection"? Our interpretation must accord with passages on which there rests no obscurity. Adopting this method, we shall be obliged to deny that the "first resurrection" is a literal resurrection, and to insist that there will be one simultaneous resurrection of the righteous and the wicked. The following Scriptures utter no uncertain sound: "For the hour is coming, in the which all that are in the graves shall hear his voice and shall come forth; they that have done good, unto the resurrection of life; and they that have done evil, unto the resurrection of damnation" (John v. 28, 29); "That there shall be a resurrection of the dead, both of the just and unjust." Acts xxiv. 15.

"All that are in the graves" are all the dead, and the natural construction of the language is, that they all will at the same time hear the voice of the Son of God, and at the same time come forth. That saints and sinners are included is manifest from the connection of the resurrection with "life" and also with "damnation." So likewise when Paul says, that there shall be a resurrection of the just and of the unjust, every one who has no preconceived theory to maintain must understand him as teaching that the just and the unjust will rise together. It will be after the resurrection that "the Son of man shall send forth his angels, and they shall gather out of his kingdom all things that offend, and them which do iniquity." Matt. xiii. 41. The language of 2 Thess. i. 7–10 has an important bearing on this point: "And to you, who are troubled, rest with us, when the Lord Jesus shall be revealed from heaven with his mighty angels, in flaming fire taking vengeance on them that know not God, and that obey not the gospel of our Lord Jesus Christ: who shall be punished with everlasting destruction from the presence of the Lord, and from the glory of his power; when he shall come to be glorified in his saints, and to be admired in all them that believe." These words are full of meaning, and they teach, among other things, that the Lord Jesus will come to punish sinners when he comes to be glorified in his saints

There will not be two comings, but one coming for two purposes.

In view of the considerations now presented, I must, of course, understand the words " first resurrection " in a figurative sense, as denoting a revival of the principles of piety exemplified in the martyrs of Jesus who laid down their lives for his sake. Andrew Fuller observes: "The ' first resurrection ' appears to me to be no other than the *millennium itself,* to which all that is said of it will well apply. During this glorious period the church will have its Pauls and Peters and Johns over again. Men will be raised up who will go forth in the spirit and power of those worthies, as much as John the Baptist did in the spirit and power of Elias. Thus the apostles and martyrs will, as it were, be raised from their graves and live again upon the earth."[1]

The thoughtful reader will see that the view any one may hold concerning the " first resurrection " determines his view of the millennium. That there will be a period when truth and righteousness shall be prevalent throughout the world, when "earth shall keep jubilee a thousand years," is one of the articles of the common faith, but whether that blessed period shall precede or follow the personal coming of Christ is the point on which good men differ. It does not accord with the purpose of this volume to go at any length into a discussion of this question. My belief that the millennium will precede the personal coming of Christ has been sufficiently indicated.[2]

[1] *Works,* vol. iii. p. 295.

[2] While holding this view, I admit that there are some plausible arguments on the other side of the question—arguments which it is not a very easy task to refute. Still, taking into account the teachings of all the Scriptures bearing on the point, I am obliged to believe that the millennium will precede the second coming of Christ. The " binding

To return to the subject of the resurrection. The coming of Christ to raise the dead will be a magnificent and glorious spectacle. "When the Son of man shall come in his glory, and all the holy angels with him, then shall he sit upon the throne of his glory" (Matt. xxv. 31); "For the Lord himself shall descend from heaven with a shout, with the voice of the archangel, and with the trump of God" (1 Thess. iv. 16); "For the trumpet shall sound, and the dead shall be raised incorruptible, and we shall be changed." 1 Cor. xv. 52.

The second coming of our Lord will be heralded by the resurrection trumpet, which will be heard in every grave and will break the sleep of all the centuries. From Europe, Asia, Africa, America, and the isles of the sea the dead will come forth. The wide empire of the grave will be depopulated, for the sea, as well as the land, will give up its dead. Millions have found their sepulchres in the deep waters, and old Ocean has chanted its stormy dirge over them for ages, but they will hear the sound of the last trumpet and live again. The day of the resurrection will be a great day—a day of wonders and a day replete with glory. Well has a poet said—

> " Ye heavens, great archway of the universe,
>   Put sackcloth on; and, ocean, clothe thyself
>   In garb of widowhood, and gather all
>   Thy waves into a groan, and utter it,
>   Long, loud, deep, piercing, dolorous, immense:
>   The occasion asks it! Nature dies, and God
>   And angels come to lay her in the grave!" [1]

It is a fact, to which I only advert, that little or nothing is said of the appearance of the wicked after their resur-

of Satan"—that is, the remarkable restraint that will be imposed on his influence—will introduce the blessed era.

[1] Pollok's *Course of Time,* book vi.

rection. One passage of Scripture (Dan. xii. 2) teaches that they will rise " to shame and everlasting contempt." Possibly, they will not only feel shame and self-contempt in contemplating their characters, but in beholding their personal appearance. It may be that the bodies of the wicked at the resurrection will be such objects of physical deformity and repulsiveness as we now have no conception of. I leave the fearful subject.

With regard to the saints, we are explicitly told, that as they have borne the image of the earthy—that is, Adam formed out of the earth—so also shall they bear the image of the heavenly—that is, the Lord from heaven. 1 Cor. xv. 49. We have likewise the words, " Who shall change our vile body, that it may be fashioned like unto nis glorious body " (Phil. iii. 21); " We know that when he shall appear, we shall be like him; for we shall see him as he is." 1 John iii. 2. I suppose that the likeness here referred to will embrace both soul and body. The last stain of sin will have been washed from the souls of the redeemed, and they will be like Christ in holiness, while their bodies will be changed into a complete resemblance of his. Without doubt, the glorified body of Jesus is the highest specimen of physical beauty and perfection in the universe, and the bodies of the saints are to be made just like it. The conformity will be so complete that the image of Christ will shine forth in the redeemed with resplendent glory through everlasting ages.

From Paul's majestic argument on the resurrection, as recorded in the fifteeenth chapter of the First Epistle to the Corinthians, we may learn the following truths concerning the reanimated bodies of the saints :

1. *They will be raised in incorruption.* They are committed to the grave in a corruptible state. They are capable

of decomposition, and are consigned to putrefaction and worms and dust. The processes that go on in the grave are processes of disorganization. The body, like a Jewish house infected with leprosy, is totally demolished. Not only do the bodily organs cease to perform their functions, but there is an entire dissolution of the bodily organism itself. All this is implied when it is said of the body, that "it is sown"—or committed to the grave—"in corruption." But the same body which is buried a corruptible one will be raised "in incorruption." There will be no liability to the wasting influence of disease, no tendency to decay, no possibility of dissolution. When it is said, that "flesh and blood cannot inherit the kingdom of God" (1 Cor. xv. 50), the meaning is that the bodies of the saints, as at present organized, are so unfitted for heaven that they cannot be admitted into its sacred mansions. These bodies must be reconstructed, and in their reconstruction every element of corruption will be left out. They will therefore rise from the grave clothed with all the glory of incorruption. An incorruptible body is an immortal body—immortal as the spirit inhabiting it. When the saints are raised from the dead the sublime words of Jesus will be true of them: "Neither can they die any more." Luke xx. 36. To die will be a blessed impossibility.

2. *They will be raised in glory.* This glory is the opposite of the "dishonor" connected with burial in the grave. Who does not know something of this dishonor? The bodies of the best Christians can be seen for only a short time after death. Friendship and love will not permit them to be long visible. The beginning of the putrefying process renders them offensive, and they are put out of sight. When Abraham was making arrangements for the burial of Sarah, who had been so beautiful, he said, "that I should bury my dead out of my sight." Gen.

xxiii. 8. Alas! how manifest the dishonor resting on the body when committed to the custody of the grave! The dishonor, too, will continue until the resurrection-day; for had there been no sin, there would have been no graves. Ignominy is inseparable from imprisonment in the grave, but the end of the imprisonment will be the end of the ignominy. The dishonor of the sepulchre will be removed. The bodies of the saints will be raised in glory, and the glory will be heightened by its striking contrast with the previous dishonor. They will be glorious bodies, perfectly suited to the world of glory, conformed to Christ's "glorious body;" and when they receive them, "then shall the righteous shine forth as the sun in the kingdom of their Father." Matt. xiii. 43. What words are these!—"shine forth as the sun." Doubtless, there will be a glory reflected from the incorruptible bodies of the saints like that which clothed the body of Jesus amid the wonders of the Transfiguration. Who can tell how much is implied in the transporting words "raised in glory"?

3. *They will be raised in power.* This does not mean that they will be raised by the power of God, however true that may be. To be raised in power from the grave is the opposite of being committed to the grave "in weakness." The powers of the body are comparatively feeble in health; they become feebler still in sickness, and they utterly cease at death. A dead body is a powerless thing. Who in looking at a corpse is not reminded of this? It puts forth no act of resistance. The feet walk not, the eyes see not, the hands move not. It makes no protest against being put into a coffin and conveyed to its resting-place in the grave. Truly, Paul labored under no mistake when he said of the body, "It is sown in weakness." But the bodies of the saints will be raised in power. This power

will include everything which is in antagonism with the weakness referred to. Fatigue follows exertion now, activity induces weariness, and disease exhausts the strength of the mortal frame. The resurrection bodies of the redeemed will be endued with such vital energy and vigor as will for ever preclude the necessity of rest. There will be no feeling of weakness or fatigue, but the body "raised in power" will be a suitable vehicle for the active, immortal spirit. The saints in their complete persons will "rest not day nor night."

4. *They will have spiritual bodies.* "It is sown a natural body; it is raised a spiritual body." We know what the natural body is. It is the present habitation of the soul, and is adapted to the present constitution of things. It therefore needs food to sustain its life, sleep to refresh it when weary, and medicine to heal its diseases. In short, it is subject to the laws which control the economy under which it now acts. But the spiritual bodies of the saints after the resurrection will be free from these laws. They will not be flesh and blood. They will not be animal bodies. They will, of course, be material bodies, for otherwise they would not be bodies at all. It seems, however, that the matter of which they are formed will be so refined and purified that it will resemble spiritual substances. But our conceptions of spirit are indistinct and imperfect. How little we know! A thousand things that we "know not now we shall know hereafter." Of these things we may be certain—that the spiritual bodies of the redeemed will be like the glorified body of Christ, and that they will answer all the high and holy purposes of companionship with the spirits indissolubly united to them. Every saint will, in his complete personality, enjoy everlasting life in the kingdom of God.

CHAPTER XXIX.

THE GENERAL JUDGMENT.

THAT there will be a day of judgment, when all the nations of the earth shall stand before the tribunal of Jesus Christ, is plain from the following passages of the word of God:

" When the Son of man shall come in his glory, and all the holy angels with him, then shall he sit upon the throne of his glory: and before him shall be gathered all nations: and he shall separate them one from another, as a shepherd divideth his sheep from the goats: and he shall set the sheep on his right hand, but the goats on the left. Then shall the King say unto them on his right hand, Come, ye blessed of my Father, inherit the kingdom prepared for you from the foundation of the world. . . . Then shall he say also unto them on the left hand, Depart from me, ye cursed, into everlasting fire, prepared for the devil and his angels. . . . And these shall go away into everlasting punishment: but the righteous into life eternal " (Matt. **xxv.** 31–46); " And the times of this ignorance God winked at; but now commandeth all men everywhere to repent: because he hath appointed a day, in the which he will judge the world in righteousness by that Man whom he hath ordained; whereof he hath given assurance unto all men, in that he hath raised him from the dead " (Acts xvii. 30, 31); " For we must all appear before the judgment-seat of Christ; that every one may receive the things done in his body, according to that he hath done, whether it be good or bad" (2 Cor. v. 10); "And I saw the dead, small and great, stand before God; and the books were opened: and another book was opened, which is the book of life; and the dead were judged out of those things which were written in the books, according to their works." Rev. xx. 12.

These are a few of the passages in the New Testament which teach the doctrine of the general judgment, and the same doctrine is taught in the Old, where it is said: "For God shall bring every work into judgment, with every secret thing, whether it be good, or whether it be evil." Eccles. xii. 14. The point is settled that the world will be judged; and to forbid the supposition on the part of any individual that he will be absorbed in the aggregate of the world's population, it is written: "So then every one of us shall give account of himself to God." Rom. xiv. 12. It is this personal account that adds to the solemnity of the great day.

Some have virtually called in question the propriety and necessity of a day of general judgment. Their view seems to be about this: that as there is at death a determination of the final state of every man, it is needless to have a general judgment. The reasoning is more plausible than conclusive, for while character and destiny are unchangeable after death, it may answer important purposes for character to be fully revealed and for the ground of destiny to be fully known. It will be admitted by all that God might, if he chose to do so, administer his government in perfect secrecy, concealing the reasons of his acts from all men and all angels. With an impenetrable veil thrown over the divine proceedings, they would still be in accordance with the principles of per-

fect justice, for a just God cannot deviate from these prin
ciples. But we must remember that God, in the administration of his government, is not only just, but that he intends that his justice shall be seen and acknowledged by
all his intelligent creatures. This is, doubtless, one of the
purposes to be accomplished by the final judgment. Its
disclosures will be the fullest vindication of the divine
character and the divine government. Whatever suspi-
cions may have rested on either will be for ever removed,
God's infinite justice as well as his infinite wisdom and
goodness will be fully recognized. Thus the judgment
will

> " assert eternal Providence,
> And justify the ways of God to men."

It is supremely worthy of remark that Jesus Christ will
be the Judge of the world. Peter said to Cornelius, " It
is he which was ordained of God to be the Judge of
quick and dead." Acts x. 42. Paul said of Jesus, " Who
shall judge the quick and the dead at his appearing
and his kingdom." 2 Tim. iv. 1. Jesus himself said,
" For the Father judgeth no man, but hath committed
all judgment unto the Son. . . . And hath given him
authority to execute judgment also, because he is the
Son of man." John v. 22, 27. As the reward of his humiliation and death, the Son of man, the Mediator, has
been invested with universal authority, that " at the name
of Jesus every knee should bow." Phil. ii. 10. The administration of the divine government is in his hands,
and is a mediatorial administration. The last act of this
administration, so far as we know, will be judging the
world, after which it seems that there will be a delivery
of " the kingdom to God even the Father, . . . that God
may be all in all." 1 Cor. xv. 24, 28. That the office of

Judge of the human race is fitly devolved on Jesus Christ appears in the fact that he is God-man. Uniting in his person divinity and humanity, it is morally certain that, while he sacredly protects the honor and the majesty of the divine government, he will make all necessary allowances for those he judges. As the God-man he will remember his experiences during his sojourn on earth. What more eminently proper than that he through whose blood countless millions are saved shall appoint them places in the heavenly mansions? What more appropriate than that the Friend of sinners shall consign to perdition those who rejected the salvation offered in his name?

As to the judicial process: We are told concerning it, that "the books were opened: and another book was opened which is the book of life." Rev. xx. 12. This language is, no doubt, figurative, for there will be no literal opening of books. The imagery employed, however, is very suggestive. It implies that everything necessary to a perfect judicial decision will be known, even as a knowledge of matters committed to books of record is safely preserved. There will be no need of witnesses to testify, for the Judge, being omniscient, will be perfectly acquainted with the characters of those whom he judges. With our finite minds we are overwhelmed with this thought. How can we conceive that our final Judge will know every individual of the multiplied millions before him, all the works performed by each one, all the words spoken, and all the thoughts indulged? There will be a perfect acquaintance with all the elements that have entered into the formation of moral character, while the character formed will be, in every case, prophetic and decisive of destiny. Works will be brought to light, even deeds of darkness, as well as deeds of mercy, performed so secretly that "the left hand has not known what was done by the right." It is plainly written that "God will bring every work into judgment." All the words that have been spoken will be, in effect, reproduced, "for by thy words thou shalt be justified, and by thy words thou shalt be condemned." Matt. xii. 37. The thoughts of all hearts will be revealed, because it is said that when the Lord comes he "will make manifest the counsels of the hearts." 1 Cor. iv. 5.

1. *The righteous will be judged.* In proof of this I need only state that when the Judge shall say to them, "Come, ye blessed of my Father, inherit the kingdom prepared for you from the foundation of the world," he will add these words: "For I was an-hungered, and ye gave me meat: I was thirsty, and ye gave me drink: I was a stranger, and ye took me in: naked, and ye clothed me· I was sick, and ye visited me: I was in prison, and ye came unto me." Matt. xxv. 35, 36. It is evident that these good works will be referred to, not as creating a title to the heavenly kingdom, but as showing it or making it manifest. Believers are justified by grace through faith, but good works are fruits of faith and proofs of justification. They are evidences of Christian character, and will be so recognized at the judgment. It is therefore to be remembered that the doctrine of salvation by grace, so far from being unfriendly to practical piety, is promotive of good works. It will, no doubt, be made known on the judgment-day that the righteous have been made righteous in Christ, not having their "own righteousness which is of the law, but that which is through the faith of Christ, the righteousness which is of God by faith." Phil. iii. 9. It will be seen that from first to last their salvation has been of grace—that God was just in justifying them through the atoning sacrifice

of the cross; and thus the honors of justice as well as the riches of mercy will be illustrated in their acquittal on the great day. Having been acquitted and pronounced heirs of the heavenly kingdom, the saints, as it may be inferred from 1 Cor. vi. 2, 3, will be appointed assessors with Christ in the remaining part of the adjudications that will be made: "Do ye not know that the saints shall judge the world? and if the world shall be judged by you, are ye unworthy to judge the smallest matters? Know ye not that ye shall judge angels?"

2. *The wicked will be judged.* We read of the "revelation of the righteous judgment of God," and this "revelation" is connected with what is called "the day of wrath." Rom. ii. 5. There will be the strictest adherence to the principles of justice when the wicked are judged. Nothing will be done arbitrarily, but all will be in perfect accordance with righteousness. The judgment will exhibit in the wicked different degrees of guilt. They will be held responsible for the improvement of all the light they may have had. This is the teaching of Christ, who says, "For unto whomsoever much is given, of him shall be much required." Luke xii. 48. Responsibility is in proportion to blessings received and opportunities enjoyed.

(a) Heathen nations will be judged by the light of nature. Paul refers to them in these words: "For the invisible things of him from the creation of the world are clearly seen, being understood by the things that are made, even his eternal power and Godhead; so that they are without excuse." Rom. i. 20. The argument of the apostle is, that men may and must infer the existence of God from the works of creation, and that their conception of a Supreme Being renders idolatry inexcusable. If, then, idolaters are without excuse, they must stand guilty before the judgment-seat. How much men may know of God without the Bible is not now the subject of discussion. The point is, that the heathen, because they can infer the being of God from his works, are without excuse. This being the case, they must be adjudged guilty and incur the consequences of their guilt. If they are without excuse, justice demands that a sentence of condemnation be pronounced on them. The comparative severity of this sentence we may not know, but of its certainty we are fully assured. It is written, " For as many as have sinned without law shall also perish without law. . . . In the day when God shall judge the secrets of men by Jesus Christ according to my gospel." Rom. ii. 12, 16.

(b) Those living under the written law of the Old Testament will be judged by it. In the parable of the Rich Man and Lazarus we have strong testimony as to the value of the Old Testament Scriptures. The rich man is represented as entreating Abraham to send Lazarus to warn his " five brethren," insisting that if one should go to them from the dead, they would repent. Abraham's answer is full of meaning : " If they hear not Moses and the prophets, neither will they be persuaded, though one rose from the dead." Luke xvi. 31. It is plain from these words that those who lived under the light of the Old Testament economy enjoyed advantages unspeakably greater than did surrounding heathen nations, who were, nevertheless, without excuse. " As many as have sinned in the law shall be judged by the law." Rom. ii. 12. A fearful condemnation awaits those who would not " hear Moses and the prophets." If the heathen are without excuse, much more inexcusable are those who neglected Old Testament advantages. The day of judg ment will be to them a terrible day.

(c) Those living under the Christian economy will be judged by the gospel. Jesus said, "He that rejecteth me, and receiveth not my words, hath one that judgeth him : the word that I have spoken, the same shall judge him in the last day." John xii. 48. I have referred to the judgment as bringing to light different degrees of guilt, but the highest degree will be exhibited in connection with the abuse of gospel privileges. The language of Christ concerning Chorazin and Bethsaida justifies this view : " But I say unto you, It shall be more tolerable for Tyre and Sidon at the day of judgment than for you." Of Capernaum he said, " But I say unto you, That it shall be more tolerable for the land of Sodom in the day of judgment, than for thee." Matt. xi. 22, 24. In perfect accordance with the spirit of these passages it is written : " He that despised Moses' law died without mercy under two or three witnesses : of how much sorer punishment, suppose ye, shall he be thought worthy who hath trodden under foot the Son of God !" etc. Heb. x. 28, 29. The sentence of condemnation pronounced at the judgment on the rejecters of Christ will be supremely fearful. It is written, " If any man love not the Lord Jesus Christ, let him be Anathema Maranatha [accursed, the Lord cometh]." 1 Cor. xvi. 22. As Paul wrote under divine inspiration, the intimation here clearly is, that those who do not love the Lord Jesus Christ will be accursed in the day of his coming. Alas for them when the curse of God falls upon them, comprehending, as it will do, " the wrath of the Lamb "! Rev. vi. 16. What a startling collocation of words ! Who knows how much is meant by " the wrath of the Lamb "? The Lamb of God, the Lamb that was slain, the Sufferer of Calvary, will be the Judge, and when he pronounces on those who have rejected him the sentence, " Depart, ye cursed," the scene will be inconceivably awful. Good were it for those whom Jesus condemns had they never been born. Through the ages of eternity there will be heard no words more terrific than these: "The wrath of the Lamb"!

The judicial decisions of the last day will fix in their final state all the millions of Adam's race. The wicked we are told, "shall go away into everlasting punishment: but the righteous into life eternal." Matt. xxv. 46.

3. *Fallen angels will be judged.* In this topic we cannot feel so deep an interest as in the topics which have just engaged our attention. That is to say, matters pertaining to the human race are more important to us than those which concern angelic beings. Still, the teachings of Scripture are not to be ignored, and from them we learn, that "God spared not the angels that sinned, but cast them down to hell, and delivered them into chains of darkness, to be reserved unto judgment;" and that "the angels who kept not their first estate, but left their own habitation, he hath reserved in everlasting chains under darkness unto the judgment of the great day." 2 Pet. ii. 4; Jude 6. Here two leading truths are stated: that these angels sinned, and that they are kept in custody to the day of judgment. To the latter truth, there seems to be reference when certain demons said to Jesus, "Art thou come hither to torment us before the time?" Matt. viii. 29. The natural inference from this question is that these evil spirits were looking for a period of augmented torment, but did not suppose that it would come so soon.

It will enhance the awful greatness of the judgment-day for the case of the sinning angels to be adjudicated There have been many useless conjectures as to the origin of sin among them, the reasons of their revolt from the divine government, the circumstances connected with the revolt, and the number engaged in it. All the facts bear

34

ing on the subject will be brought to light at the judg ment, and the intelligent moral universe will see that God was righteous in his dealings with them—righteous in holding them as prisoners of his justice for many cen turies, reserving their formal trial and public condemna tion to the judgment of the great day. When it is said, that the "saints shall judge angels," we are only to un derstand that they will concur in and approve the sen tence which the Judge pronounces. The fallen angels will, like ungodly men, know the justice of their doom, and sink in self-accusing agony to hell, to suffer the con sequences of their rebellion. The more we contemplate the transactions of the day of judgment, the more shall we be assured that of all days it deserves to be called "the great day." God grant that he who writes and those who read these pages "may find mercy of the Lord in that day"!

CHAPTER XXX.

HEAVEN AND HELL

IT is evident, from considerations already presented that the decisions of the judgment will be final and unchangeable. In accordance with these decisions, the righteous, in their complete glorified persons, will be ad mitted into heaven, and the wicked will be cast into hell. These two places will be the ultimate receptacles of al. the human race.

HEAVEN.

It is everywhere assumed in the Scriptures, and specially in the New Testament, that there is a heaven. Jesus referred to himself as having "come down from heaven," and when he ascended it is said, that he was "carried up into heaven." John vi. 38; Luke xxiv. 51. During his ministry he said in his Sermon on the Mount, "Lay up for yourselves treasures in heaven." Matt. vi. 20. At another time he spoke of the enrolment of the names of his disciples "in heaven" as the source of their highest joy. Luke x. 20. Paul in writing to the Colossians (i. 5) uses the words, "the hope which is laid up for you in heaven." In addition to this use of the term "heaven," there are many other terms and phrases equivalent to it in import, but to these I shall not refer particularly.

Some have considered it a debatable question whether heaven is a state or a place. I see no objection to the union of the two views. We may regard heaven as a state most exalted and glorious, but it is also a place. Jesus said to his disciples, " In my Father's house are many mansions: if it were not so, I would have told you. I go to prepare a place for you. And if I go and prepare a place for you, I will come again and receive you unto myself; that where I am, there ye may be also." John xiv. 2, 3. Christ has gone to prepare for his followers a place in the many apartments of his Father's house. There is one truth which for ever settles the point that heaven is a place. That truth is, that the glorified body of Jesus is in heaven. His body is, of course, a material body, composed of matter, however refined, for otherwise it would not be a body. But whatever is material is local, has relation to place. The two ideas of the material and the local are inseparable. Heaven as a place is the most glorious of all places, the select locality in the wide realm of the universe. Its attractions are unspeakably great. and the following are some of them:

1. *It is a place of enlarged knowledge.* " That the soul be without knowledge, it is not good." Prov. xix. 2. This is said of knowledge in this world. A thirst for knowledge is one of the things which distinguish men from the beasts that perish. The knowledge pertaining to this world answers important purposes, but " the excellency of knowledge " has to do with Christ and salvation. Phil. iii. 6. Saints on earth, as compared with sinners, know much; yet, as compared with saints in heaven, they know but little. There are many Scriptures which indicate the imperfect knowledge of Christians in the present state. They are said to "know in part," and not to know now what they shall know hereafter, while the assurance is

given that "it doth not yet appear what we shall be." 1
Cor. xiii. 12; John xiii. 7; 1 John iii. 2.

Limitations are imposed on the attainment of knowledge on earth which will be removed in heaven. The
intellect will no longer be fettered in its action by the
body, for the latter, as we have seen, will be made spiritual and incorruptible. The acquisition of knowledge
in heaven will be amazing. The saints in their ignorance
now cannot conceive how much they will know then.
When Paul says, in a passage just referred to, "Now I
know in part, but then shall I know even as also I am
known," it is difficult to imagine how he could have expressed more fully the vast extent of his future knowledge. To know as he is known seems to be as much as
even Gabriel or Michael can say.

The saints in heaven will know a thousand times more
about the works and ways of God than they can know in
this life. As the light of eternity falls on these works and
ways, now in great part obscured, how often will be heard
the exclamation, "Great and marvellous are thy works,
Lord God Almighty; just and true are thy ways, thou
King of saints"! Rev. xv. 3. In heaven the many perplexing problems now connected with dark providences
will receive solutions so satisfactory, so brilliant, as to call
forth the most rapturous hallelujahs. There will be a
constantly increasing knowledge of the wonders of redemption, for the subject of salvation is inexhaustible
It will be fresh when a million centuries have passed
away, and fresh to endless ages.

> "The cross, the manger, and the throne
> Are big with wonders yet unknown."

Truly, heaven is a place of enlarged knowledge.

2. *It is a place of perfect holiness.* Earth is full of sin

34 *

The effects of sin are seen everywhere, and will be seen till the earth is destroyed by fire, when from the burning mass will emerge, according to the promise of God, " a new earth " more beauteous than Eden in its primeval glory. But this blessed change is in the future. Sin is in the world now. It has dominion over the impenitent. In the regenerate its power is broken, but how bitterly they often have to deplore its polluting presence in their hearts ! Sin is their worst enemy. In heaven there will be no sin. It is a holy place. The angels are holy. The redeemed are without fault before the throne. The holiness of heaven is one of its most powerful attractions. How deeply are we impressed with the purity of the place when we remember that our souls cannot enter into it till the last stain of sin is washed from them, and that our bodies must be resolved into dust, and then be reconstructed without a taint of sin, before they can inherit the kingdom of God ! However much Christians may now be annoyed and distressed by sin, when they enter heaven they will be troubled by it no more. They will dwell for ever in the realms of perfect purity.

3. *It is a place of holy love.* In this respect, how greatly it differs from earth ! Here hatred often prevails among nations and individuals. Injustice in its many forms may be traced to it. "Thou shalt love thy neighbor as thyself " is a command the violation of which it has been the chief business of history to record. Feelings of hatred rankling in the human breast have too often made earth an Aceldama—" a field of blood." Nor can it be said that the passion of hatred is entirely extinct in the regenerate people of God. Who has not seen proofs of its existence in various forms of envy, jealousy, and evil-speaking? Alas ! love among brethren is by no means perfect on earth. But in heaven there is an undisturbed reign of

holy love. All the inhabitants of that bright world love God supremely and love one another subordinately. Every saint can there say, " I love every one of these saints, and every one of them loves me." The satisfaction arising from this consciousness will never be disturbed by a single doubt or a solitary suspicion. I do not wonder that Rowland Hill said, " My chief conception of heaven is that it is a place of love."

4. *It is a place of perfect rest and endless joy.* Earth is the place for labor, toil, fatigue, but there " remaineth a rest to the people of God." Heb. iv. 9. John, listening to a voice from heaven, wrote, " Blessed are the dead which die in the Lord from henceforth. Yea, saith the Spirit, that they may rest from their labors." Rev. xiv. 13.

> " In heaven there's rest : that thought hath a power
> To scatter the shades of life's dreariest hour."

Baxter well said, " O glorious rest! where they rest not day nor night, crying, Holy, holy, holy, Lord God Almighty !" The joy of heaven will be fulness of joy. All the faculties of glorified saints will be filled with it. There will be a rich plenitude of bliss. The joy of heaven will be endless. The joy of earth is imperfect while it lasts, and soon passes away. The joy of heaven is perpetual. Through the long cycle of everlasting years it will continue, ever increasing as the capacity of the saints to enjoy will increase. The blessedness of heaven depends much on the eternity of its joy. That blessedness would be greatly impaired if the joy were to end when ten thousand times ten thousand centuries pass away. Truly has it been said,

> " Perpetuity of bliss *is* bliss."

5. *It is a place of blessed companionships.* We are made

for society. Christianity does not destroy the social principle, but sanctifies it on earth, and will perfectly sanctify it in heaven. There are many allusions in the Scriptures to the social enjoyments of the heavenly state. The select society of the universe is in heaven. We read of angels, principalities, powers, cherubim, seraphim. These terms most probably denote the various orders of heavenly intelligences. But in addition to these there will be a multitude of the redeemed which no man can number. How blessed will be the associations of heaven! How delightful for the saints to cultivate an acquaintance with the very angels who rejoiced over the beginning of their saintship in their repentance! The social intercourse of the redeemed with one another will be productive of exquisite enjoyment. They will renew their acquaintance with those whom they have known on earth, and of whom they have heard and read, while they will form new acquaintances among the millions of unknown ones, to whom they will be drawn by the fact that they were all redeemed by the precious blood of a common Mediator. How blessed will be the companionships of heaven!

6. *It is the place in which the divine glory is displayed in the highest degree.* The glory of God is a manifestation of his perfections, or rather it is the splendor resulting from the manifestation. Hence it is said, "The heavens declare the glory of God;" that is, they exhibit such perfections as his wisdom and power. In the plan of redemption there is a much brighter display of the glory of God than is to be seen in the firmament, which is the work of his hands. There is an exhibition of moral perfections, which must ever eclipse a manifestation of natural attributes. We therefore read of "the glory of God in the face of Jesus Christ." 2 Cor. iv. 6. It is such an

exhibition as the universe never saw before—the glory of
God in the face of the crucified Christ. Now, in heaven
there is a still fuller and brighter manifestation of the
divine perfections. This is often called glory—the glory
of God. Christians are said to rejoice " in hope of the
glory of God." Rom. v. 2. Jesus prayed for his disciples,
saying, " Father, I will that those whom thou hast given me
be with me where I am ; that they may behold my glory
which thou hast given me." John xvii. 24. It is plain,
therefore, that heaven is a place in which the divine glory
is supremely displayed—the glory of God, the glory of
Christ, who is God. It is manifest, too, that the inhabitants of heaven will ever find their highest happiness
in beholding the exhibitions of this glory. That is what
the " old theologians " properly termed " the beatific
vision." It will be productive of such happiness as
language has never described nor imagination conceived.

HELL.

While it is a delightful privilege to refer to heaven as
the abode of the righteous, it is a solemn duty to recognize the teachings of the Bible concerning hell as the
place in which the wicked will be punished. The proper
tendency of the doctrine of future punishment is to deter
from sin, even as the doctrine of future blessedness in
heaven should stimulate and allure to holiness   Obviously, all that can be known of hell as a " place of torment" must be ascertained from the Scriptures. Our own
unaided reasonings are not trustworthy, and those who
die in their sins come not back from the eternal world to
tell us of their experiences there.

That there is a hell is undeniable in view of the following scriptures: " For it is profitable for thee that one of
thy members should perish, and not that thy whole body

should be cast into hell;" "And fear not them which kill the body, but are not able to kill the soul: but rather fear him who is able to destroy both soul and body in hell;" "Ye serpents, ye generation of vipers, how can ye escape the damnation of hell?" (Matt. v. 29; x. 28; xxiii. 33); 'And if thy hand offend [ensnare] thee, cut it off: it is better for thee to enter into life maimed, than having two hands to go into hell, into the fire that never shall be quenched" (Mark ix. 43); "Fear him, which after he hath killed hath power to cast into hell; yea, I say unto you, Fear him." Luke xii. 5.

These passages prove beyond doubt that there is a hell, and that it is an inexpressibly dreadful place; for we are taught that it is the part of wisdom to avoid it at the expense of the mutilation, or even the killing, of the body. That it is a place of excruciating pain is clear, because it is described as "the fire that shall never be quenched." Here, as well as anywhere, I may notice the oft-repeated assertion, that what Christ says of unquenchable fire is to be understood, not literally, but figuratively. Suppose this is conceded; and I do concede it—that is to say, I do not think that Jesus referred either to literal "fire" or a literal "worm." But what follows? That the punishment of the wicked will be less dreadful than if they should be cast into literal, material fire? By no means. The philosophy of language rather prompts us to inquire, If the symbol of punishment be so fearful, what must the reality be? Worse, far worse. It is impossible for any symbol to exaggerate the idea of pain which Christ intended to convey. Satan may try to delude men, and men may try to delude themselves, into the belief that there is nothing alarming in the miseries of hell; but it is tremendously true that these miseries defy description and surpass adequate conception. It is specially worthy

of notice that the most awful things in the Bible concerning the punishment of the wicked are the words of Jesus
He was love incarnate, but he spoke of " outer darkness,"
"weeping, wailing, and gnashing of teeth," a "place of
torment," "the worm that dieth not," "the fire that is
not quenched," "everlasting punishment," "eternal damnation." Matt. viii. 12; Luke xvi. 28; Mark ix. 44; Matt.
xxv. 46; Mark iii. 29. These are expressions of startling
significance. Indeed, the future retribution of the wicked
is a most copious as well as awful subject, which I shall
discuss only so far as to refer briefly to the words of
Christ as recorded in Matt. xxv. 46: "These shall go
away into everlasting punishment." Here two points
claim attention:

1. *The wicked will be punished.* What is punishment?
It is the infliction of pain for disobedience. Thus a
father punishes a disobedient child. Pain inflicted without regard to disobedience would be calamity, and not
punishment. Punishment has reference to sin, and under
the government of God it is the executed penalty of his
law. It is God who executes this penalty, which is
death, eternal death. Strange views on this subject are
held by some, for they think that the wicked will only
be punished by painful memories, remorse of conscience,
agony of despair. No doubt, memory has to do with the
miseries of the lost, but an operation of memory is not
the penalty of the divine law. Remorse of conscience is
inseparable from the penalty, but it is not the penalty.
Has a murderer's remorse of conscience ever exhausted
the penalty of the law of murder? Never. The thing is
impossible. Nor is the despair which lost sinners feel the
penalty of God's law. How can despair as to a change in
their doom satisfy the law, a violation of which determined their doom? The thing cannot be. All these

views fail to meet the point. The truth is, that the penalty of God's law is death. "The wages of sin is death; but the gift of God is eternal life through Jesus Christ our Lord." Rom. vi. 23. That eternal death is referred to is evident from its contrast with eternal life. There can be no consistent interpretation of the passage which does not make the death and the life equal in duration. God executes the penalty of his law. He inflicts on his incorrigible enemies the punishment they deserve. He punishes them because they deserve to be punished. This is the only true philosophy of punishment. Incidental effects may result from punishment, but the supreme reason why sinners are punished is that. because of their sins, they deserve punishment. God as moral Governor of the universe executes the penalty of nis law. This fact enables us to understand what is meant by "the wrath of God." This is a scriptura. phrase, and it denotes God's just and holy indignation against sin. This indignation arises from the fact that sin is a transgression of his law; and therefore his justice and holiness—yes, and his goodness too—imperatively require that incorrigible sinners be punished. According to the teaching of the Scriptures, they will be punished as their demerits require. This shows that punishment will be graduated by the degree of ill-desert —graduated in intensity, though not in duration; for the second point claiming attention is—

2. *The punishment will be everlasting.* The words of Jesus are, "These shall go away into everlasting punishment." Matt. xxv. 46. Of the wicked, Paul says, "Who shall be punished with everlasting destruction from the presence of the Lord and from the glory of his power." 2 Thess. i. 9. The destruction referred to is not annihilation, for it is everlasting destruction. The process of

destruction will go on for ever. It is scarcely necessary
to refer to the doctrine of the annihilation of the wicked,
for it has no scriptural support. Its advocates can give
no example of annihilation in the world of matter; and
to suppose that mind or spirit will cease to be, is as contrary to philosophy as it is to the word of God.

When Jesus says, " These shall go away into everlasting
punishment, but the righteous into life eternal," he
employs one and the same word, which in the Common
Version of the Bible is translated " everlasting " and
" eternal." The same word is used in Rom. xvi. 26,
where the apostle speaks of the " everlasting God,"
while in passages too numerous to quote it is, in its
application to the future life of the saints, translated
" everlasting " and " eternal." Now the question is this:
Does a word which, when applied to God and to the
future life of the saints, denotes endless duration, as all
admit, indicate limited duration when it is applied to
the punishment of the wicked? He who answers this
question affirmatively must do so in conflict with Scripture, reason, and common sense.

Interpretation of language is not a matter of feeling.
Sound exegesis does not permit us to consider what we
may wish any passage of Scripture to mean, but it re-
stricts our attention to the question, What does it mean?
what is the import of its words? Much that is now
(1878) said and written against the doctrine of endless
punishment is a vain attempt to magnify God's goodness
at the expense of his justice and truth; whereas God
would cease to be good if he should cease to be just and
true. In other words, his justice and truth cannot be
severed from his goodness. Alas for those who, under
the frown of God, sink to hell! They come not out of
the prison, the gloomy prison of despair. They " will be

35

punished with everlasting destruction from the presence of the Lord and from the glory of his power." What fearful words are these! Away from the presence of the Lord, his glorious presence, in which the saints will ejoice for ever !—

> " As far from God and light of heaven
> As far from the centre thrice to the utmost pole."

There is no probation after death. He that dies in his sins remains in his sins for ever. Moral character is unchangeable in eternity. The righteous continue righteous, the wicked continue wicked.

What is the conclusion of the whole matter? Jesus taught, by solemn affirmation and solemn negation, the doctrine of the endless punishment of the wicked, saying, "These shall go away into everlasting punishment," they "shall not see life," " their worm dieth not," " the fire is not quenched." These are the words of the benevolent Son of God and Son of man.

> " Come, sinners, seek his grace
> Whose wrath ye cannot bear;
> Fly to the shelter of his cross,
> And find salvation there."

GENERAL INDEX.

INDEX OF SUBJECTS.

A.

Abel, 104, 169.
Abraham, 37, 44, 104, 142.
   justified by faith, 283.
Absalom, 142.
Activity of angels, 144.
Adam, all sinned in, 169.
   and Eve sinned first in heart, 166.
   and Eve died spiritual death when they sinned, 168.
   head of all nations, 171.
   judgment on, 167.
   representative of his race, 171.
   Saviour promised to, 186.
   sinned intelligently and voluntarily, 165.
   the first brings ruin, the last brings salvation, 170.
   type of Christ, 173.
   why his descendants suffer in him, 172.
Adoption, civil and spiritual, resemblances and difference between, 291, 292.
   civil, practised by the ancients, 290.
   of Esther and of Moses, 291.
   privileges of, 292–297.
Ananias, 92.
Angel, meaning of the word, 138.
Angels, holy, 138.
   activity and power of, 144.
   are spirits, 139.
   convey spirits of saints to heaven, 150.
   goodness of God to, 53.
   great knowledge of, 142.
   guard the steps of saints, 149.
   immortality of, 141.
   increase in knowledge, 143.
   ministry of, 148.
   minister to saints at Christ's second coming, 150.
   refuse worship, 89.
   sinless obedience of, 146.
   sinful, 151.

C. did not die for fallen angels – 122 8

Angels, sinful, shall be judged, 156.
Annihilation of the wicked, no scriptural support, 409.
Annotated Paragraph Bible, 189.
Antony, Mark, 169.
Aquila, 330.
Arius, doctrine of, 73.
Artaxerxes, 191.
Atonement, antitype and consummation of all sacrifices, 238.
   appointed by God, 239.
   believers receive benefit of, 221.
   by animal sacrifices, ceremonial, 240.
   by Christ, real, 240.
   cannot be offered to fallen angels, 244.
   Christ assumes sinner's place in, 226.
   Christ, deity of, essential to, 241.
   expiation for sin, 224.
   extent of, 241.
   faith involves reliance on, 244.
   four centuries of preparation for, 239.
   Fuller, Andrew, on, 242.
   God pleased with, 248.
   gospel invitations rest on 242.
   Hall, Robert, on, 242.
   involves substitution, 227.
   Lawgiver receives it, 221.
   love of God originating cause of, 229.
   made for man, 244.
   man's unwillingness the only obstacle to, 243.
   meaning of, 221.
   measure above law, 223.
   necessity of, 228.
      how it originates, 229.
      trace to nature of God, 230.
      what it means, 229.

INDEX OF SCRIPTURES.

on points like these wisdom is silence 15

Dr. Wall; Church of England 365

Angels - fallen - no substitute 278

obscure yields to the clear 381